THE C

Modern missionary pioneering
in the jungles of the Philippines

BARBARA FLORY REED

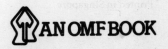

AN OMF BOOK

© OVERSEAS MISSIONARY FELLOWSHIP
(formerly China Inland Mission)
Published by Overseas Missionary Fellowship (IHQ) Ltd.,
2 Cluny Road, Singapore 1025,
Republic of Singapore

First published 1987

OMF BOOKS are distributed by
OMF, 404 South Church Street,
  Robesonia, Pa 19551, USA
OMF, Belmont, The Vine,
  Sevenoaks, Kent, TN13 3TZ, UK
OMF, PO Box 177, Kew East,
  Victoria 3102, Australia
and other OMF offices.

ISBN 9971-972-55-7

Printed in Singapore

CONTENTS

This book is lovingly dedicated to

our four children, Rick, Becky, Bob and George
whose frequent, and sometimes painful, sacrifices
made this story possible,
and whose infectious enjoyment of life
from early childhood made the recalling of it
a delightful adventure.

My heartfelt thanks

To Mother and Dad for keeping all of those long, detailed
letters since 1952, along with copies of Newsletters, Prayer-
partner and donors letters, filing them systematically as they
did those of their other two missionary daughters.

To my sister, Ann Flory, for her constant encouragement, for
reading the manuscript in each progressive stage, and for her
insightful suggestions.

To my husband Russell for his long after-work hours helping
keyboard my original scrawl and entering the changes after
each successive revision.

To Dad Reed for furnishing the computer.

T he winds were increasing, and the weathered square-rigged ships of the explorers creaked as their seams opened with the twisting of the waves of the South China Sea letting water in, and then closed again. The explorers felt confident for they were well away from land. What they didn't know was that Apo Reef lay directly ahead. When one of the ships struck, the rest turned and fled, abandoning the crew of the ill-fated vessel. Only a few of the sailors ever reached the shores of distant Mindoro Island in the center of the Philippine Archipelago.

Those few settled down with a group of the tribal people. A new language began to develop, combining a European-type grammar with the local vocabulary, and a set of unique customs gradually emerged. After three generations Taliugan, "the one with the long neck," was born.

Many dry seasons later this feared leader walked slowly along the open path through the grasslands, thoughtfully puffing on his little clay pipe that characterized the members of his tribe. With interest he watched the white sails of a large ship, not realizing it was a galleon on its way from *Maynila*, through the Sorsogon straits to Mexico. Something about the ship excited him, something of hope and also of fear.

Those white sails held Taliugan's eye so that he did not even notice the bundle of twigs planted upright at the side of the trail, nor the split end of the tallest one which held the lower jaw of a chicken, slowly whitening in the sun. It had been picked clean like the pig jaw lying nearby, a reminder of his sacrifice made before the rainy season for another shaman who had been sick. These things were common sights. White sails were a rare thing.

He was still enthralled when he arrived at the junction of the trails from the four villages. The leaders and the shaman were meeting together today at the sun shelter to discuss what to do about a group of intruders coming from the coast into their tribal area. Taliugan favored making it rain so that they would be driven back down the river to the lowlands by the ensuing flood.

At the hut only one other leader had arrived. Squatting on his heels, he, too, was watching the ship. Without taking his eyes off the sails, Taliugan softly said, "They say that the people in those boats are white, some of them as white as those sails in the sunlight, as white as bark cloth made from the *binian* tree."

Could real people, "people of the day" have skin as white as that? Old Long-Neck decided that it wasn't possible. The people he was thinking of must be spirits, "people of the night", the ones he and the other shaman would sometimes see in their dreams.

And then old Long-Neck was speaking again without even realizing it. "Some day," he said, "white people will come here to teach us. Big people. And they will know our language. When they come, we must follow their teaching."

This prophecy was passed down from father to son for sixteen generations, but Taliugan's descendants told no one else.

Three hundred and fifty years after Taliugan died, on November 11, 1953, we arrived in Mindoro.

(Researched and written by Russell Reed)

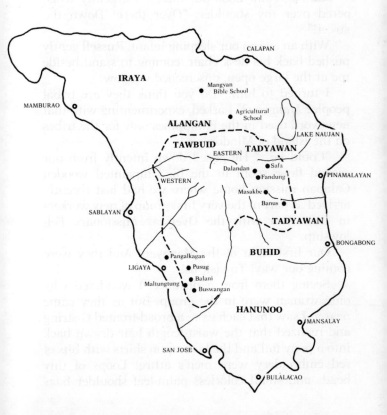

Chapter 1

UNKNOWN

"**L**ook, Hon! Look out there!" I urgently whispered over my shoulder. "Over there! Down the street!"

With an eye on our sleeping infant, Russell gently pushed back his desk chair, coming to stand beside me at the large open, unscreened window.

I turned to him. "Do you think they are tribal people? *Mangyan*?" I asked, experimenting with that new word used in the Philippines only for the tribes on the island of Mindoro.

"Could be..." He gazed down intently from our second floor room in the big, unpainted wooden Calapan mission home where we had just recently arrived as part of the very first group of new workers in East Asia with the Overseas Missionary Fellowship.

Our first sight of the Mangyan! And they were coming our way! To visit us!

Seeing them from a distance, I wondered why only women were in the group. But as they came nearer, I saw that each wore a broad-fronted G-string and realized that the waist-length hair drawn back into a pony tail and the homespun shirts with bits of red embroidery were men's attire! Loops of tiny beads and small colorless palm-leaf shoulder bags completed their simple outfits. How primitive they seemed.

Primitive! Our natural desire had always been to go to a primitive area, for we enjoyed hiking, backpacking and camping. Hadn't we spent our honeymoon in a tent on the shores of Lake Waubesa in Wisconsin?

When we applied to the China Inland Mission, as the OMF was known in 1952, we wondered where the Lord would send us, for China was closing. Reading the survey reports of the Mission's new fields in East Asia, we realized that the interior mountainous areas in several of these countries held people untouched by civilization who had never heard of Christ. We wanted to be the first to bring those neglected people the Good News. We imagined North Thailand would hold the most remote, isolated, untouched, and undeveloped groups. But the Mission leaders suggested to us tribal work in the Philippines.

That was a disappointment. We knew it would not be primitive at all — the Philippines was a highly-civilized country. But, being convinced that God guides His workers through their leaders, we accepted the Philippines as God's will for us.

And now, a year later, as I watched these simply-dressed Mangyan approaching, I thought of the contrast between them and the pictures I had recently seen of the heavily-ornamented northern Thailand tribespeople who had a wealth of long traditions and rich backgrounds. With a throb of joy I realized the men we were watching were much more primitive than any tribes in Thailand. God had brought us to the very type of people we longed to reach.

But where could these Mangyan, now at our gate, have heard of us missionaries, to come all the way from their jungle-hidden mountain homes into this bustling, frightening town just to visit us? We hurried out to the wooden-railed veranda and down the worn stairs, not to waste a minute! For surely they were interested in hearing about the Lord, or they wouldn't have come to our house. Had they learned of us from Marie Barham, our missionary in the south working with the Buhid Mangyan? Or from Frances Williamson stationed in the north reaching the Iraya tribe?

Asking questions and then listening intently to catch their quick short answers, I began to feel a sad disappointment. If we understood them right, they had never heard of any of the twelve OMF missionaries on Mindoro. Neither the recent arrivals like us, nor Dr and Mrs Broomhall in charge of the work and the Calapan mission home. They were only asking for a "Merry Christmas" at the house of these rich *Americanos*.

Someone suggested I bring out my accordian. So with the Broomhall children watching from the doorway, I played several hymns, drawing a guarded interest from the men sitting on the old cement stair landing.

But their faraway looks and blank stares as we tried to speak to them of spiritual things in our memorized phrases and stumbling Tagalog, the national language of the Philippines, made us feel frustrated and useless. When they left us to continue begging from house to house, we returned thoughtfully upstairs to our studies. God had given us an object lesson that no matter which tribal group we were to reach, we must know their very own language or we could never explain to them the true meaning of Christmas. It would just remain a day to beg.

Although we didn't know the tribal people, we did know that God was preparing our family to be mountain missionaries. Each morning, drying Ricky in his huge yellow bath towel, I had marveled at his strong sturdy body, less than four weeks old, as he pushed with his legs to stand up. And I was sure that God had given us this specially healthy child because he would have to share our pioneer life in reaching one of the tribes of hidden people in interior Mindoro.

Our first glimpse of these Mangyan filled our minds with questions. Which tribal group did our visitors represent? How many Mangyan tribes lived in the range of mountains that stretched down the hundred-mile length of this island? What languages did they speak? Were their customs all alike, or did they vary from tribe to tribe? To which tribe would we be designated? Even though we planned to spend our whole lives working with one of the unreached Mangyan tribes, they were still completely unknown to us.

Actually, information about them was scarce. Nine dialect names, placed on a Mindoro map by an American anthropologist, were later determined to be six major mutually-unintelligible languages. When OMF missionaries first arrived in 1952, two of those languages had ambiguous forms of native writing, but none had been reduced to an adequate script. I wanted us to be designated at once to one of those tribes and to go right away into the mountains to learn their unknown tongue. But I knew we had to finish the required Tagalog study before a tribal language could be begun.

Learning Tagalog was not our only difficult experience. Bending over the desk one day, concentrating on the Tagalog expressions I was trying to memorize, I suddenly heard eleven-week-old Ricky laugh out loud. That was a first! Quickly I raised my head to watch him contentedly lying on his back playing with his newly-discovered hands. He looked so darling, completely absorbed, smiling to himself, and then repeating his happy laugh.

Suddenly I felt a pang of sadness. Mom and Dad would never see him at this cute age. They wouldn't be able to watch him raise himself and roll over, looking smug and pleased with the accomplishment. They wouldn't be able to hear him entertain himself clicking his tongue or making sounds in his own private language. They wouldn't see him creeping in his basket until his head was against the end, needing to be rescued because he couldn't go backwards. They wouldn't be able to watch his surprised enjoyment when he had his first taste of Pablum.

I began to weep for all that they would miss. I wept and prayed for them, and for myself, and for Ricky and for Russell. Getting up from the desk, I groped in the cupboard for one of Russell's big hankies, but I just couldn't stop crying. I took my Bible from the corner of the desk where I had set it after my quiet time that morning. Where could I read to get comfort?

"No good thing will He withhold from them that walk uprightly." It was the Lord's word to me. He was giving us His best. He was in control, and He knew how I felt. Gradually I began to relax with a strange sense of well-being, and I knew that Mother and Daddy and our other prayer partners at home were faithfully remembering us in prayer, helping me now through this hurting crisis.

Many times during our years on the field I would face these unwelcome attacks of homesickness. Each time the Lord would speak to me through His Word, giving a special renewed joy and new sense of dependence on Him, with a realization that others were praying.

Life in Calapan could have eventually lulled us into a complacency that would have tarnished our vision of reaching the tribal people. Actually, at first there was little temptation. I even objected to the big old comfortable wooden mission home with all its conveniences, and looked with admiration at the tiny grass roofs dotting the shady green coconut plantation across the street.

In the mission home we had our laundry done, our rooms cleaned, our meals prepared and the dishes washed by house helpers to free us for study. But I gladly would have done all my own work if our small family could have lived in a neat, clean, compact, little house on stilts with a grass roof, like the one nearby. Yet as the days turned into weeks and the weeks into months, a gradual change took place in my outlook.

At the desk one Saturday trying to get caught up on correspondence, I didn't hear Russell come upstairs until he began to speak.

"It's almost lunch time, and the water's still on.

Seems like good pressure too," he said.

"Guess they meant business when they said we'd have it all day. It's so much better than the old 'magical water hours,' one in the morning and one in the afternoon," I responded, remembering how the water used to suddenly spout from the opened faucets into the empty barrels, and abruptly stop flowing after sixty minutes.

"I'm going to take a shower just to see what it feels like at this time of day!" he said, gathering up his towel and clean clothes.

And he found out. It felt really warm. Because the pipes were so near the surface of the ground, we had solar-heated water. At eight o'clock that evening the water was still coming out heated, and a warm shower as the sticky hot day cooled down was a special treat we didn't expect even in Calapan.

So every hour of the day became "magical water hour." But it wasn't long before running water lost its magic and became just an ordinary necessity. And then unconsciously we began hoping and longing for other comforts: more consistent electricity, faster mail service, a better-stocked market, more familiar food, nicer clothing, a larger room, more attractive furniture...

But our prayer partners at home were pleading daily that nothing would keep us from getting to the Mangyan. So the Lord began to work in our hearts to keep our vision bright by gradually weaning us away from our binding American habits and customs that demanded more comforts, and increasing our yearning to see the Mindoro tribes occupied for Him.

Seen through Russell's eyes, Marie Barham's struggles and triumphs among the Buhid provided the needed buffing to give our vision a new and lasting glow. Early one Saturday morning before the sun had begun to pink the sky behind my beloved coconut grove, Russell and Dr B (as we affectionately called him) were on their way south to Marie's station, bumping and lurching in the big open-sided wooden bus.

I imagined their five-hour trip would be similar to our bus ride weeks before when Russell, Ricky and I, with Bob Hanselman, had visited the Iraya work. Dust from the unpaved two-lane road had constantly swirled in our faces, relieved only when we were fording the rivers. At one crossing that relief had turned to mild panic when the fully-loaded bus mounted a rickety bamboo raft to be ferried across. In the two hours it took us to cover the 22 miles, Ricky's blanket was thoroughly ingrained with dust, our hands and faces were gritty, and Bob's hatless head had a new powder-gray wig.

Dr B and Russell, after their bus ride south, would be hiking into the mountains with Marie to a small Buhid village. We had all been praying that these Mangyan would soon invite her to teach them, building her a house among them. I could hardly wait for Russell's report when they would return that evening.

It was very late when a huge cloud of dust stopped in front of our house announcing their arrival. After a refreshing drink, Russell and I went upstairs to our room where, with a sigh of exhaustion, he plopped on the chair and began to untie the laces of his grimy shoes.

Glancing up from the sooty, blackened mess he remarked, "This is what a *kaingin* does to your nice white canvas shoes."

"*Kaingin*?" I said, mystified.

"It's a burned-over area in the jungle. To make room for their crops, the tribal people begin in January, at the start of the dry season, to cut down the jungle growth with the small trees, and sometimes big ones. Then in March or April when it has all dried out, they burn it over to make new fields for the coming year."

Still pulling at the laces, he continued, "Marie's Buhid village is way up in the mountains and it's sure rough getting there! Up one hill, down the next, up and down, up and down, through jungle growth and over open burned fields... We must have hiked about nine miles, but it seemed like ninety!"

"What about Marie? She must be twice our age. How did she do?"

"Honey, she outdid us all!" he said emphatically.

Then he told of visiting several families in their tiny shabby palm leaf and cogon grass homes, finding it hard to describe what he saw.

"The people are so pitiful. Such poor food and little clothing. And covered with sores and skin infections, and big ulcers from yaws."

"Do they want to listen to the gospel?" I asked anxiously.

"I don't think they really know what it's all about yet. They live in ignorance and superstition, just like it says in Romans, 'Without God and without hope!' They're even afraid to have Marie live in their village. She had to get a lowland farmer to build her a hut about twenty minutes hike from where the Buhid live."

He sighed and began pulling off his sooty shoes,

revealing stiff, dirt-crusted sox. I might want a home of my own, but right now I was glad I wouldn't have to wash those horrible sox.

"Even then, Marie is becoming their friend," he went on. "I'm sure they'll respond to her teaching soon. So many at home are praying."

How long, I wondered, *before God guides us to a group of Mangyan, to be their friends, to help them, to tell them of His love and care?* I was sure they would respond when they understood God's love for them. Years later I was to learn that love wasn't the attribute of God that would first captivate their attention.

Gradually we were learning that each Mangyan tribe was different. Trekking with Dr B across the jungle-covered mountains at the northern end of the island and returning by sea, Russell brought back a vivid report. After that ten-day trip, instead of blackened shoes and stiff sox, he had a pack of salt-water-soaked clothes, blistered feet, itching leech bites and a longing for a good American meal and a real bed!

The Iraya Mangyan they saw as they descended from the summit into a wide fertile valley on the northern end of Mindoro were not at all like the Buhid in the south.

"When we camped that night near two sturdy Mangyan homes," Russell said, "four healthy, well-dressed children enjoyed watching us. And their friendly parents not only sold us sweet potatoes, eggs and salt, but they agreed to guide us to the coast.

"Coming down through the grasslands the next day was pretty easy because there wasn't any jungle, so different from Marie's area. I'd guess that about a hundred Mangyan, and maybe an equal number of Tagalogs live there. Then, when we got to the coast we realized that that valley was only one of three or four similar valleys. With mouths opening close together at the sea, each one was spread fan-like back up into the mountains. And each with needy people, though the ones we saw didn't look deprived!"

With a sigh bordering on discouragement, I wondered when we would be able to go and live among them. Then I remembered the package notice from the post office. Thinking how the surprise-packed parcels from Mom and Dad had often lifted our drooping spirits, I suggested to Russell, "Couldn't you go first thing tomorrow and collect it?"

At the post office he was handed a box from Gospel Recordings. In it we found records from all the Mangyan dialects that had been cut so far, as well as Ilocano and Tagalog ones. In fascination we listened to the various tribal languages, appalled at the speed each language was spoken, for we could hardly separate any of the sounds. I wanted to rush right out and find some Mangyan to see if they could actually understand the message on those records!

The trip that influenced our own immediate future the most was Russell's visit to the Mindoro National Agricultural School with Hazel Page.

"You should have seen Hazel when we met this group of Mangyan near the school," Russell grinned appreciatively as he gave me the details. "Indefatigable! Even after our three-hour hike, which was almost a run because we were so late, she didn't pause to catch her breath. Paper and pencil were whipped out immediately, and a good discussion in

Tagalog accompanied her collection of the word list. She discovered that they were Alangan Mangyan. They seemed better related to the outside world than the Buhid in Marie's area, but not as sophisticated as the Iraya we saw in the north."

"Do they live there by the school?" I asked.

"I guess some do. But evidently the ones we met came from across the mountains to trade. Our map places the Alangan farther north than the Agricultural School, and shows the Batangan, Naujan and Pola Mangyan where the Agriculture School is located. But if the Alangan are as far south as the school, maybe that's the Alangan-Batangan tribal border. It might make a center from which both tribes could be reached."

"Well, the map does seem to place the Iraya, Buhid and Hanunoo fairly accurately," I said, for there were workers in those three tribes. "That leaves the Ratagnon, Bangon, Batangan, Naujan, and Pola needing missionaries. Where do you think we'll be sent?" But Russell just shook his head. He didn't know either. All we knew was that we wanted to work in an untouched tribe.

Finally designation day arrived. We were given our desire — an unreached tribe, the *Batangan*! With excited anticipation we again began to discuss the Agricultural School.

"It would make a good first station for us," Russell suggested. "The students, about 200 fellows and 30 girls, are friendly and open and they'd love Ricky! The grounds were jungle just three years ago, but now have concrete school buildings and a girls' dorm. The fellows live in small, trim nipa-palm houses on stilts."

"How far is it from the bus road?" I asked him.

"About ten miles inland, backed right up to the mountains," he told me. "If we lived there, I'd be able to make trips into the nearby hills to find out more about the Mangyan and probably locate the Batangan."

"We could continue our Tagalog study there, too, and make friends with the students," I added.

Dr B agreed that the Agricultural School would be a good place to start, so a request was sent to the school authorities to allow us to live there temporarily. With painful slowness the details were being worked out.

November came. Eleven long months since we had seen our first Mangyan. A second set of new workers in Calapan had replaced our original group who were now reaching out to the various tribes — the Iraya, the Alangan, the Naujan and Pola (later to be known as the Tadyawan), and the Buhid.

And we were moving to the Agricultural School hoping to locate the elusive Batangan. In our year on Mindoro we had met no one who had even glimpsed one of their members. We wondered if we would be able to find these Batangan, now merely a bold, black name lettered in a SW — NE direction across the center of our Mindoro map.

Chapter 2

HIDDEN

T he sun had not yet risen when we finally heard the lumbering roar of the motor and ran out to hail the big red wooden bus.

Dr and Mrs B in their gracious style had set aside their own busy schedules for the day to go with us, lending a picnic air to our departure and dispelling any apprehension we might have had.

Although it was an exciting adventure for me, since I had never been to the Agricultural School before, for Russell it was a serious responsibility: moving his little family into a yet unseen, only promised, unfurnished house, seven vehicleless, dirt-road miles from the nearest village, and ten miles from the motor road.

After two bone-shaking hours we climbed down at the junction, piling our baggage at the roadside. Brightening at the approach of a horse-drawn *karetela* cart, we signaled the driver, and then happily loaded our things on the high wooden-wheeled vehicle. But it seemed we had bumped along only a few yards on the narrow, dirt side-road when we came to a small broken-down bridge, and realized with a sigh that we could go no further.

By now the sun was hot. Covered with sticky dust, we were itchy, uncomfortable, and disappointed. Just then a low rustic water-buffalo cart appeared on the other side of the bridge. Crossing on foot we were able to load our belongings onto this simple vehicle. Farther on we found another cart so that I could ride holding Ricky. Perched on a footlocker, I cradled him in one arm while in the other hand I held an umbrella to protect him from the merciless sun. As we bumped and banged in our slatted wooden crate, the others walked peacefully beside us.

When we finally joggled into the forest-ringed school grounds I was charmed by the bubbling flow of water in the rocky creek bed at my left, and the rustic cogon grass hut, deserted and unkempt in its loneliness on my right. But my attention was captivated by a tiny house on stilts, beautifully constructed of nipa-palm shingles and bamboo, still a clean shiny yellow in its newness. Like those I'd admired in the coconut grove. At the Superintendent's residence, after a brief visit, Dr and Mrs B reluctantly said goodbye, for they had a long hike back to the highway and did not want to miss the last bus to Calapan.

"Did you notice that new little nipa hut on our way in?" Russell asked me quietly while we waited. My heart bounded at the thought. "It was just being built when Dr B and I visited the school and the Superintendent suggested that we could use it when it was finished."

"But that was three months ago! Do you think it's still available? It looked to me like someone's living there now," I said tiredly. Every bone in my body was aching from that three-hour shaking.

"I suppose they are," Russell answered. "As far as I know the only other empty houses are four older huts at the back of the school clearing. Either they'll put us there, or it looks like some one will have to move." Wearily we waited.

Unknown to us two boys were quickly and unobtrusively removing from their hut all their possessions, as well as those of their five companions who had gone home for the six-weeks Christmas vacation. Finally we were taken to our new home, and I was awed to find that it was the tiny, attractive nipa-palm house I had seen near the entrance. Removing our shoes at the bottom of the sturdy pole stairs, we entered the house from the lattice-work porch. Everything was delightfully shiny and new.

Two days later Russell packed his notebook, pencil and word lists into his shoulder bag, and set off to locate the Batangan. First he visited the Alangan Mangyan who lived at the edge of the school clearing. Then in the afternoon, ignoring his tiredness and the occasional showers in the heavy sultry heat, he hiked across the school fields and waded the river to contact the Alangan living over on the other side.

After two strenuous days, he had gleaned only a few bits of information from his conversations with them in their halting Tagalog. Some said that the Batangan lived on the Mongpong River, across the mountains in Western, or Occidental, Mindoro. Others thought that they were also on this side. But we were not discouraged.

On Ricky's birthday it didn't even matter that I had no ingredients or oven to make a cake. The joy of being on our first station, actively searching for the Batangan, was enough. We helped him open the presents his grandparents had sent and were as pleased as he was with the new toys and clothes.

One day when Russell had left early I gathered together the day's laundry, piled it into the flat metal washing pan, checked Ricky contentedly asleep, and headed across the path to the spring just upstream from our house.

Glancing uncertainly at the dark clouds overhead, I filled my pan with water and began to rub each piece of clothing with the long blue bar of soap. Russell would return soaked again, for he didn't wear any raingear. It merely produced more soaking by sweating. But he never complained. What really mattered to him was finding the Batangan, as well as explaining the Good News to the tribespeople he met in his search.

As I was rubbing Russell's T-shirt, trying to remove the mud spatters and sweat-soaked stains, I suddenly felt troubled about Ricky. I had carefully closed the thick palm-leaf door, so no dog or cat could get in to bother him while he slept comfortably and safely with the clever harness-bedtie that kept him from falling. But it seemed urgent that I check on him. Pulling my heavy pan up on the creek bank, I started for the house. Panic seemed to possess me and I began to run.

At the bottom of the pole stairs, I shook off my wooden-soled *bakya* and with one movement bounded up onto the porch and pulled open the door. One glance at Ricky, and my heart was in my throat.

"Oh, no! How could that happen?" Quickly I lifted his limp dangling body, turning his blue face upwards and at the same time loosening the harness at his waist that had broken away from its fastening on the wall-side of his bunk.

Immediately he began to suck in huge gulps of air,

and as I held him tenderly, my wobbly knees gave way, and I sat down hard murmuring, "Thank you, Lord. Oh, thank you!" His breath became regular as he nestled against me, and then my tears began to come.

"Lord, it seems like everything we are doing is ending in failure! Russell has been slogging through the mud, coming home soaked to the skin almost every day, and still hasn't been able to find anyone who has seen a Batangan and almost no one who has even heard of them! There just isn't anyone here who can be a language teacher for us so that we can finish our Tagalog studies. And I'm not even a good mother."

As I wept with Ricky in my arms, I thought of the phonograph. Scooting over beside it on the floor, I shuffled through the records and picked out the one labeled, "For the missionary." The only one in English. I hadn't paid any attention to it before, but now I cranked the phonograph and for the first time set that record on. Through the clear, sweet voice God spoke to my heart.

> He giveth more grace when the burdens grow greater,
>   He sendeth more strength when the labors increase;
> To added affliction He addeth His mercy,
>   To multiplied trials, His multiplied peace.
>
> When we have exhausted our store of endurance,
>   When our strength has failed ere the day is half done,
> When we reach the end of our hoarded resources,
>   Our Father's full giving is only begun.
>
> His love has no limit, His grace has no measure,
>   His power has no boundary known unto men,
> For out of His infinite riches in Jesus,
>   He giveth, and giveth and giveth again.

I thanked God for Gospel Recordings, who had lovingly cared for the missionary when they sent us that shipment of Filipino records. Many times in the years to come I would be cheered by listening to that special record.

Returning from his trek, Russell had nothing new to report. But the very next day God gave us our first piece of definite information. Tying the new bamboo eaves trough on one side of our porch roof so we could catch the rain water, Russell became aware of three students watching him.

"Good afternoon, sir," they said formally.

"Good afternoon," Russell replied. "Come on up!"

Mounting the pole stairs with a respectful, "Good afternoon, ma'am," they introduced themselves. Then murmuring something about the phonograph, they came inside and sat down beside it.

"Do you want to listen to Ilocano or Tagalog records?" I asked them.

"Ilocano, ma'am," and they seemed to relax a bit.

Whispering, fidgeting and glancing quickly around the room while the phonograph was playing told me that they had something on their minds. After Russell came in, they stopped the records and turned to us. "Sir, ma'am, have you come from America?"

"Yes, we have," Russell said. "We arrived in the Philippines about a year ago."

Seeing we enjoyed talking to them, they quizzed us on the climate in America, what our houses were like, and what kind of high schools we had, smiling and nudging each other when our descriptions seemed particularly strange.

Then Ambrosio took a deep breath, "Sir, we have

just been wondering why you are here at our school. You are not teaching or helping in the field work..."

With a smile of new understanding, Russell explained, "We are looking for a group of Mangyan called 'Batangan' and we thought that we would be able to find them in this area."

Ambrosio's eyes glanced up with interest at the mention of "Batangan" even before Russell began his explanation about the map that indicated their location, or our purpose for wanting to find them.

"Oh! They don't live around here," he stated firmly. "But we see a few now and then in my home village of Ligaya. Sometimes they come down from the hills to work for the farmers near our place. And some can even speak Tagalog! I'm still hoping to go home for Christmas, and maybe I'll even see them then."

Quickly recovering from the shock of hearing what we had been longing to hear, Russell asked, "Where is your home village of Ligaya? In English we would call it 'Joy Village!'"

With a smile of appreciation, he replied, "It's on the other side of Mindoro, on the west coast, about halfway between the northern town of Mamburao and the southern town of San Jose."

"And how do you reach Joy Village?" Russell wanted to know.

"I can take a plane from Calapan and fly south to San Jose on the southern tip of the island. From there it is sixty kilometers north along the coast to Ligaya."

"Do you take a bus then?" I asked.

"No, ma'am. There's no road along that side of the island. Sometimes we walk, or if one of the small coastal motor *bangkas* is going that day, we can take that." After more talking, and additional record playing, the boys thanked us and left.

We just looked at each other. The Batangan were on the other side of the island, in Occidental Mindoro. Ambrosio had seen them. And they knew Tagalog.

Rejoicing with this news and ready to leave at once for Ligaya, I was gently brought down to earth by Russell's wise suggestion that beginning Batangan work here in the East was much more sensible. From our missionaries in the town of Mamburao in Occidental Mindoro we had learned that transportation and communication were almost non-existent over there in the West. Only four small *municipios*, or county seats, each with its market and post office, spanned the hundred-mile western coastline. And the tiny farming villages were isolated by miles of jungle growth and bamboo. So after Christmas Russell would continue his search for the Batangan here in the East, especially along the Aglubang River.

The holidays came with constant tropical rain. Festive cards replaced the ever-present diapers on the lines in the *sala*, or main room. Lonely students who lived too far away to go home for vacation dropped by to practice their English, ask questions, look through our Christian magazines, sing carols, or play with "Boy" as they called him. We served them Kool-Aid and bananas with Mrs B's home-made fruit cake and cookies that Dr B had thoughtfully brought us a few days before. Then as each of them left, it was a joy to watch them gratefully accept one of our colorful Christmas story tracts.

Heavy rain continued to pour the day after Christmas. We went to bed that night realizing that the small placid creek near our house had already become a raging torrent bouncing logs on its foam like corks. But I went to sleep feeling safe in our sturdy nipa-palm house on stilts.

Suddenly I woke up. In the pitch darkness the sound of water swishing underneath our house startled me. Quickly pulling the flashlight out from under my pillow, I looked at my watch. Three am. Then sitting up in the sleeping bag, I leaned over and turned the beam of light down between the bamboo floor slats. I watched with horror the churning water underneath the house seemingly just inches from the floor. It was like being in the middle of a raging river.

I shook Russell awake, and together we listened to the distant roar of the torrential current punctuated by the dull thump of bumping logs. Suddenly, with a very loud thud, the house gave a sharp jolt. Instinctively I flashed the light on baby Ricky. He was still sleeping peacefully.

By this time Russell was out of the sleeping bag, and together we went back to the kitchen and pushed aside the palm-leaf door. In our flashlight beam was an endless lake of water stretching all the way, we supposed, to the mountains beyond. Soberly we left the kitchen, crossed the *sala*, and stepped out onto the tiny front porch.

The water was several feet deep and rising, so our ladder stairs were already afloat. Quickly we pulled them up onto the porch. But we were too late to save our wooden-soled *bakya* clogs which had already drifted out of sight.

We were in a sea of rising water, and neither of us had any idea which way to go to find higher ground. And anyway, who could escape in black darkness through a rushing torrent two or three feet deep?

"There's nothing we can do," Russell said quietly. "Except pray and try to go back to sleep."

He was right, of course. But sleep was impossible.

Suddenly the air rang with a series of ear-splitting squeals. "Probably just the pig next door being hauled by the ears into the house for safety," Russell said calmly while I quaked. Logs continued to slam into our house posts throughout the night, with the water swishing noisily right under the floor slats.

Finally morning came. In the first rays of light we could see torrents of water from the flooded fields behind us flowing swiftly underneath our house and joining the mad rush of our formerly quiet creek. But we were relieved to realize that the rain had stopped and that the water seemed to be receding.

With everything under water, we weren't sure how the little old grannie reached us with her welcome basket of eggs for sale and her startling news about the flood's devastation. The four old empty student huts where we easily could have been housed, as well as the entire stock of 50-gallon drums full of kerosene, had disappeared. Washed out to sea, never to be seen again. In their place was a deep gorge with a swift tumbling stream racing through it. My knees felt weak.

Unknown to us at that time, little David Todd, a member of my mother's Sunday School class in California, came to church several weeks later clutching the newsletter I had written describing the flood, for he had taken baby Ricky as his special missionary. "Look, Mrs Flory!" he said excitedly. "My prayers saved Ricky's house!"

For several months after Christmas Russell continued his exploring, meeting other Mangyan. But again he was disappointed that no contacts led to the Batangan. Finally with a fellow missionary he trekked up the Aglubang River for three days, but still he found no Batangan. The Mangyan they did meet said the Batangan were two days journey to the West, which would be across the mountains in Occidental Mindoro, probably near Ambrosio's village of Ligaya!

"It looks like the only place we can reach the Batangan is in Occidental Mindoro," Russell told me after that trip. "Maybe you and Ricky could stay in Mamburao where we have OMF missionaries, and from there I could go south along the coast to hunt for a place for us to live near Ligaya." So we faced our second major move in six months, which was fine with me, for I enjoyed new places and new experiences.

From Calapan to Mamburao across the mountain range would be a trip of only 45 miles as the crow flies, but unfortunately we were not crows. We had to go by sea around the northern end of the island.

We began this sixteen-hour trip on a Monday morning in May 1955. Just past 2:30 we heard the familiar jingle of the horse-drawn cart as the driver called for us. In the dark we climbed up into the vehicle, and swayed and jolted for twenty minutes towards the pier. There we boarded the converted mine-sweeper, the common passenger ship between Calapan and Batangas, on Luzon Island. From Batangas we took another small launch across the open sea back to Mindoro, but this time we landed on the Occidental side and boarded a bus going southwest.

Worn out with traveling and exhausted by sea-sickness, we finally arrived in Mamburao, relieved to be greeted by Doris and Cyril Weller at the door of their spacious nipa-palm home, since the bus always delivers its passengers right to the house. It was now evening, and a warm supper, bath and comfortable bed were certainly welcome. A hundred mile trip had never been so long, but at last we were on our way to the area where we knew the Batangan lived.

Cyril and Russell went to the beach the next day, dismayed to learn that the weekly boat south had quietly left three days ahead of schedule. With no boat again the following week, they decided to walk the thirty coastal miles to Sablayan to hunt for housing. We needed to get settled before the rainy season began on this side of the island. It seemed best to locate first in the municipal town of Sablayan, sixteen miles north of tiny Ligaya, until we could determine the exact location of the Batangan back in the mountains.

The two men left for that unknown area guided only by a name in Russell's notebook. But that name had been a special provision of the Lord. Four months earlier I had taken Ricky from the Agricultural School to Manila for a checkup and had myself undergone an unexpected appendectomy. Believer Rudolfo Pereno had visited me in the hospital, and then when Russell arrived from Mindoro, Rudolfo had told him about Ernesto Dapito, a fine young Christian engineer going to Thailand with a government survey team. Engineer Ernesto had asked for prayer that God would send spiritual help and fellowship for his sister and her husband, Digo, newly saved and living in the isolated town of Sablayan.

Russell had explained that we worked in Oriental Mindoro, not in the West. He had no way of knowing that in less than five months' time we would find ourselves in Occidental Mindoro, looking for housing in Digo's own town.

Arriving in Sablayan, Cyril and Russell found Digo busy at the rice mill he was managing. Rejoicing in the Lord that they had come, he immediately suggested that Russell rent the large nipa-palm house in which he and his wife and baby girl were living. It belonged to the Dapitos, his wife's parents so it was the very house that Engineer Ernesto had called "home."

About a week after Russell and Cyril returned, our furniture and footlockers from Calapan arrived in Mamburao by a large sailing *batel*, and Russell began his daily shore walks to find a small motor-*bangka* willing to take us and our household goods to Sablayan.

Just a few days before we left Mamburao, we had the eerie experience of total midday darkness during an eclipse of the sun which lasted more than seven minutes. Chickens went to roost. Dogs howled and then hid under the houses. Kerosene lamps were lit. Candles were burned to Mary and rosaries were recited as a strange sense of fear pervaded the town. But in the gradual return of the sun's brilliance, the fears evaporated and were forgotten. At least by the lowland peoples.

Later we would learn that for the Batangan this "Great Darkness" of June 20, 1955 was a never-to-be forgotten day, a marker in time. And it would prove invaluable to us to help establish a chronology in a calendarless tribe which had no way of recording even the year, let alone the day, of births, deaths or special events.

Two days after the eclipse the old ox cart loaded with all our belongings slowly trudged from the house to the beach, where a motor-*bangka* was waiting to take us to Sablayan. The sun was just coming up, and beautiful weather was the promise, for the sea was without a single white cap.

Under the awning of the 35-foot outrigger craft the three of us perched on our pile of footlockers, boxes of food, desk, cabinets, beds, table and chairs, to begin our slow smooth chug toward Sablayan. But halfway there the trip turned into a nightmare of rough seas with high splashing waves, soaking us and everything we owned with salt water.

That night in our new home Digo and his wife and her younger sister asked for a meeting. So the five of us gathered around the kerosene lantern singing, reading the Bible and praying until nearly ten o'clock. Two completely exhausted missionaries crawled under the mosquito net that night, but the prayers of Engineer Ernesto were being answered.

With reaching the Batangan heavy on our hearts, we tried to settle into our new home as quickly as possible. While Russell fixed up the kitchen and partitioned off a small storeroom, I kept busy scrubbing the bamboo slat floors in the sala, bedroom and dining room, applying paste wax and then getting my exercise by polishing them with one foot on top of a half coconut husk, bristle side down.

All this time people were coming to see us, to admire or play with "Boy," to hear our popular Gospel Recordings records, to buy Bibles or New

Testaments, or just to talk with us. The house filled with children as soon as school was dismissed, and some even ran over to spend recess with us!

We could easily bargain for food brought to the door: an egg or two, a flat basket of eggplant, sweet potatoes, squash, bananas, mangoes, or fish. But when it came to answering our new friends' many questions about spiritual things, we found it took a larger vocabulary than we possessed. In this problem Digo and his wife were a great encouragement.

But even with all these new friendships, no one was able to take Russell to see the Batangan who reportedly lived in the foothills near the prison colony. Located ten miles inland from Sablayan, the colony already had sixty acres of jungle cleared and planted in rice, vegetables and beans, even though it had been established for only a year. A 28-mile road had also been built, the only one in the entire municipality, for they had the only vehicles, two large trucks. No one from Sablayan ever hiked on the road, however, for that route took about seven hours to reach the colony, while the jungle trail took only four.

Only a four-hour hike. But every time Russell asked someone to guide him on that trail, they either had too much weeding to do in their growing rice fields, or the weather was stormy, or they didn't know the trail, or all three! The weeks began to slip by in disappointment and frustration. Finally Russell decided to go alone.

Chapter 3

FEARFUL

Russell set off early for the prison colony shouldering his pack containing clothes, canteen, lunch, tracts and his *bolo*. He wouldn't need a compass, flashlight or matches, for he planned to reach the colony before noon and to spend his nights there while trying to contact the Batangan during the day.

After he left, while Ricky took his morning nap, I was out on our bamboo platform back porch with a huge pile of weekend laundry at my feet, coaxing the water from our red pitcher-pump. As I squatted down, submerging the clothes in the cold water and soaping them, I began to pray.

"Lord, help Russell to follow the trail for the whole ten miles to the colony. Those jungle paths always have so many branches! And let him find a warm reception and help for locating the Batangan." It was exciting to think that the following day Russell could be meeting his first Batangan and learning where they lived, so we could move close enough to have daily contact.

By evening I was very tired, and went to bed just as soon as the young girl from next door arrived. I had learned that no respectable woman would ever stay alone in the house when her husband was gone.

About 9 pm I woke, realizing that Russell was calling to be let in, for no one can knock on a palm leaf door!

One look at the exhausted mud-splattered figure before me, and I knew something had gone wrong. Quickly I put our large tea kettle on the stove to warm some bath water, and began to heat up rice, get out a couple of eggs, and open a precious can of Spam.

Later, as he sat down to eat in clean dry clothes, I began with my questions. "Did you get to the colony? Were they helpful? Did you see any Batangan?"

Patiently, for he was too tired to endure much of my quizzing, he sighed, "Yes. Somewhat. And no, I didn't see any Batangan." Then a bit more brightly, "But I sure learned a lot. And not just about tribal people." I was all ears.

"You know that wide trail out from Sablayan toward the colony..." and I murmured, "Mmmmmmm," recalling that path which would be easy to follow.

"Well, I lost it in a farmer's newly-plowed field. But just then a couple of men came along and guided me. [*Thank you Lord*, I said inwardly.] After they turned off, the trail divided, but the branch I chose began to get pretty small, so I went back to follow the other one which went along a swamp. Later at the colony they told me that those swamps swarm with crocodiles! A professional hunter had shot fifty over six feet long, as well as fifty smaller ones!"

I shuddered at the thought!

"Well, after the swamp I was lost again. At a house nearby they told me how to get to the next farm. When I got there, no one was at home, so I wandered off across a field and just happened on a road [*Thanks again, Lord*] which led to the Mong-pong River across from the prison colony. The water was only a couple of feet deep, so crossing over to the colony wasn't too hard."

"What about the Batangan. Are they close?" I asked.

"No, they're not. And the nearby Mangyan who could have led me to them were away. So I visited with the colony staff for a while, and then started home. Back across the river, I was able to give out tracts in Hinaya village."

"It must have been getting late by then," I suggested.

"It was, so I began to hurry. After about half an hour I didn't recognize the countryside, and couldn't find my earlier footprints either, so I knew I'd taken a wrong turn. So I had to go back to try to find the right trail.

"About twilight, I got to the swamp. With no flashlight I plowed my way along the edge through gloomy dense bamboo thickets. Pretty soon it was jungle-dark. I had lost the path and knowing about the crocodiles sure didn't help!

"I knew I should go west, so at the next open field, I looked for the Southern Cross and the Big Dipper to get my directions. I walked back and forth along the overgrown edge of the field and every time I ducked into what looked like a trail opening, the jungle clutched at my feet and arms with its tangle of vines and branches, and I had to go back into the open and try again. It was only the Lord who helped me find it. [*You're great, Lord!*] And then it was lost again in another plowed field and I had to start all over." He sighed. "Looking at the stars again, I knew I was going in the right direction even if it wasn't the trail I had taken this morning."

"By now you must have been dead tired!" I interjected.

"It was too much! But once when I sat down to rest, a loud crashing noise in the bamboo thicket made me decide it was time to move on! I wasn't sure exactly which way to go, but when I heard the ocean breaking on the beach a few miles away, I knew that was the direction of Sablayan.

"Finally I began to hear the swarms of dogs barking. And then I got to that old broken-down bridge at the end of our lane and I knew I was really home!"

I sighed with relief.

"You know, Hon," he continued, "for all the slipping and falling, and all the mud, the Lord kept me from really getting hurt. [*You did it, Lord! Thanks!*] But from now on," he added sheepishly, "I'll always carry a flashlight and a compass. And start home earlier."

"Are you thinking of going again pretty soon?" I wondered aloud.

"Next week if this rainy season lets me. I'm sure I can find a guide from the Mangyan living near the colony who could take me into the hills and introduce me to the Batangan," was his optimistic reply.

Russell left on Monday. Tuesday, with Ricky in his stroller, I took the six-block walk to the post office and was rewarded by a packet of mail. Tuesdays as well as Fridays the mail carrier arrived from Mamburao after a difficult two-day hike involving many river crossings.

Losing my loneliness for Russell in my absorption with our far-away family and friends, I happened to glance up just in time to see several little playmates giving a second-hand piece of candy to Ricky. Quickly I jumped up to intervene, then tempered my approach, for they were lovingly sharing. In this place his guardian angels would really be kept on their toes!

As I was fixing supper that evening, Russell arrived. He wasn't a bit muddy this time, but I noticed a wound that had been well painted with iodine. Returning to my cooking I asked, "Whatever happened to your hand?"

"You should see my side!" he said, teasingly. I swung around from the stove, but his grin set my heart at ease, ready to hear the details.

This second trip had been even more eventful than the first. Besides the nasty dog bite on his side, he experienced flooded river crossings resulting in a good soaking and a lost *bolo*; the opportunity to share the gospel and give tracts to the 150 prisoners at roll call; the privilege of leading devotions for the colony staff; the meeting of Alangan Mangyan Leon; the two-hour mountain trip with him to find a guide to the Batangan; the introduction to that guide; the disappointment of his refusal to go until after the rainy season in three months and finally the pleasure of being taught a few words and phrases that this would-be guide and his wife had learned from the Batangan.

With amusement we tried to pronounce, "*Sinumufud. Laglagyu. Malukmeaw.*" (Who is your companion? Don't run away. I am kind.)

"Maybe we are going at this from the wrong

place," Russell said suddenly.

"You mean learning Batangan? I agree! An Alangan Mangyan isn't the ideal source!"

"No, I mean trying to find the Batangan from the colony. We are sixteen miles from Ligaya where Ambrosio has met them. Maybe they're not this far north."

"You'd need to go to Ligaya to find out about that," I said hesitantly.

"That's what I've been thinking," he agreed. "But first I want to return to the colony in ten days to be sure that dog doesn't have rabies."

Hiking to Ligaya on the unfamiliar six-hour coastal trail, as well as finding someone there who knew about the Batangan, was not as difficult as he feared.

Following his usual custom, he gave Tagalog tracts to every home he passed on the way. In Ligaya the Santos family, glancing at the colorful tract, introduced themselves and invited Russell into their home.

"We are Methodists," they told him warmly. "But there is no Protestant Church here in our *barrio* of Ligaya. We can only attend when we are in San Jose." Then they asked hopefully, "Will you be having services here?"

"Well, no," Russell answered. "We are really trying to reach the Batangan to teach them about our Savior. But we haven't been able to contact them from Sablayan where we're now living."

"There's an Ilocano family here that has a farm in the hills at Pangalkagan where the Batangan live," they said, not realizing the impact of their words. "They probably aren't home right now, but this evening we could take you over to meet them."

"Could I come again some other day and meet them?" Russell asked. Thinking of the new baby on the way he added, "My wife wasn't too well when I left this morning, and so I need to get back."

Less than a week later Russell made a two-day trip to Ligaya. Because I was so sure he would be meeting his first Batangan, I could hardly wait for his return.

Arriving home, he first gave Ricky his welcome hug, and then without a word pulled a sheet of notes from his pack. His eyes were shining as he handed it to me.

"Batangan words and phrases!" I said in admiration, trying to read the phonetic script. Then I added, "The first time any Batangan has ever had his language written down! Tell me *all* the details."

He had arrived in Ligaya after lunch, warmly welcomed by his new friends, the Santos family. During the rainy afternoon, he had entertained them with Tagalog Gospel Recording records. Then when the rain let up, he gave out gospel tracts to each home.

At 4:30 the next morning the youngest daughter began cooking the rice. Even before he ate, Russell's host went to the Ilocano section of the *barrio* to find the promised guide. After breakfast the young farmer arrived to take Russell to the Batangan.

The two of them hiked for about an hour along the dikes with the heavy heads of rice brushing their clothes, then up over hills covered with bamboo thickets and through several small streams. After passing the guide's farm house, they began to hear voices ahead of them on the trail.

"It's the Batangan," the farmer told Russell. "We're not very far from their houses." He went on ahead to meet them while Russell waited breathlessly.

Suddenly breaking through the overgrown trail, seven Batangan men appeared. It was Russell's very first sight of these much-prayed-for people, and their first sight of an *Americano*! While his guide spoke reassuringly to them in Tagalog, Russell stood motionless lest he frighten them into running away.

Unhampered by excess clothing, although two of them had added T-shirts to the traditional G-strings, they all carried *bolos* hanging from a waist-cord. One was smoking a tiny clay pipe, while another was carrying glowing embers in a small four-inch green-leaf cone. Responding to the farmer's persuasion, they reluctantly consented to return home, taking Russell and his guide with them.

"They were just on their way to the Mongpong River to catch wild pigs," the guide explained to Russell.

The leader's home was a simple palm-leaf shelter, walled on two sides, with a sagging bamboo floor eighteen inches above the ground. No other houses could be seen. While his wife squatted low over the ground-level cooking fire at the back, trying to be invisible, the leader began to wipe off a place on the smudgy floor for Russell and his guide to sit.

Then he relaxed in his tiny woven rattan hammock while his six men arranged themselves against the back wall, as far from Russell as possible, ready to push aside the palm leaves and escape at the first false move.

Unobtrusively removing his paper and pencil

from the small canvas shoulder bag, Russell began quietly to ask in Tagalog for Batangan words and expressions, or to point to objects if his Tagalog was not understood. As the leader, covered with a whitish scaley skin condition, answered each query carefully, Russell wrote down his words. While they talked, Russell became aware that over in the dark corner was a young man, perhaps the leader's son, with a large sore on his lower leg. But he kept on writing.

After an hour of concentration, Russell casually asked, "Has he had that sore very long?"

"*Ken, sama,*" he replied in Batangan. "Oh yes, friend. He can't even walk now."

If only I had some medicine for him, Russell thought to himself.

But out loud he asked, "*Sama*, how many people are living in this area?"

"Well, *Sama*, we are about twenty here, and many others are living a day's journey away."

Feeling he had quieted their fears of him as a total stranger, Russell took a small brightly-colored Wordless Book from his pack, and turned to the men. Quickly they drew back, obviously very much afraid of the booklet. He waited a moment, then gently went ahead with his explanation in Tagalog.

"This black page is the color of soot and dirt, and it has a special meaning. Every page in this booklet has a meaning. This one means that everyone has sin. We have all done things that are wrong. God says we are not clean."

He paused, realizing by their questioning stares that they understood nothing he had said. Then the leader calmly began to explain to his men, but his Batangan was too fast for Russell to write down the words. He only hoped the meaning came through. When he was finished, Russell went on to the next page.

"This red page is the color of blood. God says that the only way we can get rid of our sins is that a sacrifice be made." Russell didn't realize it then, but the Batangan knew all about animal sacrifices to atone for displeasing the evil spirits. "God's son, Jesus Christ, died for us. He was the sacrifice so that we could get rid of our sins."

Again the leader gave an explanation in Batangan to those listening. But again it was too fast and too involved for Russell to take notes.

"If we ask God to take away our sins, and if we believe what He says, He will take them away, and we can be clean and white inside, like this page." And again the leader's words followed Russell's.

After the interpretation of the blue page, Russell handed the booklet to his host, who did not seem to fear it. Noting that he carefully placed it between the palm-leaf shingles of the roof, Russell silently prayed that he would understand this message, and that soon he would truly believe.

Stiffly getting up from his two hours on the floor, and stooping over to avoid the low slanted roof, Russell made his way to the edge of the floor and walked down the pole to the ground.

Then trying out his newly-acquired Batangan, he carefully pronounced "*Glo kwan*. I am going now," hoping that this traditional goodbye phrase would please them. For they had certainly pleased and thrilled him. To think that after almost a year of searching he had seen the Batangan and was actually writing down their words!

When he had finished telling me the whole story, we went over the word list together and then he carefully put it on top of his desk.

The next morning, going to his desk for the list so he could record each word on a separate slip to begin a Batangan dictionary file, Russell was mystified that it wasn't there. "Hon, have you seen my word list?" he called to me.

"The one you showed me last night? You put it on your desk," I said from the bedroom where I was helping Ricky dress.

"But it isn't there!" Tension and disappointment were in his voice. And although he searched in the desk, under the desk, out the window, under the house, and over by the fence, he never found it.

Keenly feeling the loss, Russell was more determined than ever to make one more quick trip to see the Batangan before we had to leave for Manila for our baby's birth.

"I guess I'll just go directly to the Ilocano's home, to see if he'll go with me," he told me the night before. "I could go alone, but maybe the Batangan wouldn't be so frightened if I'm with someone they know."

It was dark when he left, and dark when he returned. Although exhausted, he looked happy enough. At the supper table he told me about his day.

He had arrived at the Ilocano farmer's home just after lunch. When they got to Pangalkagan the men and their leader, named Ilmidio by his lowland friends, were pounding their newly-harvested rice. Russell approached them, repeating the usual Batangan greeting, "*Lag kalimu. Lag lagyu.* Don't be afraid. Don't run away." Their interested glances showed pleasure.

In the two hours with them, Russell was more than able to make up for his losses, filling his notebook with new words and expressions. But no women appeared except the leader's wife, which suggested that they were still too fearful.

When Russell asked about the young man with the ulcer on his leg, Ilmidio told him that now he had a sore under one arm and on his chest, and that he was very ill. How much Russell would have liked to help him, but he had little knowledge and no medicine.

Because we needed to determine exactly where we should permanently locate, Russell decided that while Ricky and I were in Manila after the baby's birth he would visit the coastal *barrios* south of Ligaya. Perhaps from these, other groups of Batangan could be reached. It was our tribal workers' policy to locate where a welcome to the gospel was evident, and we were not sure if Pangalkagan was that place or if there were other Batangan more eager and ready for our message.

Together with Alex, a believer from Oriental Mindoro, Russell went along the coast handing out tracts with a word of witness to almost every home, from Ligaya south to Calintaan. At the same time they asked for information about the Batangan.

The interior areas of three rivers were also explored as far as the last lowland settlements, often cattle ranches. Where they did not see the Batangan, they sought information that was first-hand and authentic. The Batangan homes were expertly hidden in the jungle interior and they never did find any, even though they met several fearful Batangan on the lowland farms.

Finally Russell concluded that the Batangan were more accessible from Ligaya than from any other coastal *barrio*. We realized also that a beginning had already been made in Pangalkagan, where Ilmidio seemed to know enough Tagalog to help in the initial stages of language learning.

We returned to Sablayan from Manila in January 1956 with bundles, boxes, shopping bags, two-year-old Ricky and baby Becky, much to the delight of Digo's family and all our neighbors. But we had to tell them our time in Sablayan would be short, for we would soon be moving to Ligaya.

A few days earlier I had written to Mother and Daddy that sometimes I was so discouraged that I wished I were home where we could live a normal, happy life with conveniences and comforts. But that first evening back in Sablayan Ricky set the right tone. As we sat down to eat, he repeated after us his usual "Dear Lord Jesus, Thank you for this nice supper." But then, instead of saying "In Jesus name, Amen," he began to add, "And thank you for Mama, and Daddy, and Becky, and spoons, and plates, and glasses, and..."

I glanced up to see if he was being funny, but he was dead serious, something that was hard for Russell and me to be about then! "...and for food, and rice, and eggs, and ...." When he finally got to the "Amen," we realized that he had captured our feelings of thankfulness, too, for all the Lord was doing for us.

The following week Russell visited Ligaya and

was able to rent a suitable, sturdy new wooden house, in that *barrio* of fifty homes. So we began packing to be ready for the Barge, an old World War II Landing Craft, that left Sablayan each Saturday for *barrios* to the south.

But that week the old Barge did not make the trip. The *San Nicholas*, a smaller motor-*bangka*, arrived on Thursday, but again we were terribly disappointed for they refused to take us.

Finally the following Friday, when we heard the distinctive sound of a motor-*bangka* docking in the river, Russell rushed down to find that the *Dos Commadres* was quite willing to take us the next morning before daybreak. That evening we hastily stuffed our last-minute things into woven palm-leaf bags and cardboard boxes, and went down to watch the loading of our furniture, household goods, personal belongings, and food supplies. Then the squeeze came as we all, including Ricky and baby Becky, attempted to sleep on the boat that night.

But we were rewarded, for it took just over an hour to get to Ligaya, and at that very early hour the sea was like glass. Everything we owned arrived dry, and was piled up on the pebble-covered beach, while Russell went into the village to find a water-buffalo cart.

"Guess what?" Russell said, looking rather weary as he returned alone. "Ligaya doesn't even have any *carabao* carts. Just the tiny sleds, and they can only take about two footlockers at a time!"

"Did you find someone to help us?" I asked.

"The trouble is all the *carabaos* are out in the fields working," was his discouraging reply.

As we watched Ricky under his sun hat happily

playing with the fallen palm fronds and stones on the beach, and kept an eye on Becky to see that the umbrella I was holding kept her from the sun's burning rays, we asked the Lord to help us get to the house.

Suddenly, breaking through the trail down the beach was a *carabao* hauling a sled piled with sacks of rice. The driver then began to stack them on the beach, waiting, no doubt, for the arrival of a boat. Immediately Russell headed in his direction, and soon arrangements were made for him to take our things back to the *barrio* on his return trips to get more sacks of rice.

It was very late when the last load safely arrived at our new home. The next day the owners continued to move their things out of the house while we arranged ours inside.

On Monday several women stopped to talk as I was squatting down vigorously soaping our huge pile of laundry on the bamboo-pole floor of our open back porch.

"Did you hear the news?" they wanted to know.

"What news is that?" I asked them.

"The motor-*bangka* called the *San Nicholas* sank last night. Have you heard of that boat?"

Had I heard of that boat? It was the very one we had begged to take us to Ligaya, and had felt so bitter about when they refused!

I'm not sure how much she understood of my explanation of the way God had saved us from being on that boat, but I know I could hardly wait to go inside and share the news with Russell, who was busy making kitchen cupboards from the wooden boxes that had contained our food supplies.

Chapter 4

SUSPICIOUS

Each morning at 5:30 Russell left our little Ligaya home and followed the cow-path trails to the foothills to visit the Batangan. On the first trip from our new home to Pangalkagan in March, he asked the Ilocano farmer to go with him again, to be sure the Batangan would not be afraid.

That morning after he left, I not only did my shopping at our door, buying an egg, a squash, and some bananas that were brought by the house, but I was also kept busy with many curious visitors who listened to the phonograph, played with the children, chatted with me, and gladly took the Tagalog gospel tracts I gave them as they left.

We had finished our lunch, and baby Becky was cooing a "lullaby" to Ricky who was fast asleep. The Wham! Wham! Wham! of the wooden paddle that spanks the clothes clean was coming from the neighbor's back yard. Across the street wood shavings were collecting under the house as a new boat rudder was being made, and I was waiting for the teakettle to boil so I could wash the dishes. Just then Russell walked in the door, drenched with sweat, hungry and thirsty.

"Well, how'd you do?" I asked, handing him a glass of Kool-aid.

"I didn't get lost, anyway, even coming home by myself. Takes about an hour to get there, and the trail wasn't bad at all. Really dry right now."

"What's it like after you get past the rice paddies just outside the *barrio*?" I wanted to know.

"There's a stretch of grasslands, about shoulder high and really wet first thing in the morning. I got soaked! It's this cogon grass that's used for our thatched roof. Then it's jungly, partly bamboo thickets and partly tangled undergrowth, with some streams to cross. But they're really small now that it's dry season. Then the last part is a matter of finding the tiny little trails to where their house is hidden."

"Who'd you see?" I wondered if the women were bold enough to come around.

"Just the leader and his wife. Oh, and a glimpse of a young girl. They sure act suspicious of me, like they really can't figure out what I'm up to."

"Whatever are they suspicious of? You've never done anything to scare them," I commented defensively.

"I know," he sighed. "And when I'm up there, I just relax in the doorway with my notebook on my knees. I don't even try to go inside. Maybe in time they'll get used to me," he added wistfully.

"Were they much help on the language?" This was especially important to me, because while Becky was so small I wasn't able to go with Russell, But he could share with me the things he had learned.

"Well, yes, but Ilmidio doesn't know as much Tagalog as I thought. I really wonder now if he understood that Wordless Book message. Anyway, besides the words and phrases I asked for, I was able to write down some expressions they used between themselves, even though I'm not sure of all the meanings. But it's a start."

The second time Russell went by himself, anxious to see if he would be well received. Ilmidio seemed about the same, but no one else came around. He felt that even Ilmidio wasn't really trusting him.

Thinking that the phonograph would make a pleasant diversion, he took it with him the following day, although he realized that Ilmidio might not understand the Tagalog. But no one was home.

This happened again the next day, and I wondered if they were trying to avoid him. But Russell felt they were either busy in their own distant fields or were working for some lowland farmer. He decided to use this time to explore the foothills for other groups of Batangan.

With his ever-present bundle of tracts, he set off each morning at 5:30 returning in the late afternoon. It was slow and frustrating. At one lowland farm he saw four Batangan he had not met before. Carefully keeping their distance, they wouldn't answer his questions or even look in his direction. On another day he met a more friendly group, but they were leaving for their mountain homes so had no time. When he found several men who were persuaded to help him with a word list, they quickly became bored because they didn't understand much Tagalog.

Encouragement came when Russell met "Berto" (his lowland name) on the trail. He wasn't afraid to talk, and appeared to understand some Tagalog, giving Russell many Batangan words and phrases and showing a real interest in the message. But his home was in distant Buswangan, too far away to be of permanent help.

At Pangalkagan their Tagalog was generally very poor, and ours was only one stage better, so it was hard to make God's wonderful plan of salvation clear to them. But to learn their language we needed someone who was willing to spend time regularly with us. Perhaps if Ilmidio and his people weren't so suspicious, they would be willing. Why did he doubt us, and how could we show him we were completely trustworthy?

In the lowlands, however, Ligaya was living up to its name, Joy Village. The people were friendly and helpful, especially the Santos family, and we loved our little thatch-roofed home sitting five feet off the ground on those huge sturdy posts. Actually it was two tiny houses put together with a short, wide walkway between.

The wooden front house contained a bedroom just big enough for our three beds, and a tiny *sala* exactly right for the thirty who attended our Sunday School. The adults sat on the four newly-painted black and red footlockers lining two of the walls, while the children used the floor space between the desk by the window and the book and clothes cupboards in the corners. Through the large window openings that could be covered by nipa-palm shutters when it rained, we had a brisk breeze from the ocean to relieve the intense heat of the day, and a delightfully cool one from the mountains for comfortable sleeping at night.

The wide plank floors, which I kept waxed and polished, made it possible for us to use the space under the house. Here Russell put up clothes lines for the coming rainy days, and built Ricky a sandbox which attracted all the welcome neighborhood children as well as all the unwelcome wandering pigs!

The small back house was our kitchen with walls and roof of nipa-palm shingles. Here a traditional bamboo slat floor had the advantage of being cool as well as easy to clean. Spilled milk just ran down to the ground between the narrow floor slats which then could easily be washed off, and no dustpan was needed when sweeping! It was not so easy, however, to recover dropped spoons that slipped between the cracks or to reclaim a sack of spilled rice!

One evening as I looked at the calendar, I realized that Becky should have her shots soon. I told Russell, "I can't bear the thought of taking her all the way to Manila, or even as far as Mamburao on one of those motor-*bangkas*, though I don't suppose the medicine is available there anyway."

"Maybe we ought to have one of our OMF nurses visit us," he said, half teasing. Then more seriously, "If one of our tribal nurses like Margrit could come, she'd probably be a real help medically to the Batangan. By this time she must have had plenty of experience with tribal illnesses."

So we wrote our letter and weeks later were delighted with the answer. Margrit would welcome a quiet time for Tagalog study away from her busy station among the Iraya, and an opportunity to use her medical knowledge for the Batangan. But she couldn't come until after our annual OMF conference in May.

In the meantime, Ilmidio returned to Pangalkagan after being away for eight long weeks. He was still unwilling to have Russell know the location of the other Batangan homes, although he did take him to his own *kaingin* fields on the Mongpong River. Russell now would know where to find him when he wasn't at Pangalkagan. If only they would really trust us, the progress in teaching them about the Lord, as well as in studying their language, could go so much faster. And the women could become involved too.

We came back from our annual missionary conference and vacation with a tiny three-cubic-foot kerosene refrigerator, a DZAS "Portable Missionary" radio and Margrit. All three were to prove their value in the coming months.

Margrit's Tagalog language teacher was Ruperta Santos, a delightful arrangement for all of us. And her bedroom was the curtained-off end of the kitchen. The landlord, seeing we had a special visitor, made some promised improvements, too. The pump was lowered, giving more water with each push of the handle. A tiny shower room was built on the back porch. A new cogon grass roof was promised for the kitchen. And the railing was finished around the front porch. School children coming to play the phonograph could be out there with no threat that they or Ricky would fall off.

But the most exciting change was that Margrit had volunteered to give a whole day of her precious language study time to care for Ricky and Becky, so I could go with Russell to the hills!

At the end of that week Russell made the two-hour hike to visit Ilmidio at his *kaingin* on the Mongpong River. Not only was he able to spend several hours getting new expressions and practicing old ones, but he also arranged for me to go back there with him on Tuesday to get language help, and

Margrit on Saturday to give medical help.

Monday night I was so excited that I could hardly get to sleep, but at 4:30 the next morning we were jolted out of bed by the relentless alarm clock. In the dim light of our small kerosene lamp, we ate breakfast. We had put on our oldest clothes, for the mud and rivers are merciless on them, and we wore our tennis shoes with heavy sox. In the shoulder bag were Tagalog and Ilocano tracts, our little first aid kit, some hard candies, notebooks and pencils and our canteen.

The dawn was bright and clear, promising another hot day. Our two hours' trek was mainly through grasslands, wet with the morning dew and sharp enough to cut our legs. Two days of dry weather had left the trail in relatively good condition with deep, thick mud in only a few places, and rivers and streams that were only ankle or knee deep.

Arriving at Ilmidio's palm-leaf house, and trying to get comfortable sitting on the uneven pole floor, I noticed a leech crawling on my ankle. Quickly Russell got rid of it before it could fill itself at my expense. As I was beginning to feel very itchy from my wet clothes and tired from the hike, I kept changing positions to ease my aches, when suddenly Ilmidio began to speak.

I sat stock still. I was hearing, for the first time, a Batangan speaking his own language. And I was seeing, for the first time, a Batangan and his wife. His body was whitish with a scaley skin condition, and his wife had several large sores on her legs. Immediately I thought what a wonderful place heaven would be for them, with no sores, no sickness, no tears, no dying. If only we can make the message of

God's love and salvation clear!

Russell guided the conversation, constantly taking notes, and by the end of our visit even I had several pages of what I hoped were accurately recorded Batangan words. As we told them goodbye, Ilmidio said that on Saturday Margrit and Russell should come to his home in Pangalkagan. Glad that they wouldn't need to hike all the way to the Mongpong River *kaingin*, neither of us even gave a thought to the reason for the new arrangements nor to its possible results.

On Saturday, armed with penicillin, sulfaguanadine, malaria tablets, and other medicines, Margrit and Russell took the hour-and-a-half hike to Pangalkagan. When they returned, Russell announced with his teasing grin, "I could have brought home two chickens for you!"

"Did they want to sell them?" I asked.

"No, Ilmidio actually brought them to us as a gift. For Margrit's medical help," he explained.

"You must have really felt good about that!" I said appreciatively.

"But it was too much pay for what little we did. Even one chicken would have been too much," he commented. Then he added brightly, "And guess what! All the wives and daughters were there!"

They had finally emerged from their jungle homes! It was such good news I could hardly believe it.

"At first I thought they came for medicine," Russell went on, "but none of them were sick. And they didn't really act frightened or suspicious of me, either." And then he told me his conclusion.

When Ilmidio saw that Russell truly had a wife

and then told the other men about me, they knew that he would not be wanting to take their wives or daughters as other Batangan and outsiders had done. Margrit's baby-sitting, as well as her medical help, had allayed their suspicion, answering our prayers! And it all began from a needed injection!

Three days later down in Ligaya the new grass roof was put on our kitchen. "Making it," Margrit said, "like sleeping in a hay loft!" And it was just in time. For if the old termite-eaten roof poles and thatch had not been replaced, they would have been blown off just a week later when the first typhoon of the 1956 season crossed Mindoro.

At that time we were especially thankful for the DZAS radio which not only broadcast messages and Bible studies that we and our neighbors could enjoy, but also gave weather bulletins and storm warnings.

Six more typhoons followed in quick succession, keeping us isolated in the Ligaya area for the next two and a half months with uncrossable rivers and waves so huge that no boats could land. During that time we had plenty of activity as well as anxiety.

From one of the occasional trips to the hills which were possible between typhoons, Margrit and Russell returned with new excitement. They had been taken, for the first time ever, to three of the well-hidden jungle homes where Margrit gave medical help and Russell tried to talk to the families about the Lord. The Batangan were really beginning to trust us!

"And it's a wonder they do!" Russell had said with a mischievous grin after one of his trips. "Remember that bottle of chalky diarrhea medicine I gave them for their children? When I went up the next time, they asked for more, indicating it had been very effective. And then I saw the children with their thickly coated white tummies!"

A few weeks later during another lull between storms, Margrit again took care of Ricky and Becky so I could have another "language lesson" in the hills. This time Russell had compiled a long list of useful Batangan questions which I had been learning, and now I wanted to hear the people say them so I could mimic their pronunciation.

On the trail we met the leader and several other men just leaving to work in the lowlands. As they looked at me with friendly curiosity, the leader told us we would find his wife at home. Arriving at his house, we greeted his wife in our practiced Batangan, and then sat on the floor and began looking over our word lists. I started by asking the leaders's wife in Batangan to repeat for me the words, *Dada dalan*, which means "Where is the trail?"

Instead of repeating the expression so I could hear it spoken, she proceeded to answer the question, launching into a long and involved explanation that I couldn't even begin to follow. It was the same with every one of the expressions, though some of the answers were more concise. "Where is the house?" "Where is my *bolo*?" "What is this?" "Who is with you?" So I never did hear any of the questions repeated in Batangan. But I wrote down enough answers!

When I asked in Tagalog the word for "love" and "God loves all men" the leader's wife looked blank, for she didn't know the word. How could we tell them of God's great love and His wonderful salvation, with no written language and almost all monolingual tribespeople? We were thankful for Ilmidio's knowledge of Tagalog, although we were beginning to realize that it, too, was severely limited.

When we arrived back in Ligaya that afternoon my neck was fiery and itching, and even a good hot shower didn't help. Russell took one look and with a comforting hand on my shoulder sadly informed me, "Looks to me like you got into some *lipa*." The "nettles" of the Philippines! That night my calamine-lotioned neck persisted in itching and burning, and when I did get to sleep, Becky would fuss restlessly, for she seemed to be coming down with some kind of diarrhea.

We knew it was only the Lord that had kept our children well, for they were exposed to so many things. Ricky playing outside with the other children, surrounded by the many wandering animals, often came in with fleas or bites. And any scratch got infected so easily.

Nine-month-old Becky in her playpen upstairs always had several children who delighted in watching her constant exuberant antics, playing with her and talking to her. Sometimes during those rare moments when she was relatively still and my back was turned, they would gently put their fingers in her mouth to see how many teeth she had!

When her diarrhea began, we were glad Margrit was with us. She was a nurse and could advise us, as there was no medical help in Ligaya. First we gave Becky one of our diarrhea medicines for children, and eliminated some of her solid foods. When she didn't get any better, we changed to another diarrhea medicine and eliminated all solids. But her diarrhea and weight loss continued, and she became pale and listless. Because of the series of typhoons we were having, there was no way to get to a pharmacy or take her to a doctor. We simply continued praying, comforted by the knowledge that others at home were praying too.

At the end of the second week of Becky's illness, the rain stopped for a few hours, so Russell and Margrit took another trip to the hills. When they returned, Russell went straight to the baby crib, looking down on quiet Becky in sad silence. With a deep sigh, he told me of their experience that morning.

As they had passed Dampitan's, the last lowland home on the trail to Pangalkagan, they heard him calling out, "Mr Reed! Mr Reed! There are some Batangan here at our house!" He was standing in the doorway motioning to Margrit and Russell.

As they left the trail, Dampitan urged them to come into his house, even though the Batangan were standing outside. Adjusting to the dim interior, Russell could hear a strange sound like a pig breathing heavily under the floor. And then he saw the source of the noise.

Little three-year-old Washington was dying. Margrit immediately recognized the "death rattle." Russell had never heard it before. The distraught parents asked for medicine, and although Margrit knew it was too late, she felt she could not refuse this comfort to the parents. Gently she explained that it might not help their little son.

As they continued on their way to Ilmidio's, Russell couldn't get his mind off Becky. With no medical help here, how many children die! It was hard to concentrate on his language learning, for he was anxious now to return home.

And so he looked down at Becky, finding her condition just the same. No spark. No activity. Just lying there.

Early the next morning I was drawn into Dampitan's tragedy when Washington's two small cousins came to the house to ask for colored paper for the little casket. As I searched for something suitable, my eyes constantly returned to the crib where Becky lay.

About noon the church bell began its dull bong-bong-bong, bong-bong-bong. Soon the hasty, disorderly procession was making its muddy way to the graveyard located about fifteen minutes out of the *barrio*. The little casket, lovingly decorated with the gift-wrap and tissue paper, was carried between two men leading the way, while others came behind with the shovels, followed by the grieving family and friends.

After three weeks of tenderly caring and constantly hoping, we knew Becky could not last much longer. Continuing to hold down liquids, she wasn't completely dehydrated, but she was thin and lifeless. As we battled the terrible depression, Russell was wondering what he could use to make the tiny casket.

At the beginning of her fourth week of illness, the Lord put the thought in our minds of trying the Terramycin pediatric drops which we had on hand, but hadn't considered for diarrhea. We could hardly believe her immediate improvement, and then her slow steady progress back to health! What thanksgiving to the Lord! We felt that she, like Ricky two years before, had been snatched from death.

Later my mother wrote me that one night she had been awakened, as if someone had roused her, with an urgent need to pray for Becky. Heavily burdened, she had pled with the Lord to take care of her tiny granddaughter, though she had no idea of anything that could be wrong. After praying, she felt completely at peace and went back to sleep. The next morning she shared her burden with Daddy and they both felt Becky must have been in real danger. It was weeks after that that our typhoon-delayed letter reached her telling of Becky's near-fatal illness just at that time.

During these days of our isolation, when the weather was clear, Margrit would study at the beach, with the waves, normally non-existent, breaking noisily on the shore because of the typhoons. After she had been with us for about six weeks, she finished her studying and took the language exam that she had come to "quiet Ligaya" to complete. But it was a number of weeks later before the sea became its usual lake-calmness allowing boats to land and pick up passengers, and she was able to return to her station among the Eastern Iraya Mangyan.

Returning from the hills one afternoon, Russell brought back the news that old Fufuina ("Grandmother") had died. Driven by their wretched fear of the ghost of the recent dead, everyone abandoned the village, including her large, new house which would later be burned. Off into the jungly interior they fled, to flimsy field houses that had to be repaired to be made liveable. Sadly we realized that although their suspicion of us was gone, they had not yet understood our message of God's love and care for them, and so had not yet learned to trust Him.

Even Berto from far-away Buswangan. He had been so unafraid, so interested and seemingly able to understand when Russell, months before, had talked to him in Tagalog on one of his trips. But later we heard that when his wife and new-born infant died, in desperate panic he deserted his house and fled to the beach to hide, as far away from the death scene as possible. If only he could have experienced the comfort God can give!

Surprisingly, encouragement came to us through old Fufuama ("Grandpa") whom we thought could hardly hear and surely did not understand. "I know that even if men are sinners," he told Russell one day, "if they will only believe in Jesus they can have life without end."

But no one else was as bold as he, for the Batangan follow their leaders, and Ilmidio did not believe our message. They no longer feared us, but we saw how they lived in constant fear of ghosts and evil spirits. The only answer was for us to have a house right with them, to learn their language well, so they could clearly understand our teaching and put their trust in the Lord.

We knew that because of deaths and clearing new fields, frequent moving was their way of life. If we pushed ahead too quickly, before they welcomed the idea of our living among them, they would just quietly disappear, putting together new palm-leaf houses at another location in the jungle. How could we persuade them to allow us to live in their village?

While patiently waiting God's timing for us to have a house among the Batangan, we basked in the warmth of their new friendship, snatching at every opportunity to increase our language ability. When Ilmidio suddenly appeared at our door in Ligaya, Russell was mystified, but I was elated. *Someone to help me with Batangan*, I thought.

After talking to Russell and having a good look round, he seemed happy to teach me. In one hour of fierce concentration I added 136 new words to my vocabulary list!

"I wonder why he came?" I asked Russell later.

"I don't know. He didn't ask for medicine, or give me any special news."

"He sure had a good look at everything, including the kids! I wish we could have asked him about a house for us," I said longingly.

"I think you're going too fast," he answered cautiously. "It might seem like we're trying to push him. But I still can't figure out why he came."

One morning two months later the mystery deepened. Russell, dripping with sweat and completely exhausted, had returned surprisingly early from one of his daily visits to Pangalkagan. When he got his breath, he asked, "Has Ilmidio been here?"

"I haven't seen him," I told him.

"Well, when I arrived in the hills, he wasn't there," Russell began to explain. "I thought he was probably pig hunting or fishing or visiting some other area now that the weather is drier. The trouble is, when he's not there I don't learn much Batangan. Anyway, his wife Nati, as the Tagalogs call her, told me he had gone to the *barrio* to see me!"

"He hasn't shown up yet," I said unnecessarily.

"That's good. Because I stayed for a while trying to get some new words. When I left I really made a run for home, hoping I wouldn't miss him." Glancing at his watch he added, "It only took me 45 minutes!"

After lunch, Ilmidio appeared with three Batangan Russell had never met. It was hard to believe how unafraid they were. Talking freely in Batangan, they asked to hear the phonograph and listened to record after record, all in Tagalog, though we were sure they understood very little. Then before they left, the one with the festering sores asked for medicine, which we were delighted to give.

"Who are they, and where are they from?" I asked Russell.

"They didn't say, and I didn't feel I should ask. I'd guess from somewhere in the interior above Pangalkagan," he said.

Two days later Russell learned the heart-warming answer to the mystery. At Ilmidio's he had seen the three men again, and Ilmidio had told him, "They want you to be the government agent for the Batangan."

"Oh, Hon," I said enthusiastically when he told me, "What a privilege! They must really trust you."

"I had to tell them that the government wouldn't

allow it since I'm not a Filipino," he said resignedly. "But think of the progress this shows since my first visit over a year ago, when fear could be seen in every move they made!"

"Maybe we can ask about a house now!" I suggested.

"Maybe," he said, a bit uncertain. "But Ilmidio still won't show me the trail to Pusug. There must be at least thirty people there, and maybe another hundred in the surrounding area. Guess he doesn't want to be responsible for bringing me to homes of Batangan who want to remain hidden."

Ilmidio did suggest a lowland farmer who knew the way. But he proved unwilling, saying there were too many leeches on those jungle trails, which Russell knew to be only too true!

Near their houses one day, he discovered footprints in the sand coming from the thick wall of brush beside the stream. Following them back into the jungle, he could see a trail going in the direction of Pusug. At Ilmidio's he learned that some Batangan had come from Pusug the day before, so he knew that was the trail.

Two days later he followed it for three hours, and arrived at two houses where he was actually welcomed, unheard of among interior Batangan. They even told him there were six more houses in the area, information they normally do not share. Although he had never been there before, the men were friendly because they had met him months ago at Ilmidio's house! As Russell wrote home, "God's hand can be seen in each advance."

To learn more about the interior Batangan, Russell

planned a trip with OMFer Colin Tweddell and Pastor Tolentino. With Mrs Tweddell, they arrived in Ligaya on a Saturday. Sunday the pastor gave a welcome Tagalog message for the eight adults and 24 children gathered in our sala, and then the following day the men left for a six-day trip.

When they came back Russell wanted to hike up to Pangalkagan and I was thrilled to be able to go with him, for the Tweddells had volunteered to care for the children. Only a few of the Bantangan were at home but still I filled several pages of my notebook. Old Grandpa Fufuama and Russell talked at length, and I marveled how fluent he was. Except for the expression, "What is this?" I was still almost completely tongue-tied.

After that visit the men left again, this time to explore the Batangan area south of Ligaya, and then cross the mountains to Oriental Mindoro.

Just a few days after they returned and our guests had left for Mamburao, we saw three Batangan shyly approaching our house accompanied by one of the farm women. As she told us their lowland names and then left, I glanced at Karlus' face covered with sores and knew why they had come. But my interest was centered on Kabilugan's tiny wife.

While Russell got the medicine, I boldly sat down beside her and began at once using the few Batangan expressions I knew. But she hid her face permanently behind her husband's back.

Oh, I thought, *If only I could speak this language. I'm sure we could be friends!*

As I watched Russell's calm approach and quiet words my eyes were suddenly opened. His characteristic gentleness was just like theirs, making me realize that God had specially equipped and chosen him for this particular work. My natural enthusiasm kept us encouraged, but I knew I must temper my approach to these timid and cautious people.

Kabilugan and Karlus listened carefully to Russell and felt free to talk, but as soon as the medicine was given, they quietly left the house and disappeared on the path into the interior. Russell turned to me, "Kabilugan is the first Batangan that any of our missionaries had ever met. Colin Tweddell saw him in a small *barrio* not far from here almost two years ago! And he is from Pusug. How I'd like to reach that village for the Lord!" And then he added thoughtfully, "But even if we had a welcome there, we don't know Batangan well enough to make the gospel clear. I guess we really need that house in Pangalkagan."

The very next day he set off for Pangalkagan, thinking of asking Ilmidio about a house for us near theirs. But no one was there. He just retraced his steps home again.

Every morning Russell faithfully plodded to the hills. Sometimes the Batangan were at home and sometimes they were not. But Ilmidio didn't appear. Then one day Russell walked in the door with news.

"Ilmidio sure doesn't look very good," he said, setting down his sweat-soaked shoulder bag. "I wonder what's wrong with him? And I couldn't get anyone enthused about building a house for us up there."

"I wonder if I'll ever get a chance to learn this language?" I sighed.

"I think you will. Do you remember the one they called Makisig? I noticed his old abandoned house sometime ago, so I suggested they let us stay there. And guess what?" he teased.

"They'll let us!" I was losing my dejection now, and began wondering what it would be like living in the hills.

"They'll let us, and I think it'll be ok. Just for four or five days at a time. That's about all the food I'd be able to carry up there anyway," was his practical comment.

"What's the roof like?" I asked, thinking of the children.

"Seems pretty good. Those buri-palm leaves are fairly recent. But there are no walls. And the floor is just large bamboo poles tied together as close as the joints allow," he trailed off, thinking.

"Sleeping on a floor like that'd take some getting used to! Even with our thick sleeping bag." I commented.

"I know. And besides, it's filthy. Cooked sweet potatoes have been mashed into it and people have spit through it... Maybe I could go up a few days early and make a split bamboo floor to go on top of the old one. We could use it for sleeping at night and for Becky to play on in the daytime. It'd keep her little feet from getting caught between those uneven bamboo poles."

To make the flooring, he had to chop down the bamboo, split the lengths into eight strips, lay them close together, and weave rattan ties over and under them securing them at each end. "And I made a cute little bamboo fence around the new flooring," he told me enthusiastically, "to keep Becky from crawling onto the other part."

"How neat!" I said in admiration. Then, handing

him the list I'd been making, I asked, "Could you look at this, Hon? It seems so long, but I've really tried to keep it simple."

"The day before we all go," he volunteered, "I'll take up a box with our sleeping bag, and some clothing and food, like the dried fruit and powdered milk. If I wrap it in heavy plastic, it should be ok."

Returning from that trip, he sadly reported, "I guess I cut the bamboo too green. It's all beginning to curl as it dries out."

"Oh, it'll be ok," I said lightly. "At least it's new and clean!"

To beat the intense heat of the day, we got up at 4:30, pleasing three-year-old Ricky who loved to eat breakfast by kerosene lamp. At first light Russell shouldered the heavily-filled pack, with Ricky proudly taking his place beside him, while I hugged fifteen-month-old Becky against my hip supported by a woven shoulder strap.

The hike took three hours, including all the candy and gum stops and the numerous sips from the canteen. Ricky proved to be a sturdy hiker, for even on the last half mile straight up the dry stream bed he doggedly continued climbing over the boulders until we got there.

Our new wall-less home, firmly planted against a bamboo thicket, with its picturesque palm-leaf roof and eighteen-inch-high floor looked beautiful, cool and inviting. The two neighboring families had evidently gone to their fields, but just the closeness of their houses was reassuring. I could hardly wait for my first Batangan conversation!

With Becky in her bamboo play pen and Ricky

resting on a big rock, I unpacked the large saucepan to boil some drinking water. Russell took the long bamboo water tube he had prepared the day before, and filled it at the little pool in the almost-dry stream bed.

After scouting out some wood, he built a fire on the ground in front of the shelter, balancing our big saucepan on three carefully selected stones. I began scrubbing the bamboo poles that had not been covered by his new flooring. In the quick-drying weather, I was soon able to unpack our clean clothes, for we were hot and sticky and longing for a cool bath, and to locate our lunch.

Our neighbors returned late. But because they carried their fire with them for the tiny clay pipes that even the children smoked, they soon had a blaze under their big black pot of sweet potatoes.

Everyone was friendly, including the children who came over to our shelter and shyly peeped in, so it was easy to visit. I mean we listened, wrote and tried to look intelligent when they spoke to us. Mangena, ("woman"), the widowed mother of four, brought us sweet potatoes in exchange for medicine and gave us the disturbing news that Ilmidio, whose house was across the valley, was ill. We had no medicine to relieve his suffering, and without him our teaching about the Lord would be severely limited and our language study would have to be monolingual.

That night on our slightly humping flooring all four of us slept together in the huge double sleeping bag with the big mosquito net tented over us. What a joy to wake up the next morning to the sounds of spoken Batangan! From our open palm-leaf home we could hear every word of our neighbors' conversation, even if we couldn't understand it. We would repeat each expression, try to write it down and note the circumstances. Sometimes Russell would recognize a word or two, or we would call across and the speaker would try to give a Tagalog word which hinted at the meaning.

After breakfast, Mangena perched on her stone doorstep, while I sat nearby on a mound of hard clay. My data board with the blue word list of two hundred nouns was balanced on my knees. As we began our struggles, for she knew almost no Tagalog, Ilmidio surprisingly arrived, disappearing into Grandpa Fufuama's old house next door. As I gave the Tagalog word, hoping Mangena would know it, he helped her by calling out the Batangan from inside the house. If neither of them knew it, I tried pointing to the object, for many were common words or parts of the body.

Becky, showing signs of getting a cold, was fussy, and Ricky was often in the bamboo enclosure trying to cheer her up. I quickly learned, "The little one is crying," and "The brother and sister are playing." I also heard, "The children are going to carry water and bathe." For although when we arrived the neighboring children looked like they hadn't bathed for weeks, they kept sparkling clean while we were there. Then about noon everyone left for the fields, to clear weeds, dig sweet potatoes, or plant new stems to get more produce.

The following day, Ilmidio did not come, and I was trying to get a list of two hundred verbs. I asked Mangena in Tagalog for the word meaning "bow the head," but, like all the other Tagalog words, she didn't recognize it. So I proceeded to bow my head, but then I wasn't sure if I got the word for nod, or bow. The next word, "bite", was easy to illustrate. Or did she give me "eat" instead? "Blow" wasn't too hard since I had learned the word for wind the day before, and when I put the two together, Mangena and her married daughter smiled broadly. Peals of laughter greeted the acting out of such verbs as cough, call a person, whistle, spit, smile, laugh, and blow the nose. And even more merriment when I illustrated the cat's meow, the cow's moo, the pig's grunt, and the dog's bark! Cheery friendliness surrounded me no matter how many times words had to repeated for my dull ears or slow pencil.

But then I was stuck! How could I illustrate invite, help, forget, think, remember, and a great many others? Since I couldn't act them out, I used the Tagalog, but found I was getting the same expression, "*kunasaful*", for a number of unrelated words. I called Russell over to help. He looked at my paper and a quiet grin spread across his face.

"That expression," he said with laughter in his eyes, "means 'I do not understand.'"

With the lesson over, I dug out the colorful Tagalog picture-tracts of the Lord's resurrection, wanting to give copies to everyone. Mangena's daughter hugged hers to herself, but the others did not seem to want the paper. I tried to explain the story in Tagalog, but no one could understand. And I could not tell it in Batangan.

I taught them the Tagalog song, "How precious is Jesus to me," explaining that the word *mahal* meant "precious." I knew they understood for I heard them singing it constantly. The next day when I asked them what *mahal* meant, they replied in Batangan, *Maori way*, or "evil." I was devastated. And then I remembered that "mahal" also means "very expensive," and for them, an inflated price is evil.

On our last evening while we were trying to marshal enough courage to ask if we could come back in another week, they told us, "We are all going to the Pusug area for two weeks to hunt for *nami* (wild yam)." We knew that it took a long time to find and dig that root, and then slice it thin and soak it in running stream water for several days until the poison was all washed out, so it could be cooked and eaten. But Russell's perceptive eyes had noticed evidences of spirit worship, like the bundle of nine sticks carefully tied with a vine and planted upright in the ground. With Ilmidio failing fast, he thought it likely that they would be performing more spirit rituals, and for that we knew we would not be welcome.

Thankful for their warm friendliness that was sending us home with full notebooks, we got up at 3 am on Saturday and after a sweet potato breakfast, left before six. By 9:15 we were home, with the children ready for another breakfast and their beds.

As we tucked them in, our hearts were heavy for our new friends in the hills. If only they would turn to the Savior who could free them from this bondage of worshipping the evil spirits! But we still lacked the language to tell them clearly.

Transcribing our notes, analyzing the expressions, putting new words in our dictionary file, and memorizing our material filled those two weeks while we impatiently waited to go again to the hills. Packages from home that Russell collected when he walked the sixteen miles to the post office in Sablayan delighted us. And we were encouraged by our Sunday meetings in Ligaya which had increased to 33 children and eleven adults. But our eyes, minds and hearts were focused on the Batangan.

When we arrived for our second stay in the hills, everyone was as friendly as before, and, although Ilmidio did not appear at all, we again had well-filled notebooks by the end of the week.

On our last day a heavy downpour made us slowly migrate toward the center of our shelter as the rain, splashing through our invisible walls, dampened the outer floor area. The roof was tight, but it was a real trick for Russell to keep the outdoor fire going that was cooking our sweet-potato stew. The rain stopped about dark, but the trees dripped the rest of the night. Russell's foresight in cooking our breakfast rice before we went to bed kept him from battling with the dripping foilage at our early rising hour.

Our pre-dawn start for home was wet and slippery, especially down that first steep bank into the stream bed where the mossy rocks felt well-greased. Russell carried Becky while I slithered along behind Ricky. Three hours later we safely arrived at our "Palace" in Ligaya. As Russell took Becky down from his shoulders, I noticed a scratch above her eye.

"A tiny sharp tree branch must have jabbed her," Russell said, gently examining the puncture wound. "Thank the Lord, it wasn't just an inch lower! It would have gone right into her eye."

We had been home in Ligaya only a few days when we suddenly heard "Batangan! Look! A Batangan couple is here!" Quickly we went to the porch, and saw Kabilugan and his little wife coming up the path outside our yard.

"*Sakboi*! Come up!" I called with deliberate gentleness.

Climbing our wooden stairs, they sat gingerly on the edge of the porch bench. We invited them inside, away from the neighbors' staring eyes, and brought them each a glass of water. They soon made themselves comfortable, squatting on the floor rather than sitting on the footlockers!

"*Nataw am fakailatun*," Russell asked them in Batangan. "What can we do for you?"

"*Karlus ke dailan dawdaw*," Kabilugan said quietly while staring at his feet. "Karlus is very very sick."

After Russell asked about his symptoms and went to the cupboard for medicine that might help, I slowly turned toward his tiny wife and said quietly in Batangan, "Have you come very far today?"

Frightened eyes suddenly looked into mine, and then darted away, as they pled with her husband for help. But she didn't hide behind his back this time!

"Yes, it was very far," was his friendly answer on her behalf. "We started early this morning."

After giving the medicine to Kabilugan, Russell switched to Tagalog, "What will happen to Karlus if he dies? Will he go to heaven?" We were glad Kabilugan could understand some Tagalog.

"I don't know," he said simply.

"God loves everyone," Russell explained, "and He wants everyone to enter heaven." He then explained God's gift of salvation, and that it was for all who truly trust in Jesus.

With eyes wide, Kabilugan told him, "That is just what we want. That is the very thing that we need!"

As far as we knew it was only the second time he had heard of the Savior. Russell tried to make clear what trusting Christ meant, only wishing he could explain it in Batangan.

As Kabilugan started to leave, he turned to Russell, "Do all the people here in the *barrio* believe in Christ? Have they all put their trust in Him?"

When he told him that they hadn't, he seemed at a loss to understand why they did not feel the need of a Savior and a way to heaven.

After they left, Russell remarked, "This is the first time I've ever seen the gospel given such an open welcome by any Batangan."

"Do you think we are seeing the 'first fruits' among them?" I asked. "Maybe the gospel will get into the tribe through Pusug instead of through Pangalkagan. Even though Ilmidio has been friendly, he's never really wanted to accept our message."

"But I wonder," Russell said thoughtfully. "Do you think Kabilugan really understood? Guess we'll never know until we're more fluent in their language."

On one of his daily trips to Pangalkagan, Russell decided to pass by our borrowed shelter and was startled to see it standing alone and forlorn, with the houses on either side of it cleaned out and deserted! Why had the people moved, and where had they gone?

As he went on toward Ilmidio's, he noticed one of the big woven-leaf sunshade capes slowly working its way across the field like some huge caterpiller, and knew Mangena was busy with her sweet potatoes. Crossing over to see her, he first talked about her work, and then casually asked, "Where are you living now?"

"Over there," was the noncommittal reply. He sensed she was ill at ease about the move, so he changed the subject.

"I'm just going to see Ilmidio," he told her, and was surprised when she answered, "Oh, no one is there."

"No one is there? Where are they? Where is Ilmidio?"

"Oh," she said almost too nonchalantly, "Maybe he is in Ligaya." When she saw Russell's incredulous look, she added, "Or maybe he is in Suriagao."

Suriagao? Russell knew that was far up in the center of Mindoro, so he began to suspect something was wrong. "When did you see him last?" he quietly asked.

"Oh, maybe a few weeks ago," she shrugged, continuing to uproot sweet potatoes with her long *bolo*.

After leaving her, he met some of the boys, but they couldn't tell him where Ilmidio was either. Then just before reaching Ilmidio's old house, he saw Nati. As he talked with her, she finally told him that her husband "had been taken."

"Dead!" I said, horrified when Russell told me. "He was still young. About 35, don't you think? Now Nati's a widow. And the people have no leader. And we needed his help. Will Makisig take his place?"

"I suppose so," Russell answered. "I wonder if he'll be open and friendly now that Ilmidio is dead? I didn't see him, but I told Nati that we wanted to stay again in the little shelter, and she didn't discourage me."

"How far away did they move?" I asked him.

"I found them across the valley in a well-hidden ravine," he said. "Those tiny, hastily-built houses sure blend right in with the forest growth, but I guess it's their only protection from outsiders now that Ilmidio is dead."

Arriving for another five-day stay, we found the roof of Mangena's house next door was being removed palm-leaf by palm-leaf to provide more roofing for the new homes. As we settled into our shelter, feeling very much alone, we decided that each day we would take turns making the twenty-minute walk to their new houses to visit them and study the language, so one of us would always be with the children. But before nightfall that arrival day, Makisig with his wife and young son had moved into Grandpa Fufuama's old house, right next to ours.

Feeling that Makisig knew some Tagalog, Russell asked him the next morning if he would help me, and he agreed. I brought out my blue word list of adjectives, and as I carefully pronounced each Tagalog word, he came right back with a Batangan equivalent. Trying to write them down, I became confused with his mushy pronunciation. As I watched his mouth when he spoke, I noticed all the teeth on one side of his upper jaw were missing! But I persisted for nearly two hours, pleased to find how far we had gone with Makisig knowing nearly all the Tagalog words.

After he left for his fields, Russell brought one of the young boys over so I could hear the words on my list spoken clearly. Cleverly recognizing each Batangan word as I tried to pronounce it, the young lad repeated it back so I could correct the toothless version on my blue paper.

The next day Russell took my list back to Makisig for a second check. As he repeated the Batangan word I had written down, asking what it meant, Makisig gave him a Tagalog word with an entirely different meaning from the one on my list. Over and over, all down the list, it happened. Evidently he had just guessed at the meaning of the Tagalog words, instead of simply saying "*Kunasaful.*" Almost the whole list was worthless and my hard day's work was wasted.

In desperation we decided to spend the rest of that visit concentrating on listening, repeating, writing and asking questions about the things we heard.

The children and I had been in Ligaya for a year without seeing a paved road, a car or bus, a faucet, an electric light, a market, but most of all we missed the familiar faces. So a break for our 1957 Mission Conference and annual vacation was welcome and refreshing. Then in the remaining months before furlough God gave us some poignant memories that would go home with us when we left, and bring us back a year later.

In Ligaya a group of young girls began earnestly memorizing Bible verses to earn New Testaments, an offer we had made months before. Our Sunday School had grown to a record-breaking 45 children, with fifteen adults regularly attending the simple service that followed.

Three to four hours away in Pusug, Russell had been able to find Kabilugan's isolated home. He was thrilled with his continued interest in the gospel, although he made no outward commitment.

In the hills at Pangalkagan we concentrated on

getting as much Batangan into our heads and into our notebooks as possible. The people, now under Makisig's leadership, were still friendly, so that we not only had full language folders to take back to the States, but also a bow and arrow they had thoughtfully made for us.

But we had nothing to leave them, even though we had known them for a year and a half. Nothing in writing, for although we had now formed an alphabet and had written out simple Scriptural truths, they were afraid of paper and would not learn to read. And there were no gospel records in Batangan, for we had no way of making them. Our aching hearts found expression through Mary Jane Dick's poignant lines:

Little boy with body brown,
    toasted golden in the sun,
Smudged with black from sooty fire —
    bathing never spoiled his fun!
        Little boy, don't run, don't run...

Little boy with ready grin,
    impish eyes 'neath straight black hair —
Who would dare to say him "Nay"
    though he loved to site and stare.
        Little boy, stay there and stare...

Little boy from jungle green
    thought those mission'ries so queer,
Hardly spoke his words at all,
    but their smiles soon chased his fear.
        Little boy, come here — don't fear...

Little boy was always there,
    watching how they cooked their rice,
Listening to the magic box —
    all so strange but oh, how nice!
        Little boy, how nice, how nice...

Little boy who loved to eat,
      always seemed to wish for more;
Stole some little cans of fish,
      thought they wouldn't miss those four.
                  Little boy, 'twas more than four...

Little boy who did not know
      Jesus would forgive his sin,
Wash his heart and make him good,
      Open heav'n and let him in.
                  Little boy, your sin, your sin...

Little boy with runny nose
      hardly sick, then was no more.
Missionaries did not know —
      they had left the day before.
                  Little boy, hearts sore, so sore...

Little boy, where are you now
      (body buried in a tree)?
Did you understand at all?
      Did God help your heart to see?
                  Little boy, did He? Did He?

F our o'clock, and the ocean liner's stacks were beginning to bellow the characteristic smudgy smoke. The small yellow tug had come alongside and its cable secured. Brightly-colored paper tapes streaming from our hands to the hands of loved ones on the dock were being broken. And gradually the waving of goodbyes faded as the people on the shore grew smaller and smaller.

Reluctantly we turned to look out ahead as we left the Los Angeles harbor en route across the Pacific. Anxious to serve the Lord, we still felt inadequate, remembering that our first term ended with no definite response from either the Batangan in the hills or the Ligaya folk in the lowlands.

The most important thing God had done for us during furlough was not Russell's complete restoration from typhoid, nor the children's healthy, happy development, nor the valuable help we received during our ten weeks at the Summer Institute of Linguistics. But it was the prayer partners He had led to work with us. Some were from our first term, others newly committed to this responsibility.

After three restful weeks aboard ship, we arrived in hot, sultry Manila. That evening as I kissed Ricky and Becky goodnight and carefully tucked the edges of the mosquito nets under their mattresses, I told them, "Daddy will go to Ligaya first to get our house ready for us and to visit the Batangan. Then we'll all make the trip together when he gets back."

Ten days later Russell returned with good news from the hills. "Everyone seemed glad to see me! Really friendly, just like old times. Makisig's still their leader, and there are several new folks in the group. It's almost a village now, with five or six houses. And guess what? Binsulna, that's Mangena's married daughter — you know, they're beginning to tell their names now — well, she and Karias have a nice fat baby girl."

"That's the first baby up there in years! And she, I mean Binsulna, always seemed the most interested in the gospel. I remember during our very first stay in the hills giving her a colorful children's tract," I reminisced. "She hugged hers when the others were almost afraid to touch theirs, though she couldn't speak any Tagalog to tell me how she felt."

"There's sadness, too," Russell added. "Nati has died, and old Grandpa Fufuama. Do you think they knew enough to trust Christ?"

As we boarded the little inter-island steamer in Manila for its regular trip to San Jose in Occidental Mindoro, God's word to us was from Zechariah 4:6, "Not by might nor by power, but by My Spirit, says the Lord Almighty." Arriving there after a smooth sixteen-hour trip, we transfered to the *Lady Mina* motor-*bangka*, which left for Ligaya after dark. For a crowded, uncomfortable three hours we were kept in uneasiness and suspense as she ran the entire trip without lights!

Once we had settled in, good weather made it possible for Russell to go to the hills each morning, and our new tape recorder made it possible for him to bring spoken Batangan home to Ligaya. This accelerated my language learning, improved my pronunciation, gave accurate text material for our further grammar analysis, and supplied us with additional vocabulary, always a constant search. With our five-day visits in the hills and constant study at home we were slowly reaching our goal of fluency in the Batangan language.

On Sundays after our morning Sunday School and adult hymn sing in Ligaya, we had lunch and then Russell packed his canvas shoulder-bag with the new compact phonograph, the Tagalog Gospel records and his notebook and pencil. Hiking in the unrelenting midday heat, he arrived in Pangalkagan to give the Batangan a Sunday service. Attendance was never a problem, for even without spiritual interest all who lived there enjoyed the novelty of a meeting.

About four months after our return, Russell came back from the hills one Sunday with a light step and a broad smile. "When I got up to the houses today," he began, "they had a visitor from the interior. I took the phonograph out of my pack, wound it, put on a Tagalog record and set the needle to play. The newcomer watched intently, carefully keeping his distance. When a man's voice suddenly came out of the box, he froze! You should have seen his face. Disbelief and awe were written all over it! But the Pangalkagan crowd, probably remembering how they felt when they first saw this strange phenomenon, began to giggle quietly behind their hands.

Really enjoying themselves!"

And that day after all the records had been played, and familiarity had diminished the visitor's fears, Russell preached his first real sermon in Batangan. Not lengthy or complicated, but in their very own language. He had been pleased that he now had enough vocabulary so he didn't need to ask their help in the middle of his message, even though he still didn't know the Batangan for words like love, forgiveness, authority, grace, and hope.

Binsulna's eyes had shown special interest when he spoke of God removing our sins. But she had said very little, probably because Makisig was there. The Batangan are very careful to show interest only if their leader does.

Between hill visits Russell made occasional trips into the surrounding area. One memorable day in May he started from the house at 4:30 am to miss as much of the heat as possible on the long and difficult hike to Pusug River interior.

When he arrived at the eight scattered, well-hidden homes in the Pusug area about mid-morning, not a chicken clucked or dog barked. He couldn't tell how long the "village" had been deserted, but his guess was that everyone was higher up the mountains making rice fields, where he had found them on his last trip. On that visit he had talked to them about God who created the world, and about His Son who could take away their sins. They had listened attentively, but he wondered if they really understood. At least they didn't run away!

Deciding now to visit other scattered homes in the area rather than climb the mountain again, he hiked along the trail, heard some ambitious chopping, and came upon two Batangan cutting down palm leaves for house roofs. Squatting down to talk with them, he asked about their families, homes and fields, even though he realized that fear often keeps them from answering such questions truthfully.

Soon a third Batangan came along and two men asked him, "*Sama*, where is your companion?" For it is rare that one travels alone.

"Ah, *Sama*, I have no companion," the newcomer answered, squatting down with them.

"I wonder, men," Russell interjected, "if you know my Companion, *Hesus* (Jesus)?"

"Oh, yes, *Sama*!" The reply startled Russell, but the speaker went on to explain, "He lives out in the lowlands, and has a farm where some of my friends have worked."

Russell realized with chagrin that *Hesus* was a common first name all over the Philippines. So he tried another approach. "Well, men, do you know my companion *Dios* (God)?"

"*Ken, Sama*. Yes, we know that man, too, although I have never been to his place near the coast," was the reply.

Again realizing that DeDios is a common lowland family name, Russell began to explain, "No, my friends, this One is not a man. *Dios* lives in heaven, not in the lowlands. And He is the One who made the earth and the sea and everything in them. Even people. It is His Son that is named *Hesus*. If you just ask Him, *Hesus* will take away your sins, and when you die, your spirit will go to heaven and not to hell."

Questions followed, and soon he was trying to describe heaven and hell. How he wished that his language ability permitted him to explain the atoning death of Christ, the exchanging of our sinfulness for His sinlessness, and the life that was possible with God caring for us. But at least they now knew that He exists.

"Well, friends, I am going now. Don't have gas on your stomach," Russell told them, rubbing his in true Batangan style as he left.

Walking along he realized that if he knew their word for God or a Good Spirit, it would be so much easier. Hadn't someone mentioned the name *Funbalugu*? Literally it means the trunk of the *balugu* vine, but it had been applied to a good spirit.

While he was gone, I had spent the morning studying. Five-year-old Ricky came over to the desk with a tiny rocking chair he had designed and made from the metal girders, plates, corners, screws, and other parts of his Erector Set. Praising it enthusiastically, I watched fascinated as he set Becky's eight-inch doll comfortably in it, much to her delight. He had made it just for her!

Fondly observing them play and share together, I thought of the fast-approaching day when Ricky would be going to our OMF Chefoo school in cool Baguio City, three hundred miles north of us. As a close-knit family we would face our first long separation. Russell and I would miss Ricky terribly but it would be hardest on Becky, for he was her constant companion.

Ricky's eagerness to go to school relieved some of my anxiety. Not only did he enjoy studying, like his math- and reading-readiness books here at home, but he also looked forward to being with the other missionaries' children he'd played with at conference time.

Russell and I both felt sure we could never endure the separation, even with the prospect of having Ricky home for a four-week vacation after every three months at school. But when the time actually did come, we experienced the Lord's peace, knowing that our partners at home were praying and that a constant flow of letters to and from school would help keep us close.

Becky's loneliness was relieved by the friendly neighborhood children in Ligaya. She had abandoned her effort to teach them English and now used only Tagalog. Learning to make mud-pie *suman*, a rice-delicacy, to sing Tagalog folk songs, to call the neighbor's pigs at feeding time and to chase the hungry chickens from the unhusked rice drying in the sun kept her busily happy. But her big brown eyes really filled with smiles and twinkles when we told her, "Tomorrow, Honey, we're going up to the hills again!"

"Oh, please, Mommie," begged our four-year old, "Let's go while it's still dark!"

"Well, at least we'll get up in the dark," I assured her.

The next morning, after leaving behind the sleeping houses of Ligaya and balancing our steps on slippery dikes between the flooded rice paddies, we came to the *carabao* trail. Here we gingerly picked our steps, for a miscalculation meant sinking in the mud to our knees. Like thin ice at the beginning of winter, the dry surface quickly breaks when weight is put on it and underneath is deep gooey mud.

The sun peeked over the top of the ridge as we arrived at the last lowland house and picked up our carton of hill supplies left there after our previous trip. In another twenty minutes we broke through the tangled vines, and our little home for the next five days came into view.

From across the fields we could hear a call, "*Tam lagbe kadasug wan*! Our cousin is here!" Ever since we had returned from furlough and had concentrated on speaking and teaching them exclusively in Batangan, they had been using that special name *lagbe*, or cousin, for Russell. Like a new sign of acceptance.

And then Salidayna, Mangena's second daughter, began to use a special name for me, too. She had thoughtfully taken me down to a hidden nook in the stream where I could bathe privately, staying with me so I wouldn't be lonely. After we came back, her mother asked where she had been. "Oh," she answered, "I was showing our special bathing place to our sister." Our sister! I was thrilled.

I began to think of God's promises to those who leave their loved ones for Him. Our parents, brothers and sisters were far away, and now even Ricky was not with us. But these friendly helpful Batangan had made us part of their family, without even knowing that God was in it!

By the time I had hung our laundry on the pack-rope clothesline, some of the young people were at the house to greet us. With ball-point pen and data board I began by asking, "*Nataw am fakamulun?* What is your work today?"

Writing as much of the conversation as possible and asking questions about new words or new uses of old words, I carefully watched for openings where I could talk about the Lord. Of all the young people, my "sister" Salidayna and Fufuama's young son,

Kiagum, were our two best language teachers.

The following day as I approached Mangena's home, I could hear Fufu's baby voice chanting her version of a lullaby. In the background her mother, Binsulna, was making soft encouraging noises.

While Becky played outside, learning how to build a doll-sized stick house complete with woven leaf roof, I ducked through the low door onto the ash-covered bamboo floor. Two logs extending from opposite corners of the room met on the central hard clay fire-hearth where the ends were glowing brightly. I perched on the highest one, laughing at Fufu as she imitated her elders.

"*Seyuk magdanun?*" I asked. "How many moons is she now?" With the writing down of Mangena's answer, my Batangan "lesson" began. Trying my new words and phrases in conversation and putting into my notebook everything I heard or observed kept me busy for several hours.

Then I told Mangena and her family that they had taught me well, and now I would teach them! Each day I had a brief, carefully-prepared lesson about creation, or heaven, or God's care for us and His willingness to take away our sins. Russell was doing the same thing over at Makisig's house, or perhaps he had followed him to the fields and was talking to him there.

A good visit with the family often included a lesson in basket weaving or making a braid-of-eight used for women's skirts. Or perhaps Ginluman, Mangena's youngest son, would show me how to carve or play a Jew's harp. Or they would burst into giggles as I tried to learn a Batangan "song" in the high falsetto that comes so naturally for them. By the end of my visit my heart and notebook were both full, and I returned to our shelter with a determination to work even harder on their language, and pray even more for their souls.

In the afternoons I visited them in their sweet potato fields, or watched them spread their unhusked rice on mats to dry in the sun, or pound the husks off in the big hollowed-out log using long wooden pestles.

Not long after that visit, Mangena confided that she would like us to live in the hills always. But we knew the leader must first give his assent. Although willing for us to visit, he had never shown the friendliness and enthusiasm the others had, especially when permanent housing had been mentioned.

That Christmas of 1959 brought a delightful interlude between hill visits. From Chefoo school Ricky was escorted home to Ligaya by my sister, Ann Flory, also a missionary with OMF. Although she had arrived in the Philippines more than a year before, had spent some time with May Roy among the Western Iraya, and was now permanently assigned to the Hanunoo in the south of the island, she had not yet visited our home in Ligaya. For the next month Joy Village was filled with Joy!

Ricky's happiness at school was apparent as he related details of his new life, making Becky long for the day she could join him. But it was the parting that tore at our hearts.

Ann told us later that as she and Ricky boarded the little coastal boat and it chugged slowly out to sea, Ricky's attention was riveted on the shore where we were waving goodbye. Finally turning to her with tears in his eyes, he said helplessly, "I can't see them any more, Auntie Ann! I can't see Becky's face any more!" We were glad it was his very own auntie who could comfort him.

We continued our short visits to Pangalkagan. Our friends moved often, and we always tried to find a house close to theirs. An old abandoned hut, a small field shack or perhaps a rice storage shelter.

Between two of our visits the people moved twice! Once because of the death of Makisig's wife, and the second time because there was a week of typhoon weather (our Ligaya rain gauge showed fourteen inches of rain in seven days). Afraid that the trees surrounding their houses would fall, they chose an open site and built a sturdy new longhouse, the first we had seen in Batangan territory.

Five families, including Mangena's, lived side by side in one long line. Each had a ten-foot-square room with its own floor and fire-hearth. But the partition between each section was just a single pole across the division about shoulder height, so you could look down the entire length of the house.

For our next five-day visit, a tiny harvest shack on stilts right beside their house became our home. Looking out the open side of our hut, we could see the thick grass roof that covered the entire length of their longhouse, reaching almost to the ground at the front as well as at the back of the structure.

While Becky was being taught how to use a new bamboo spring-loaded rock-shooter the children made for her, and Russell with Kiagum's help was deep in language study, I walked up the small pole to enter Makisig's house. His home was a leader-worthy elevated addition to the longhouse, but I had to stoop almost double to get in the tiny end door. I hoped to study with my "sister," Salidayna, who had become his new wife.

After my eyes got used to the dim light which the one small window-hole allowed, I saw Makisig's young, almost-blind step-daughter Ligdayna putting her long *bolo* in her big basket ready to go to the fields. Her new husband, Dayumian, an orphan raised by Grandpa Fufuama, picked up his leaf-wrapped *yabokan*, a smoldering piece of decayed fire wood. Tucking the flattened end of the green leaf under his waist band, he left the house with Ligdayna, while Makisig's ten-year-old son followed them. I sighed, for Ligdayna, especially, had listened attentively to the gospel, but had made no outward sign of interest, probably because of Makisig.

Turning to Salidayna I began, "*Nataw am fakamulun?* What is your work today?"

She was fun to chat with, helpful with the language, and attentive as I talked about the Lord. But since becoming Makisig's wife she warmly welcomed me only when he was absent, for he had never shown any real interest in our teaching, although he had given us the little field house on stilts.

One morning we were sitting on the edge of its platform floor when a couple of Batangan from the longhouse stopped to visit. My opportunity to get those two needed words for the parable I wanted to teach!

"What is your word for someone who has many, many things?" I asked. "Large fields, a big harvest, a lot of food, a big new house, lots of bark cloth, a good cooking pot and a long jungle knife."

I was trying to get the words for "rich" and "poor," but since money was used only for ornaments, I needed this long explanation. All their needs were supplied from the jungle or from working for a lowland farmer for such items as a *bolo*.

"Why, we don't have a special word," was the answer. "We would just say he has many, many things."

"And what is your word for a person who has just a tiny field, a poor harvest, not enough food to eat, a small old shaky house, hardly any bark cloth for his clothes or bedding, a cracked cooking pot and a short, broken jungle knife?" I hoped my description was clear.

"Oh, that," he said with the light of understanding in his eyes, "is *momuy*." I had to suppress a grin. The adjective he used was "lazy."

In Ligaya our Sunday meetings and incidental witness continued, but our time and energy were dedicated to the Batangan. Then, about halfway through our term, God showed how He could work through the prayers of those at home even when the missionaries' time and ability were severely limited.

A young Christian worker came from Manila for a week of special meetings in Ligaya, and thirteen people publicly confessed faith in Christ. Less than a year later the Philippine Missionary Fellowship placed three permanent workers in the *barrio*. Soon forty adults were regularly attending services, more than twenty were ready for baptism and plans were being made to build a small chapel.

Now we were truly free to spend all our time with the Batangan. On our next hill visit we sadly learned that young, almost-blind Ligdayna had fallen on a jagged tree stump, puncturing her abdomen and losing her unborn baby. We gave her medicine for the wound and tried to comfort her and Dayumian. But how would they remember that God always cares when no one was there to remind them?

Russell decided to translate and record on tape some very simple gospel scripts for the people to hear when we weren't in the hills. Using his dictionary file and the sentence forms he knew, he began putting the English message into Batangan. When he couldn't continue because of lack of vocabulary or sentence forms, he had to back up and reword the original scripts. It took most of a day to translate a script which would last only three minutes playing time. After laboriously checking them with his brightest helper, Kiagum, the scripts were recorded by Mangena on our small tape recorder.

Because she could not read, Russell had to read the first line to her and have her repeat it once for practice. Then he immediately told her, "*Dogi ap.* Repeat it again," as he quickly turned on the recorder to catch her words, turning it off the minute she finished. The process was then repeated for each sentence in the script, taking about an hour to record the brief message.

The most delightful part was playing the tape back to the Batangan and watching their amazed expressions when they heard it as a whole. We felt sure that very soon the whole village would decide to trust Christ, for some had already indicated an interest, and even Makisig had been enthused with the recordings.

Russell then left the tapes with Makisig to be

played while he had to be in Manila for a week. As soon as he returned, he hiked up to Pangalkagan, planning to study with Kiagum and to make arrangements with Makisig for another nine-day stay in the hills.

After he left, I quickly did the dishes and straightened the house, watching Becky with her friends happily at play in the gnarled *baliti* tree. I would be able to finish making my new vocabulary cards for the words collected on our last hill visit. English to Batangan on one card, Batangan to English on a second card, with any sentence examples I had collected. Then a duplicate copy of the English-Batangan for the file at our Calapan headquarters in case our originals were lost by fire, flood, or typhoon.

I was deep at work, figuring I still had two more hours before Russell returned. Suddenly he appeared in the doorway, looking horror struck.

"Three of the folks up there have just died, and a fourth one is dying," he said quietly with pain in his eyes. "They moved after each death, and I sure had a hard time finding them."

"Oh no!" I gasped, unbelieving. "Who are they? Who's died?"

"Bandigaman. And Barako's wife who had the three-month-old baby. And," he added softly, "Salidayna."

"Salidayna? Oh, not Salidayna, too!" Sick at heart I thought of that first day when she had called me her sister. And of the friendship we had shared since. And of her important help in our translation and language work. I couldn't believe it!

"How did it happen?" I finally asked. Then thinking of the unusually cold weather we had been having, "Was it pneumonia?" But could it be? Four people all at once out of a village of about thirty? It didn't seem possible.

"They said it was colds, but I'd guess it must have been more like pneumonia," he said over his shoulder with his head in the medicine cupboard. "They seemed to have a lot of chest pain. I'm going right back. Maybe I can save Rigwayon." Then he added resignedly, "but it's probably too late. He was really bad."

With a lump in my throat though the tears didn't come, I swallowed hard and said, "I'll fix you something to eat, and then..."

"It'll have to be quick," he interrupted. "I want to get right back to help the ones who are still alive." Gulping down his lunch and then stuffing his pack with the medicines, some sugar and candy, and his refilled canteen, he was off again.

Toward evening he came home. Defeated. "Rigwayon died and was buried even before I got back."

"Buried?"

"Well, set up in the roots of a tree, I'd guess, the way they do. With a fence built around it." He sat down heavily on the bench at the kitchen table. "Everyone is so full of fear! They have moved three times in three days! And now they'll move again because of Rigwayon," he added helplessly.

He had told them to be sure to eat and drink. "Even if you don't feel like it," he admonished them. "And remember always, if you trust Jesus, you do not need to fear the *legan*, the ghosts of those who have died. God will help you and take care of you."

The following day Russell returned from the hills

saying Bandigaman's wife looked terrible. No coughing, no chest pains, no fever. But huddled in a corner she refused to eat or drink. "She is dying from stark, horrible fear," he concluded. And a few days later she, too, was "buried" in the big buttressed roots of a large jungle tree.

After his next visit Russell described to me the fear-dominated group huddled together in two tiny newly-erected huts on the hilltop overlooking the longhouse. To be sure the *legan* did not gain entrance, the well-covered doorways were only two feet square and every crevice in the grass walls was stuffed and re-stuffed with branches or leaves. A fire was kept burning all night and most were afraid to sleep lest the *legan* come. Such was the terror in which Satan was keeping them.

Their welcome to us was cool for the first time. Our hearts ached for them. Besides the first four deaths, another life had been lost because of fear. A sturdy beautiful home was deserted. Protection from rain and cold was gone. Food growing in the fields of the dead was abandoned. Sleep was lost. There was no end to the sadness and heartache. And they had seemed so close to trusting in the Lord Jesus.

Weeks later reluctant permission was given for us to use the abandoned longhouse, which was sturdy enough to weather coming typhoons, making semi-permanent hill residence a possibility for the first time. We boldly told them, "We are not afraid of the *legan*, for God will take care of us." Wanting this to become a testimony of God's power, we were actually disappointed when they said, "Oh, the *legan* don't bother the Tagalogs," inferring that we too were exempt! But we knew if we or Becky became ill while living in the longhouse, the *legan* would be blamed.

Hiking into the hills, we arrived at the empty longhouse. Shock and sorrow were evident everywhere. Even Mangena hardly wanted to talk, though she did sadly tell us how she missed the long conversations with her daughter. And then she murmured, "And now Makisig has no one to dig his sweet potatoes!" Not one person was interested in helping us anymore. No one even cared whether we were there or not.

About six weeks later Harold Withington left his work at the OMF Publishers in Manila for an eleven-day trek with Russell to several interior villages seen previously from an aerial survey. They returned elated that they had met 103 Batangan, mostly in small groups, and had been able to speak to a large number of them about the Creator God and His Son. But they were mystified with the attention given them by two Batangan they met on the second day of their trek.

Harold had been resting his sore city-feet in camp, when he heard a strange heavily-accented voice say in English, "Where have you come from?" Startled, he had looked up and found himself gazing into the eyes of two grinning Batangan. When Russell arrived back in camp, the talkative one said that his companion was his older brother, Matalaka Sirut, a shaman. His few English expressions as well as some Tagalog had been learned from a lowland farmer who had also named him "Teacher."

They stayed around the camp, listening attentively as Russell talked to them about the true God and His salvation. The shaman told them not to visit his village, and then asked nonchalantly if anyone had died in the Pangalkagan valley.

"Yes," Russell answered. "Five have been taken."

He made no reply, but went over to the fire, and squatting by the bubbling rice kettle, removed the lid and peered in. Seeing he was watched, he left the camp quickly without a word.

"Strange," Russell mused. "Looking into another's cooking pot is something a Batangan would never do."

Evidently assigned the job of keeping an eye on the men, Teacher was constantly reappearing for an "English lesson." To show off his ability he brought some of his friends along, giving Russell a wider audience.

On the second morning Teacher questioned Harold in Tagalog, "Where is your companion?" Learning that Russell had gone up river, he had quickly asked, "Is he after our children?"

"No," Harold had assured him, "he doesn't want to take your children."

The following day when Teacher appeared, Russell asked him where the shaman was so they could say goodbye. "He is so terribly afraid of you that he can't even leave his house!" Teacher had told them.

"Afraid? Why?" But Teacher mysteriously remained silent.

After Harold had returned to Manila, we went again to Pangalkagan. During the eight days in our private longhouse we felt the cold winds of rejection. We did learn, however, more details of the five sudden deaths, and were able to piece together the ghastly truth.

A leader from the Pusug area had arranged for a

shaman to perform a sacrifice in Pangalkagan at his son's wedding, so his own dying wife would recover. The shaman demanded that the Pangalkagan people have a pig sacrificed for themselves as well. After the pig was tied and swung from the ceremonial poles, he made the usual requests for payment, which were unreasonably heavy.

He asked Karias, Binsulna's husband, for a *bolo*, eight chickens and some sulfur, which he gave. From Rigwayon and Bandigaman he had requested *bolos*, but they refused. He demanded that Makisig's wife, Salidayna, and Barako's wife go home with him to carry the "loot" and become his wives. They also refused.

The pig was killed and cooked as usual by the shaman, who personally served it to each person in this all-night affair. The next morning he left early, and by afternoon the four people who had refused his requests became seriously ill. In three to five days all were dead, suffering extreme pain, climaxed by labored breathing.

Later the Pangalkagan folk were told that the shaman had "cursed" those four by "burning a candle against them." But the details indicated that they had been poisoned, a method of eliminating opposition. The two men who died were the only ones in the Pangalkagan area considered knowledgable about sacrificing, worshipping, or singing to the evil spirits.

That shaman was Matalaka Sirut who with his younger brother had come into Russell and Harold's camp. Had he been hoping to slip some poison into their rice while it was boiling? Had he been afraid because of the evil he had done? Had he felt that the power of God with them was greater than his own power?

We never learned the answers, but we felt the effects of his evil. My "sister" and language helper was dead. Fear controlled everyone. No longer were we warmly welcomed. To add to those sorrows, the prison colony was preparing to take over the valley. And soon Becky would be leaving us to join Ricky at school. Death! Fear! Rejection! Defeat! And coming loneliness.

As I lovingly labeled and folded each item of Becky's school outfit, I wondered how we could manage without her sparkle which had kept us happy even though we had desperately missed Ricky, and had cheered us when we were overwhelmed by discouragement. I had written in my newsletter that month, "Our God is all powerful." Did I really believe it? Our friends at home did, and they were faithfully praying.

Then before we left for Manila with Becky and vacationing Ricky on their way to school in Baguio, a letter arrived with astonishing news and a thrilling request.

Chapter 7

SEEKING

Batangan had been found in Oriental Mindoro!
Dr B had written that Caroline Stickley and her
partner, while teaching the Tadyawan Mangyan in
the hills along the Banos River, had been visited by
tribal men that the Tadyawan called "Batangan."
These tribesmen had asked for teachers who could
speak their language, and Dr B wondered if we could
arrange to visit them.

The Banos River was further south than Russell
had gone from the Agricultural School when he
searched in vain for them more than six years before.
Why had no one directed him there then? Why had
God not let us find them? The only thing we had
accomplished in the West was to learn their language.

In Manila that May of 1961, as we and the other
parents waved the Baguio-bound bus out of the
station and tried to dry our eyes with our little "white
flags," emptiness overwhelmed me. But when I
realized that Ricky and Becky and the rest of the
chattering children were in God's care and would be
active and happy at school, and that our visit to this
new group of Batangan was imminent, God's peace
calmed my heart.

We left Manila with our carefully-packed Batangan Bible stories, choruses, recorded tapes and paraphrased selections from Mark and Genesis. Questions filled our minds as we sped along in the bus to Batangas and then crossed the channel to Calapan. Would the language be the same? Would they be able to understand us? Would they be afraid? Could these possibly be the ones we had been praying for who would leave their old ways and follow God's way? If they asked for teachers who knew their language, they surely must want to be taught.

Going south from the Calapan pier, we enjoyed the fast forty-mile bus trip, in contrast to the slow motor-*bangkas* in Occidental Mindoro. At the missionaries' base home in Pinamalayan, getting our packs filled and ready for the hills was easy. Not only was there electricity, running water, a post office and a telegraph station, but also a large open food market, several bakeries and a variety of small and large shops.

At supper that evening Caroline painted a background for our visit. The Banos River Tadyawan, beginning to respond to their teaching, had built a house by the river where missionaries and tribal people could live together for a month at a time as they studied "Our Father's Words." Not only was it easier for the missionaries to reach than their palm-leaf homes on the hilltop, but many tribal people, including the Batangan, passed by in their travels up and down the river.

Each time new ones came by, the responsive Tadyawan faithfully chatted the gospel with them, or brought out the Two Roads poster to explain the way to heaven. One of their visitors, called Gorio, was a big, gentle Batangan leader. He was the one who had asked to see the teachers who could speak his language.

Reaching the Tadyawan house-by-the-river took six hours, but we didn't have to walk all that way! From Pinamalayan we travelled south for eight miles on the main road by jeepney, an elongated jeep used as a short-trip bus. At the Langgang junction a horse-drawn *karetela* took us to the end of the cart track where the Tadyawan men met us and carried the ladies' packs.

On the four-hour hike we did not have to climb any steep hills, or fight off the ever-hungry jungle leeches. Instead the trail went first through the grasslands, then beside the river with an ever-so-gentle ascent. As the trail became impassable on one side of the river due to sheer rock cliffs or impenetrable jungle, it crossed to the other side, until it became impassable there and recrossed back to the original side.

In all, we made 25 knee- or hip-deep cool, refreshing crossings under the blazing tropical sun. Although the Tadyawan are less than five feet tall, the strong grip of their hands and their sturdy movements were reassuring in the swift, deep current.

Suddenly the grass roof of our tiny home-for-the-week came into view. The rest of the Tadyawan, already gathered at this house-by-the-river, welcomed us with hot fragrant rice and boiled sweet potatoes, and showed an eagerness to hear more of "Our Father's Words" from their own missionaries.

On the second day we had our first Batangan visitors. But they did not call themselves *Batangan*. They were the *Tawbuid, taw* meaning "men," *buid* meaning "interior." *Men of the Interior*. Perhaps that was why we could never find them in the East in those early years of searching! Had we actually met some who did not want to answer to the name *Batangan*?

Hearing Russell's first tape, our visitors told us with wide grins, "*Ken, Sama.* Yes, that's our language!" But as they listened repeatedly to all the messages, they said, "We do not understand."

As they began discussing among themselves what it could mean, we picked up a number of differences in vocabulary and grammar between the Eastern and Western dialects. But we ached to understand all that they were saying.

"The teaching is good," they told us at first. "We want our sins taken away, so that we will never be sick and will live to be old and gray-haired!" We explained that sickness would not be eliminated, even if their sins were removed, for they would still be living in this evil world. But they didn't seem to understand.

As Russell continued to teach, they listened attentively. But after conferring again, they told us they could not yet believe our words, for we might force them to go into town, or kidnap their children and take them off to school! We quickly assured them this was not so, and we really felt they were not afraid of us. Some even made a return visit during the week, although they were hesitant to make a commitment.

Husky, gentle Gorio, whose request had brought us there, showed a lively interest when he finally put in an appearance on the fifth day. During the chat with him he explained to us, "Our word for *Dios* (God) is *Funbalugu.*" As we inquired further he told us that *Funbalugu* was a good spirit and was involved in the creation of the world.

Gorio came only that once, reporting that his people were all too sick to visit us. And we had no way to reach them. Had they received a bad omen and been afraid to venture out? Even during this short stay we saw the grip of superstition and darkness on the tribal folk.

During our last night with them an old Tadyawan grannie had a bad dream about the lowland people. This was such an important omen that although the Tadyawan had huge bundles of rattan prepared to sell in the lowlands when they took us out the next day, their leader allowed no one to leave. Even the following day, when three of the newly-believing Tadyawan guided us to the outside, they were prohibited from carrying out their rattan!

We had been thrilled with the interest of Gorio and the other twelve Tawbuid we met, but although they seemed to be seeking, they didn't seem to accept what they were hearing. We could only pray that the Word of God would continue to do its work in their hearts.

Going back around the island to Occidental Mindoro, we battled discouragement. We had so hoped the Tawbuid in Oriental Mindoro would have been more eager to listen. Arriving in Ligaya, we found our home disturbingly quiet, for we hadn't realized how much we would miss the children! Knowing that our prayer partners were faithfully continuing to uphold all four of us, we plunged into the first of three special projects we had planned.

Gospel Recordings was ready to cut records for

the Tawbuid in both the Eastern and the Western dialects. We were to make the tapes and send them to their headquarters in Los Angeles.

Following the completion of the tapes, we planned to begin translating the Gospel of Mark. Many stories from Mark and Genesis had been written out and taught to our Pangalkagan friends as well as to those Tawbuid in the East. But now we wanted to begin serious translation work.

Our final goal was to live more permanently in the hills. We were sure that all three projects would easily be within reach.

After weeks of carefully translating the scripts and checking them with the people, we took them to the hills with the recording equipment. But no one was willing to be the speaker. We asked the group as a whole. We asked individuals. Because of those terrible deaths, Satan was still keeping them in bondage.

We were not the only ones affected. The young widow of one of the men who had been poisoned gave birth several months after her husband had died. We were not in the hills at the time so on our next visit I went to see the baby. But it wasn't there. I was told that it hadn't moved or cried, and decided it had been still-born.

But now, during this visit, one of the men told Russell that it was evil if a baby born with no father was allowed to live. "There is no one to care for the child. And besides, when the child gets older if anyone says, 'You were born with no father,' the child will sicken and die. So why should we take care of such a child now?"

We could hardly believe what we were hearing.

The Tawbuid dearly love their children! No one seemed very happy that the baby had not been allowed to live, but all were apparently afraid to go against the custom and save the tiny life. How our hearts bled for the mother and her precious little one.

Although they had refused to do the recording, they were not unfriendly. They felt free to confide in us and to ask our advice. As we conversed, we asked them about the term *Funbalugu*. "He is good. He was involved in creating the world," they told us. "But no one knows much more about him." Tentatively we decided it would be a good name for God if accompanied by additional teaching from the Scriptures. We wanted to use as few foreign terms as possible in the Bible translation.

Our unused recording equipment seemed terribly heavy as we lugged it home again for its eventual return to Manila. All we could do was wait and try again.

Carefully Russell prepared for our next hill visit. Thoroughly studying and researching the verses of Mark 1 that he would cover, he drafted a preliminary translation in Tawbuid along with an explanation of each verse. He hoped that Kiagum, who knew only his own language, would be able to understand the preliminary translation and put it into accurate, colloquial Tawbuid.

But when we arrived at Pangalkagan the mournful clack, clack, clack of the bamboo *taraktak* could be heard on every trail. We were again surrounded by sadness, sorrow and fear, for sixteen-year-old Kiagum was dead. And now no Batangan would dare go out of the house without constantly shaking this clapper to frighten away the dreaded *legan*. For the only way a lonely ghost can have companionship is to "bite" someone so that he will sicken and join the dead one.

How can someone so kind and gentle as Kiagum produce such an evil ghost that the strongest of men are controlled by the fear of it? Their village had been deserted, and far away from the death scene, one large structure to sleep everyone had been quickly thrown together. There we found the Tawbuid when we arrived and learned of the boy's death, probably from tubercular hemorrhage.

Another dear friend and helper gone. Had he understood our teaching? Did he believe? Our sadness was compounded because no one else was as bright nor as capable of helping us put God's Word into their language.

Without realizing it, they cheered our aching hearts by thoughtfully supplying us with squash, rice, sweet potato, bananas and eggs in payment for simple medicines. And we tried to brighten their days of grief and fear with our choruses.

They listened attentively, trying to mimic our words and music. Later we even heard strains of "Jesus' Words Will Always Be True," with their personalized Tawbuid "tunes," as they put their babies to sleep in the tiny rattan hammocks, or vanished down the trails to their fields.

On Sunday morning we had prepared a special surprise, replacing Russell's usual Sunday visit. Crowded around the mysterious flannelgraph board, everyone exclaimed with great delight as they saw the Bible story illustrations appear, the first time most of them had seen any pictures. They had to be shown how the two-dimensional figures represented three-dimensional people! Immediately they turned the figures over to see what their backs looked like!

Through the whole story they sat enthralled. That was something for folks who couldn't sit still for two minutes, even if they could dig sweet potatoes all day long without getting tired!

But whether they were really able to "read" the pictures or not, they chuckled at the way Adam blamed Eve for his sin and Eve in turn blamed the serpent. Though the punishment of being driven from the garden was severe, they agreed it was justified because of their sin.

Like their counterparts in Oriental Mindoro, they believed if a person had no sin (and they had sacrificial ceremonies to get rid of it), he would never be ill! All we could do was write to our prayer partners, "Pray with us that they will understand that Christ has already paid for their sin, and that cleansing is available to them, not by pig sacrifices but by faith in Christ."

At times we were elated when someone assured us that he believed, or that Salidayna, who had died in the poisonings, believed and was in heaven. But discouragement came when we heard about their spirit rituals.

Their abundant rice harvest brought the Tawbuid no happiness. Their entire crop had been exhausted by the purchase of eleven pigs from local lowland farmers. The pigs were small, but prices were so high that large debts would have to be paid off later by working on the farms.

These pigs had been offered in the terrifying *Taraun* Ceremony held at full moon, to placate the spirits of those who died in the poisonings. When the deaths occurred one pig had been offered for each person. And now, just after harvest, a second one had been sacrificed. The eleventh pig was for Kiagum's spirit. Everyone, including a few interior visitors, took part in the fearful midnight feast of pork, rice, cassava, taro root and sweet potato.

When they told Russell, he realized that they knew this *Taraun* Ceremony was not according to God's teaching. They could repeat the truths of God's protection for those who followed Him. Yet they were so terrorized by evil spirits and interior leaders' demands, that they continued their life-long practices lest negligence bring sickness or death.

While we were in agony over the Tawbuid in the hills, our house in Ligaya was getting a new look. Everything was being cleaned and polished. The children's beds were being put up. Their books, toys, hill clothes, and wooden-soled *bakya* were set out for their arrival. Then as the house again rang with childish voices and laughter, we praised the Lord for His loving care during the months of separation while Becky had been in first grade and Ricky in third.

Happy to be in the hills, where the low ceiling cross-beams made good monkey bars, they played with the children, learned more Tawbuid, and became concerned for the people. Some were sick with colds and malaria, and one night the two-year-old baby girl of Binsulna and Karias had fever and convulsions, thoroughly frightening the parents. Together we prayed for them, and together we all praised God for the baby's recovery, as well as that a threatening cholera epidemic did not reach Pangalkagan.

Our hill visits gradually developed into stays of more than a week. In the shelter of our sturdy tight-roofed longhouse, we had left two footlockers containing all our hill belongings, now protected against creatures and climate. Our dream of staying two to three weeks would soon be a reality. More time to be with the people in their homes, on the trails and in their fields. More time to hear those words we needed. More time for teaching and translating. We even discussed taking more equipment, perhaps another footlocker for a typewriter, some of our files, and additional supplies.

With a head full of ideas for the quicker progress of our work, Russell left for Pangalkagan after the children's departure. But his return was somber. "I went by our longhouse on my way to the other homes," he began. "Our stuff was scattered all over the floor, and the footlockers were wide open with nothing left in them!"

"What'd you do?" I asked, in shock.

"Cleaned up the mess," he answered tiredly. "I put the stuff back and hid the footlockers in an old overgrown field, covering them with some brush. But there was a lot missing. Clothes, dishes, the mosquito net, the flashlight, most of the medicines."

"Nothing up there was really worth much," I said, trying to cheer him. "It was all so old."

"But it'll be such a bother to replace," he said realistically. "You should see how they opened the padlocks! Just one small mark on each one where it was given a hard sharp blow. They were good locks, too. Must have been done by a professional!"

"From the prison colony?" I asked.

"I suppose so. You know what some of them told Makisig? If any prisoner gets hurt in one of his wild-pig spear traps, they'll come and kill everyone in the village!"

I shuddered.

A week later, taking our pack full of replacements, we set up housekeeping again in our hill-home. Sunday morning, as usual, we climbed the nearby hill to the Tawbuid houses carrying our flannelgraph board and Bible lesson. With no way to lock the doorless house, we simply prayed it wouldn't be "visited" while we were gone.

Before we started the meeting, I went over to the dark corner where Mangena was lying, so ill she spoke in gasps. "Oh, oh, I..don't...want...to die. Oh, Uh, I..I...just...just...want to...stay...on earth. Uh, Uh, I...I...don't want...to become...a spirit!"

Reminding her again of the Lord's precious promises to the believers, I prayed they would bring comfort to her. She was still seeking. Had she found Him? Was she ready to trust only Jesus?

The flannelgraph board went up displaying the Sea of Galilee. The children squatted as close as they could while I told the story of Jesus stilling the tempest. Each sentence was repeated after me by Binsulna. Repeated, that is, in good Tawbuid. Quickly Russell found his pencil and notebook, and writing as fast as possible, tried to capture it all on paper.

Following the story, we began singing the new Tawbuid choruses, when suddenly there was a furious barking. Outsiders had arrived! Everyone in the house began furtively to hide their food. Then they peeped out to see who had come and what they wanted.

"Mister Reed! Mister Reed!" A couple of prison messengers handed him a note. He was to return to Ligaya where a letter was waiting for him from the Colony Superintendent.

At noon we arrived back in Ligaya. The letter said that three prisoners were in the guard house and our belongings were at the colony office to be claimed. Russell left early the next morning for the three-and-a-half hour hike, returning with an overflowing pack! He was thankful to be allowed to bring our things home without having to go to Mamburao and testify in court as the Superintendent had at first requested.

Returning to the hills the following day, we enlisted Binsulna's help in a thorough recheck of the eight Gospel Recording scripts, and asked if she would be willing to do the recording. In about two months a couple of our OMF missionaries would be coming to Ligaya in a second attempt to make the tapes.

As the week ended, we were thankful to the Lord for the completed scripts, for a willing attitude to record them later, for another hidden field-house in which to safely store our footlockers, and for fun and laughter as well as serious teaching with our friends.

One hot morning Neville Cooper and Roger Snyder arrived in Ligaya with the recording equipment. At breakfast, they described their forty-mile walk to reach us, which had taken all the day before as well as several hours early that morning. If only the boats were more dependable!

I hastily put a lunch together and three of us set off for the hills. Roger's swollen, blistered feet dictated a day of rest for him in Ligaya.

After a lengthy search through the fields near the village, we finally located Mangena and Binsulna. But they were strangely cool to our proposal that they help with the recording. Puzzled by their behavior, we had a friendly chat with them, but could find no reason for their changed attitude. Disappointed, Russell went up the hill to talk to some of the boys working there. "Makisig has forbidden us to record for you," they told him. Was the reason connected to the five deaths the year before?

Our prayer partners were praying and God had even a better plan than using Binsulna. Nardo, a young new arrival in the group, seemed to do as he pleased without arousing Makisig's opposition. Although the women could not record, he said he would do it.

With his brightly-colored jungle rooster tucked under his arm, and accompanied by the leader's young son, he arrived at our hill-house to see what he was supposed to do. His clear masculine voice, his bright mind and his ability to follow instructions made him a choice speaker for this work. He was even willing to go with us to Ligaya that afternoon where the other eleven recordings could be made more easily, without the frequent crowings of the village roosters under our house.

Two days later with the precious tapes in their packs, Neville and Roger returned to Mamburao by boat and jeep. And were their feet thankful! That Sunday as we played copies of the tapes at Pangalkagan, everyone beamed their enjoyment, including the leader!

"You know what I'd like to do?" Russell said to me, prompted by Makisig's pleased reaction to the recordings. "I'd like to take these tapes up to interior Tagisian, where Mangena's old mother and sister live. I was up in that area once before."

"How far is it? More than a day?" I asked.

"Not that far. I suppose it's three or four hours. I could go up and try to locate their village, and then the next day take the recorder and tapes."

When he returned from his second trip to their cliff-top village, he told me that in the clearing of the seven houses were fifteen men and one woman. She immediately disappeared, but the men had actually stayed! Five listened carefully, even though the others seemed too frightened to keep their minds on the teaching. And their leader, Ligaydi, listened to the nine three-minute messages twice with rapt attention! Were these people in the interior seeking to know more about the Lord?

Several weeks later Ligaydi's adult son surprisingly appeared at our door in Ligaya, asking for medicine for his badly-ulcerated legs. After taking care of his sores, we had a good chat with him before he left.

Was God telling us we should consider reaching the interior? From the air Russell had seen a large settlement in the very center of the Tawbuid population and he had considered hiking there to look for an opening among them. An alternative seemed necessary, for not only was Makisig unresponsive but also his whole village might soon be forced to leave Pangalkagan. The prison colony now had more than a thousand prisoners and was expanding into that tiny valley, designated by the government for colony use.

Or should we consider the Pusug area where

Russell had found some interest? Somewhere, we felt sure, there were seeking Tawbuid prepared by God. For from the very beginning of work among the Mangyan the OMF workers had asked God to open hearts, pledging ourselves to go to those who were seeking Him.

Already our missionaries had seen five churches organized among the Eastern Iraya and three among the Western Iraya, with more than a hundred baptized believers. In the Alangan church at Ayan Bekeg over fifty believers were meeting, with another congregation at Balingoway. Buhid believers gathered at both the Batangan River Village and Apnagan, and among the Hanunoo in the south of the island three churches had been established. The most recent tribe to be evangelized was the Tadyawan on the Banos River where we had seen the new believers reaching out to the Tawbuid.

But in the nine years we had been on the field, we had not seen any active seeking that led to commitment among the Tawbuid, nor even any group that wanted regular teaching. Those at Pangalkagan allowed us to be there, became our friends and taught us their language. But their allegiance was still to the old customs and spirit worship that they had always known. Even the ones on the Banos River in Oriental Mindoro had disappointed us by their lack of response.

During this time of heart searching, we received the news that the Tawbuid in Oriental Mindoro were again asking for teaching in their own language. So we sent some scripts and choruses to Caroline and a letter to our prayer partners: "Pray that the Tawbuid may receive the teaching they desire, and that we will know the Lord's will for us."

A few months later Dr B urged us to consider teaching again in Oriental Mindoro. He quoted a most surprising and urgent letter from Caroline which began, "Surely something is happening among the Tawbuid in this area." The Tawbuid had visited them while they were teaching the Tadyawan on the Banos River, and some were so hungry for the truth that they had even spent a night or two with them. Eight adults and seven children had come to one Sunday meeting and ten adults attended the following one. But all she could do was read them a very brief sermon and sing them four Tawbuid choruses she had received from us. After months of quiet suspicion, all were so eager to hear God's Words that she felt someone should "make a concentrated plunge into their area" at this opportune time.

Could this be gentle Gorio again and his village? Or was it another group altogether? Finally we decided to make another visit to the East. Based on the booklet "100 Questions Answered From the Bible," we began the gigantic task of writing out 54 lessons starting with the Creation, explaining who God was and how our world began, and progressing to the New Testament teachings of the Savior. We had three lessons a day for eighteen days of evangelistic Bible studies.

But we were determined not to abandon our friends at Pangalkagan, a decision reinforced by Russell's last visit there before we left for the East. He had seen Mangena working in her field and had gone over to speak to her. But she had merely grunted and would not converse, a mystifying change from the usual friendly woman who told everyone that Russell was her *lagbe* or cousin. Wondering what was up, he had gone on to the houses where he had found Binsulna, her married daughter, in a very friendly and cheerful mood.

"Have you seen my mother today?" she asked.

"Why, yes, I saw her in her field," he told her.

"Did she talk to you?"

"Well, no. She wouldn't talk,"

"Ah, yes," Binsulna had smiled appreciatively. "She is angry with all of us and won't speak to any of us! It was my youngest sister who made her angry by disobeying, and now she won't speak to anyone in the family!"

To anyone in the family? And Russell was included! Rather than being treated like an outsider whom she would be afraid to ignore, he had just been included in her anger with the rest of the family!

Then Binsulna had asked him, "When will you be coming to live with us again?" And Russell had explained that it would be many weeks before we would return to their village, for we were going to the other side of the mountains to teach some Tawbuid there who want to hear God's words.

"Hurry back!" she told him. But we both longed that they would want us for our teaching and not just as a good luck charm. They desired us to be with them but were clinging to their old spirit worship while tentatively reaching out toward the teaching of God's Word. But we would not forget them. We would be coming back.

Chapter 8

LISTENING

The last day of May 1962 will remain in my memory forever. It was about 3:30 in the afternoon when Caroline, Dode Pack, Russell and I made the last crossing of the swift, deep Banos River in Oriental Mindoro and saw on the bank a new and much larger house-by-the-river.

"The Tadyawan built this end of the house," their missionaries explained to us. "And the Tawbuid built the far end. That way there's room for everyone to stay when we come to teach."

As we climbed the bank, brown bodies tumbled out of the sturdy palm-leaf structure, grinning and staring at our approach. "And these," said Caroline with a majestic wave of her arm, "are the Tawbuid!"

I couldn't believe it! Not the eight or ten we had expected, but at least thirty crowded around, from the wrinkled old grannie to the tiny two-month-old infant in his mother's arms.

"Bagu ami kadasug," we greeted them. "We have just arrived."

More grinning! More friendly staring! It was love at first sight! How different from our reception the year before! Those Tawbuid had just casually dropped by, didn't stay long and had evidenced suspicion and fear. But this group, open and warmhearted, had been showing continued interest for months in "Our Father's Words," as the Tadyawan phrased it.

These Tawbuid understood almost no Tadyawan, although several of the Tadyawan believers knew enough Tawbuid to pass on some of the teaching. But they faithfully came and attentively listened to the missionaries, trying desperately to understand. And now their eager welcome was so refreshing we almost forgot how hot, sticky, itchy and tired we felt.

After a refreshing bath and swim, we walked up the tiny pole and entered our new home. What a unique interior! Across one end of the Tawbuid section was a platform about six feet deep with its split-bamboo floor raised eighteen inches above the rest of the flooring. Their leader, whose lowland name was Tiban, proudly told us that the platform had been built for us, their teachers. Remembering their custom of elevating the leader's floor, like Makisig's in the Pangalkagan longhouse, we felt humbled, especially later when Tiban slept on the lower floor with the other Tawbuid.

As we pulled sleeping bags, enamel plates and lesson materials from our packs, they delightedly watched every move we made. Not in the proverbial fish bowl, but on stage! Suddenly a thoughtful hand reached up, offering us a kettle lid of newly-husked rice. And then they even volunteered to cook it for us!

The others patiently sat, quieting their children, waiting for us to finish our unpacking and begin teaching them. Although I was thrilled at their eagerness, I was simply too tired to think of even talking. I only wanted to lie on my sleeping bag, my head on the clothes-filled pillow case, and pass into oblivion.

But not Russell. Knowing what they wanted, he began at once. Their abounding enthusiasm and rapt attention was unbelievable. Low mumbling could be heard as they tried to repeat Russell's phrases to be sure they would not forget what he said. After the lesson they put every effort into singing the chorus for that evening, even though our western music was so foreign to their four-note scale.

Although we did not ask them, "Are you believing now?" if we had, they would have answered, "We are listening." To them that meant hearing what was said with the purpose of obeying it.

Even that first evening, we became aware of more and more differences between the Eastern and Western dialects which were to constantly try our ingenuity and patience as we sought to be clearly understood.

Every time Russell used a word in his lesson that was not in their dialect they stopped him. If they recognized the Western word, they gave him their equivalent. If they did not know it, they asked him its meaning.

Quickly grabbing my notebook and pencil, I wrote down each correction as Russell continued to teach. And he did the same for me when it was my turn. On one section of 45 sentences we had 61 changes recorded! But nothing was going to stop these earnest Tawbuid from learning and obeying everything we had to tell them from God's Word.

Although we didn't realize it until months later, that obedience began during the first week. The lesson was the creation of Adam and Eve, one man for one woman, God's divine order, to be husband and wife for life.

The Tawbuid customs allowed wife-exchange, giving your unwanted wife to a younger brother, sending her back home with the pacifying gift of a jungle knife, or strangling her if she refused to go. All of these had been done in the past by this group of listeners. But when they heard "God's Words" about the permanancy of marriage, they "froze" their marriages as they were that day — the snarled threads of the past could never have been untangled — and never again resorted to their old ways.

On our second day, after we had finished the two morning sessions, the strong, burly interior leader of the whole area came by, his falsetto voice betraying his fright. Tiban told us his name was Balinguy. He did not stay long, and he did not want to listen, but he brought a sense of fear and evil. With a sigh of relief we watched Balinguy leave, not realizing how often during this visit we would feel his malignant influence. How comforting to know that our prayer partners at home were fighting this battle with us on their knees. And how cheering that very day to have one of the Tadyawan believers arrive with a huge basket of bananas, liberally giving them to us and the Tawbuid.

Several days later our Bible lesson was " Trusting God in Times of Fear" accompanied by the chorus, "I will not be afraid." Hastily we rewrote part of it, for one of the words we had used for "fear" was not understood here in the East! That song and the verse from Psalm 56:3 "When I'm afraid, I will trust in Thee," were diligently memorized, for fear is the dominating factor in the life of every Tawbuid.

"The Tawbuid farther in the interior," they told us, "are very much afraid of you! They think you want to bring outsiders into their area, or force them to come out into the lowlands. We tried to tell them that it wasn't true." But all kinds of rumors, like darts thrown by the enemy, continued to fly.

After class, one of the very young wives shyly pushed her friend toward me to be her voice. "Is it good," the Voice began hesitantly, "Is it good to give this one some medicine?" And she brought the young wife forward showing me a large raw sore on her side just below her waist.

She was so sooty from the ashes rubbed on her body in an effort to keep warm the night before, that I knew the effect of the medicine would be lost. So I told her to go first to the river and wash thoroughly. "*Malanu wa malanu*," I said. "Get clean, really clean!"

Her elderly husband asked timidly, "All over? Even her head?"

"Oh, yes!" I enthused, looking at the matted mass of hair. "Even her head!"

A large group went with them as they left and I thought with satisfaction, "Look what I've started. Now they're all going down to the river to bathe!"

Soon after, Tiban came over to us, handing Russell a square leaf-wrapped package. As he removed the fire-softened banana leaves, inside he found a hard block of white starch.

"What is it?" I asked.

"It's *yudu*," Tiban explained. "When we are hungry, this is our food."

"Where do you get it?" Russell inquired.

"We wash it out of the fibers that are inside the trunk of the sugar palm," he said. Then he described the all-day work of cutting down the tree, splitting the trunk, pounding out the fibers, washing them in bark troughs at the river, catching the washing water and letting it settle until the starch collected at the bottom of the troughs.

"But how do you cook it?" I needed a Tawbuid recipe book! His wife brought out the huge heavy lid of their rice kettle, and blowing the cooking fire into a blaze, she balanced her instant frying pan over the flaming ends of the two big burning logs. Breaking off a chunk of the white cube she powdered it onto the hot lid until it was about half an inch deep.

As she worked Tiban remarked to Russell, "Many of the people are leaving today."

Startled, I turned quickly toward him. For it suddenly dawned on me that the large group with the young wife and her husband had not gone to the river. They were leaving! *They must have been offended by my demand for a clean body before medicine could be applied*, I thought miserably.

"Why are they going?" Russell asked quietly.

"They are hungry. So they've gone back to their fields in the interior to dig sweet potatoes, and get their bananas and squash," he said. Then as an afterthought, "They'll be back with the food tomorrow." Suddenly I completely relaxed.

With a ladle Tiban's wife was expertly turning over the big *yudu* pancake. The powder that had been on the bottom was now cooked into a solid mass. After a few more minutes, interspersed with peeking at the underneath, she presented it to us. Rubbery on the outside and powder dry on the inside, it still tasted good!

But they were feeding us on rice, while not even having enough food for themselves. "Lord, bless these generous and loving people," I breathed. "Give them real joy as they trust in You." In less than 24 hours I would see that trust graphically illustrated.

The next morning after our lesson of The Visit of the Wise Men, Pakubas (as we had named him) approached Russell. Shyly he asked, "Would it be good if we prayed to our heavenly Father so that it won't rain?" Had he seen how God guides by stars and applied that authority to controlling the elements? Even though Russell had some misgivings, when he saw Pakubas' childlike faith, he joined him in praying that there would be no rain while he was out at work.

After he left, Tiban came over and squatted by Russell who was busy writing notes about the new words he had hastily jotted down as he heard them that morning. "What does *Funbalugu* mean?" Russell asked, deciding to test this word again to see if it would really be suitable to use for "God."

"Oh, that's our word for *Dios*," he began, using the Tagalog for "God." Then he explained it was a good spirit who was involved in the creation of the world.

"Would it be good," Russell asked him, "to use that instead of *Dios* in our songs and in our teaching?"

"Oh, yes! It is really our word! *Dios* is not Tawbuid," Tiban said.

Trying out the new expression, Russell told Tiban, "*Funbalugu* has brought you here to learn more of His words."

Tiban immediately asked, "Have you heard why we came to listen?"

"No, I haven't," Russell answered and waited for Tiban to tell him what was on his heart.

"Many years ago," Tiban began, and shifted his position to a more comfortable log nearby, "my father told me that a new teaching was to come into the interior, and that when it came I was to listen and to obey it." He glanced down, picked up a little stick and playfully chased away an advancing spider. "He wasn't even sick, but after only a half-month, he died." He stopped as if the memory shocked him still.

Later we learned that the time of his father's death was one dry season after the Great Darkness. That placed it more than six years ago, during our first year in Ligaya. Petitions that our prayer partners brought to the Lord as long as eight years before, when we had fruitlessly searched for the Eastern Tawbuid, were now being answered!

We knew the last charge of a Tawbuid parent before his death becomes "law" to the son. And as Tiban continued his story, we saw that he had taken his responsibility seriously.

"Many dry seasons passed. And then just one dry season ago I heard about the *Duena*, the two white women, who had come into the Banos area with a new teaching. I wondered if this was what my father spoke of. So several of us went down to listen." He gave a deep sigh, as if recalling the problems of those visits.

"The teaching was in the Tadyawan language," Tiban continued, "and we didn't know what it meant. The Tadyawan who spoke Tawbuid tried to explain it to us as best they could. Each time the *Duena* came to teach, a number of us would go down to listen. But there was so much we couldn't understand."

Russell and I exchanged glances, thinking of the letter Caroline had written about "their hunger and desire to know the truth." Tiban had engendered enough interest in his own village, composed largely of his brothers' and sisters' families, that in spite of their fears they had gone down with him to hear this New Teaching. Then we were asked to come over and teach them.

But even before we arrived, opposition from their interior leader, Balinguy, began to mount. He already had a quarrel to pick with Tiban's family because the wife they had given him, Tiban's older sister, was barren. Following Tawbuid custom Balinguy gave her to his younger brother. But the brother didn't want her either, for she was nearly thirty years older than he. And now this unwanted wife was listening to the New Teaching! Feeling his power as interior leader was being threatened, Balinguy angrily demanded that all listening stop.

But Tiban was not to be stopped. When he heard from the *Duena* that teachers who knew his language were coming, he decided it was time to seek an omen of confirmation for his plan to listen to them.

"Do you know our custom of chicken sacrifice for guidance?" Tiban asked, continuing his tale. As Russell answered in the negative he explained, "If a calamity has occurred, we behead a chicken with everyone squatting in a circle around it. As the body flaps, it will come to rest in front of the one responsible for the tragedy."

Drawing a long breath, he continued, "We wanted to know if it was good for all of us to commit ourselves to the New Teaching, to come down to the Banos River when the teachers came who knew our language — that was you — or if we should stay in the interior. The decision was so important that we sacrificed three chickens. One flapped off toward the interior, but two flapped toward the lowlands. So we

all came down to meet you!" he concluded triumphantly.

We were awe-struck. Speechless! For nearly seven
years God had been preparing this group to receive
His Word, beginning when we had first moved to
Ligaya and had started to study their language. We
had done nothing to promote this. God had done it
all. And not only that, but how did a shy, fearful
Tawbuid receive enough courage to tell these tribal
secrets to strangers he had known less than a week?

With a heart too full to speak, I just bowed before
our Almighty loving God, thanking Him that by His
guidance we now knew enough Tawbuid to teach
these people so uniquely prepared by Him.

Pakubas was also showing trust in God. He
returned that afternoon in time for the evening's
lesson on the raising of Jairus' daughter from the
dead. During the prayer time as Russell finished
thanking the Lord for holding back the rain, Pakubas
quickly added to the prayer, "This also, Our Father in
Heaven. Please do not let it rain yet, for many of our
people are still on the trail coming back from the
interior!"

After the meeting Pakubas approached us. "Many
of the interior men are afraid of this New Teaching,"
he said. "The stairs on a number of homes are pushed
away from the door so the angry evil spirits cannot
come into the houses and bite the children!" More
fiery darts of the Wicked One from rumors and
reports.

"And," he added significantly, "two of our group
with their little boy did not come back with us to
listen." We knew he meant the Tawbuid who wore a
pig tooth on his necklace, and among ourselves we

had referred to him as "Pig-Tooth." He was afraid. So we prayed that God's superior power, able even to raise the dead, would be understood.

Slowly we began to realize that the Tawbuid were not so much moved by God's love as by His *power*. They needed to know the power of God, who is all good, to overcome the powers of the capricious evil spirits that have constantly dominated their lives.

Before dark the rest of the Tawbuid began to arrive from the interior. Watching them squat down until the heavily-laden baskets on their backs were resting on the ground, we were delighted to see the supply of sweet potatoes, bananas, squash, and taro root. Tied here and there on the outside were little green leaf packets containing their protein: succulent grubs, tasty little lizards, tiny fish, and several large white snails.

But my eyes were searching for the young wife who needed medicine for her wound. Suddenly I saw her. I was aghast. There she was, sparkling clean, clothed in new bark-cloth. But her head was completely bald! Shaven clean!

"Oh, no!" I wailed inwardly. Too late I remembered that *malanu*, the word I had used for clean, when applied to the head means a bald one! Recovering from the shock, I quickly got out the medicines, salves and bandages, only too glad to begin to cure her neglected wound, and somehow make up for the loss of her hair which was my fault. Afterwards as she walked away with her contented, shy smile, I was relieved that her shiny head didn't seem to bother her as much as it did me!

On the second Sunday "Pig-Tooth" and his wife and little boy returned. Pedro, one of the Tadyawan, was busy making sugar cane juice to use as "wine" and roasting a sweet potato for the "bread." For that morning the first Tadyawan baptisms would take place, and then the Lord's supper would be observed by the newly-baptized believers and the missionaries.

At the regular Tawbuid afternoon service which followed, Pig-Tooth told everyone, "We have decided we will follow the words of our interior leader, Balinguy, and not listen to this New Teaching." Promptly he, his wife and little boy left. Fervently everyone began to pray for them.

"They have gone," the others told us, "because Balinguy and the other interior leaders are making threats and sending curses down the river." I shivered as we remembered the five deaths in Pangalkagan caused by an angry shaman.

By the next day the sores on my legs caused by grass cuts were getting worse. To keep them dry I had to forego the usual refreshing swim. Then it rained most of the afternoon, and while we were house-bound, chatting, someone asked us, "You know Balinguy's first wife that he gave to his younger brother?"

"Yes, we know that one," I answered, dodging the drips from the leaky roof. "She is Tiban's older sister."

"Well," our informant said, "the younger brother is here and wants to take her back into the interior when he goes. But she is afraid. She thinks they will kill her. What are Funbalugu's Words about that?"

How could we possibly answer? To be truthful might be to sign her death warrant. Hesitantly we had to tell them, "He tells us that a man and wife should be together." But God intervened. She had severe chills and fever and was unable to accompany him, and he went alone.

The following afternoon our lesson was on the Holy Spirit, and there was unusual freedom and understanding. Someone, surely, was praying for us as we taught. This helped prepare us for the news that Balinguy had sent word that his former wife was not to be baptized under any conditions!

Why did he keep opposing and hindering? But we continued teaching. These eager listeners were memorizing all the verses, choruses, and now the ten commandments. Each day we taught one command-ment, illustrating it with a New Testament story. They tried to learn all these stories, too!

On our last night with them the pungent odor of the leaf-wrapped resin torch filled the air, for the little kerosene bottle lamp with its rag wick just wouldn't light. Between scrapings of the torch, as it spit and smoked, they told us, "We are sorry you are going. We might forget the teachings, the songs, the Bible verses and the stories."

"Oh, those stories," someone added, "they are the hardest to remember! We forget the names of all those people!" Later we learned that they knew the Bible stories were true accounts of real people because they all had names!

"How soon can you return? We want to hear more!" another added.

So that night before going to bed we studied the calendar. "Three weeks," we told them, "will give you time to weed and care for your fields, and give us enough time to prepare more lessons."

We were torn between the hungry, eager listeners

here in Eastern Mindoro and our needy, yet uncommitted, friends on the Western side. During part of the three weeks out of the hills Russell and Bob Hanselman with two Buhid church leaders hiked to the west to visit Pangalkagan.

The Buhid believers were excited to meet Makisig, the object of their prayers for several years. But response to Russell's teaching was the same polite listening, with the request to be sure and come back.

As we began our hike into the hills for our second teaching trip, both Tadyawan and Tawbuid met us to carry our packs and help us through the many swift river crossings. I was light-hearted. The rain had stopped, the sun was out and we were going to teach an eager, interested, loving group of people.

We had covered about three-fourths of the trip, and as I looked at my watch I was pleased to see that we were making good time. We'd be arriving at the house-by-the-river quite early in the afternoon, so there'd be plenty of time to get cleaned up, organize our things, and even have a rest before the evening service.

Then, without any warning, the men set our packs down on the stones at the river side and began wading in the water, as if to test its warmth. I was glad for the few minutes' rest this would give us.

After some examination accompanied by shouts and laughter, they began to pile rocks in the water forming a line at an angle to the shore. I enjoyed their fun but after about half an hour I was ready to go. I was tired and hot. I wanted to finish the trip, have a cool bath in the river and relax. Surely they would leave soon? But as I reluctantly watched, it was clear that they were having too much fun.

"Whatever are they doing?" I complained to Russell.

"They're fishing," he told me simply. "That's a dam they're building out of those stones and leaves. It'll divert the water from the main part of the river, making a side-stream. When the water in the main part is low enough, they'll reach under the rocks and catch any little fish or eels they can find. It's the fun way of fishing!"

"Well, I wish they'd have their fun some other time!" I said crossly. By now the sky was beginning to cloud over, and I wanted to call out, "Come on! Let's go! We want to get there before it rains!"

Two hours went by and I really became upset. But I tried not to show it. Why didn't they take us there with our packs and then come back and fish? We were wasting so much time! Finally they came out of the water joking and laughing. How dare they? Nonchalantly they picked up the packs and we all set off.

Stiff, sore and terribly weary I got off my rock and plodded along, rebelliously. Suddenly the sky let loose. Rain began to soak us as we quickly got out the plastics to cover our packs. How could they be so thoughtless? If they hadn't stopped we'd be there now and in the shelter of the house. I was steaming, and not just from the sultry tropical rain!

Somehow we arrived, cleaned up and got ready for the evening meeting. I didn't even feel like being congenial. I was weary, cross and in no mood for anything. After the song time, verse reciting and prayer, Russell began a review of the Fiery Furnace lesson. And God spoke to me.

What a price those men had paid to serve God,

and what opposition they had endured. And yet how loyal and true they had remained. And I was unwilling even to get wet! How unworthy I was even to be here! I bowed my head in shame, blew my nose, and asked God to forgive me. I don't know if the Tawbuid learned much that night, but I certainly did.

We had two new lessons each day and one review, using large Sunday School poster pictures to add color and interest. Having seen almost no pictures, everyone would gather round after the lesson to examine the many details of animals, houses, utensils and dress. Some would shyly lift up the picture to look at the other side for more details of the backs of the people. Just like their Pangalkagan counterparts!

The only way they could learn the choruses was to sing several words behind us, repeating what we sang. After several days one clever lad was able to sing three words ahead of us!

When we introduced the new song "Daniel was a man of Prayer" everyone beamed! Later we learned it had their own Tawbuid seven-beat poetical rhythm. But at the time we thought the word-story was the reason they enjoyed it, so we wrote additional verses on Noah, Moses and Jonah.

Attendance and attention were excellent in spite of much sickness. One young couple was very concerned for their newborn daughter, as she had an open sore on her back. Nurse Dode lovingly dressed it each day, although we wondered if it would be possible for this extremely tiny newborn to live.

One afternoon I found one of the men lying on a piece of bark under the house close to a small open fire. Shaking with chills and fever, he could hardly grasp the malaria tablets I handed to him.

Later the wee baby's mother was unwell, too. I gave her hot sweetened tea, a new taste, and medicine. Then several days after that, Tiban, his wife and little daughter became ill, as well as the two children of Mr Squint, (as we later learned to call him).

But no one performed any sacrifices for the sicknesses or sang to the evil spirits. We prayed with them and gave medicine where we could. And we praised God for their new trust in Him. We could not help wondering, *would it be the same if we were not here?*

After this visit we started back to Ligaya with Rick and Becky, now on vacation from school. On the way we were detained a week in San Jose as two typhoons hit in succession, but it didn't affect our joy-filled month together.

When they returned to Baguio, we again headed for Pinamalayan for a third and last visit to Banos River before our furlough. What a delight to see the remodeled house-by-the-river, with new flooring, new walls and a new roof! And even a larger, but still too high, stage for us.

A new family, too, had joined us, the sister of evil Balinguy, and her husband, whose name we later learned was Bumblebee, with their two youngest children. They went back again into the interior to fetch their oldest son from her brother's village, and when they returned Balinguy's sister's eyes were wild with fear.

"Wicked! Wicked! He is very, very wicked," she cried out hysterically about her brother. "His words are wicked. He is a very wicked man!" He had ordered them not to stay at the Banos and listen, but with what threatening curses, we didn't ask.

That night a wild thunderstorm struck, causing terrible fear and anxiety. Defiance of one who has power and authority is not taken lightly by any Tawbuid. Russell reminded them of God's unsurpassed power, and then in his practical way began to explain how thunder is simply caused by two masses of air coming together. I'm not sure they understood, but his quiet calmness could be felt, and the verse they had memorized, "I will trust and not be afraid" put their eyes on the All-Powerful God.

The next morning the Tawbuid moved our cooking fire under the house, for it was too rainy out in the open. They not only laid it, but lit it for us, piling beside it a fine stack of wood for our use! And then one by one the different families began to bring fragrant newly-harvested rice, roasted pumpkin seeds and one even offered us a tiny lizard for our breakfast.

Late that night we could all hear someone singing to the evil spirits. The people were upset and concerned. "That is bad," they told us, an insight that came from the Lord. Everyone was fearful. Someone was disobeying *Funbalugu*. But it was not one of Tiban's group of listeners.

And then they began to examine their own lives. "Is it bad to *Funbalugu* if we smoke our little pipes?" one asked us.

"Why do you smoke?" Russell inquired.

"It keeps the mosquitos away, especially when we are working in the fields," they told him. We had noticed that few had tobacco, just a live coal or papaya leaves would do.

"You ask *Funbalugu*," Russell suggested, "and He will put the right thoughts into your mind. And then be sure to do as He says." And as an afterthought he added, "But don't hide what you do, for that is bad."

And later, "Does it please *Funbalugu* if we make baskets?"

If they make baskets? Why, what could be wrong with that? And then we realized that we did not make baskets, and some baskets were used for cursing. Perhaps that is why they asked. We were able to assure them that basket making was an art we would like to master!

Reading had not progressed beyond the syllable stage, but we were pleased when Squint's wife could actually recognize several syllables. That is, until her husband came in. And then she didn't seem to remember any of them! Later we would see many times this special regard and love that wives showed to their husbands, being careful they never appeared to outshine them!

Finally the last day of our visit arrived. Rain poured outside. Inside the four walls, with two cooking fires under the bamboo slat floor and one on a hearth right in the room, I felt like I was in a choking smoke-house. But no one else seemed to notice.

That morning's lesson was Christ's Temptation. After forty days and forty nights he hungered. *I hunger, too!* I thought in self-pity. *After fourteen days I'm hungry for clean crisp sheets on a real bed, for nice clothes, for some exercise not in the rain, for food besides rice and sweet potatoes.* Continuing my self-centered thoughts, *And after four years on the field I'm hungry for a nice home with our children always near, so we can enjoy real family life. No one really appreciates all I've given up to be here!*

And then God spoke to my heart. Jesus could have made bread from the stones, but it wasn't God's time. One day he would be a bread-maker and feed five thousand people. But not today. And it wasn't God's time for me to have these things. I looked around at the wet muddy floors and drab walls and then I saw the eager faces drinking in God's Word as Russell taught. It was enough.

In the evening, after the story of Cornelius and before Russell made any application, he asked the group, "What is the meaning of Peter's dream, that he was to eat all the animals in the sheet, even if he had never eaten any of them before?"

Tiban wisely replied, "We are to leave all of our old customs that are not good, and do everything that pleases *Funbalugu* even if we have never done it before." What joy filled our hearts as we listened.

It was hard to believe that this was our last visit. For our furlough was due. What would happen to these babes in Christ while we were gone? They didn't have a single book of the Bible in their own language, and they couldn't have read it if they had.

Dode and Caroline would be there for several more months, but when they, too, went on furlough would the Tadyawan be able to help these new believers? Would some bad omen frighten them away? Would they return to their old customs when tested by sickness or death in our absence? We could only commit them to the Lord, and ask our prayer partners to continually remember them too.

Chapter 9

RESPONDING

F urlough! Exchanging our palm-leaf house for a spacious, well-furnished, three-bedroom American home, our summer cottons for winter sweaters and jackets, our Philippine clogs and sneakers for leather shoes and rain-boots, our rice-centered diet for one of interesting variety, and the hot sticky climate for coolness! We enjoyed many delightful moments.

Transfer from the Mission's Chefoo school in Baguio with its fourteen pupils to the public school in Orange, California with over three hundred students was a tearful experience for Rick and Becky at first, that winter of 1962. But soon it became a pleasure.

Leaving the house one rainy morning, Becky was swinging her pink lunch box with its black-painted poodle, her braids sticking out stiffly from under her plastic rainhat and her red rubber boots hurrying so she could catch up and walk with Donna. Instinctively I bowed my head and thanked the Lord for her and for all His loving care, praying her bubbly spirit would show her playmates what it meant to love Jesus.

Then Rick, after practicing the piano for a half-hour, grabbed his jacket and green lunch pail, decided boots weren't necessary today, and hopped on his bike for a quick trip to school. Again I bowed in thankfulness to the Lord. I prayed that he would do well in his school work and would speak a word for his Lord when he had the opportunity, like he had spoken to Bruce just a couple of days before, and they had been good friends ever since.

Basking in the warmth of loving relatives, a caring church, thoughtful friends, faithful prayer partners, and a precious closeness in our own family, I pushed from my mind thoughts of the Tawbuid and our return to Mindoro with its inevitable separations. Secretly I was hoping I would not have to leave my utopia.

Then one day as we were arranging our slides for presenting the tribal work to interested churches, we came across the picture of a brilliant orange life preserver floating on an ocean of deep blue. And God spoke to my heart.

The photo had been taken on our way home, just a few hours before our ship docked in San Francisco. Someone on deck had shouted, "Man overboard! Man overboard!" and the bright orange ring had been thrown into the sea to mark the spot. For four hours the ship circled, trying to locate the missing person. But in the end it was found to be a false alarm, initiated by some young fellows longing for excitement!

God used this memory to open my eyes. If a large steamship company considered that great outlay of time and money worthwhile to save one person's life, surely it was worth the outlay of our whole lives, to look for the Tawbuid and bring them the news of eternal salvation!

Although I knew it would be heart-rending to end

our privileged family closeness, we began to prepare, praying and trusting God, for our return to Mindoro. As we thought of Makisig's group on the Western side, we prayed that their eyes would be open to the truth of God's Word. And for Tiban's people at the Banos River on the Eastern side, that no bad omens or catastrophes would turn them back from their new-found faith in *Funbalugu*.

After we had left for furlough, the Tadyawan missionaries and believers taught and cared for the Tawbuid on the Banos River. Welcome news came from them that Tiban wanted to be baptized. Also, that when his first son was born, he broke with Tawbuid fear-prompted tradition, not only by naming him immediately but also by announcing his name publicly!

When the Tadyawan missionaries also went on furlough a few months later, only the newly-believing Tadyawan were left to teach and encourage the Tawbuid. And now we were returning to Mindoro with no news of them for more than six months.

As our Pinamalayan-bound bus sped along the two-lane Oriental Mindoro highway, I was fighting tears of loneliness for Rick and Becky who had gone straight to Baguio. Will they really enjoy Chefoo school as they did before? Will they resent this separation after our priceless year together? How can we ever be happy without them? "Lord, take care of those two precious children."

As my thoughts shifted to the Tawbuid, I wondered again what had been happening in Pangalka-gan on the West and at the Banos River here in the East. As we neared Pinamalayan, I realized we had no way to send Tiban news of our arrival.

Turning to Russell, I asked, "How will we ever find Tiban's group? We never did learn exactly where their village was. And they won't be meeting in the house-by-the-river because there've been no missionaries to go in and teach them. It's probably even fallen down by now!"

"We'll just have to hunt for them," he said, quite undisturbed. And I knew he meant he would simply trek into the interior trusting in the Lord's help.

Although we planned to visit and teach these Eastern Tawbuid first, later we would be going to see our Western Tawbuid friends at Pangalkagan. Would we settle again in Ligaya to reach them, or move permanently to Pinamalayan to minister to Tiban's group? The people's response to God's Word would be one main guiding factor.

The day after we arrived in Pinamalayan, Russell took the long, lonely trek into the Banos River interior. The following afternoon he returned accompanied by Bumblebee and Tiban! What boldness for these interior men to come all the way into the bustling town just to help us.

"How did you ever find them?" I asked immediately.

"I was hiking along the Banos near the old house-by-the-river," he said, "and the Lord just sent one of the women from Tiban's group right across my path."

It was as simple as that!

"Then she must have gone up to their village and told everyone," he continued, "for that night they all came down to the old house. They even killed five chickens, so we had quite a feast. Then they asked me to teach them more of God's Words."

After Tiban and Bumblebee stayed the night with us, Russell helped them find the right jeepney at the market so they could return home. Each one carried a load in preparation for our coming the following day.

After they left, Russell suggested, "Maybe they will take us right into their village to live!"

"Oh, Hon, that would be great! We could learn so much more and teach them so much better that way." And then, wondering, "Is that what they told you?"

"No, they didn't really say much about it." Then thoughtfully, "But the old house-by-the-river is really dilapidated. We slept in it, but I don't think they're using it any more."

We went in the next day escorted from the end of the *karetela* track by several Tawbuid. After the three-hour crossing and re-crossing of the Banos River, we were disappointed when they began to lead us uphill on the south bank. Russell had learned that their village was somewhere on the north side, though he had no idea how far. But our disappointment turned to amazement.

For more than sixty Tawbuid, children and adults, as well as the three Tadyawan believers who had been teaching them, were waiting to greet us as we finished that hot sticky 45-minute climb from the river to a new large hilltop house. Stooping to enter the welcome dim coolness, we were motioned to a generous section of the bamboo flooring that had been laboriously scrubbed to a glistening golden yellow. A special high shelf had been built above it to hold our things, with even a full can of water in the corner!

Big plates of steaming rice, quickly followed by another of hot boiled *ubi* root, were put into our hands. Feasting on their food and their love, we relaxed, chatting happily as we exchanged news with them.

"Will you begin teaching us tonight?" they anxiously asked. They couldn't wait! So our first ten-day Short-Term Bible School (STBS) began immediately that evening with materials prepared before and during furlough. Full of questions and comments, they showed an interest and desire for God's Word that was deeper and more real than it had been a year ago! That night, completely exhausted but joyously happy, we crawled into our sleeping bags and dozed off to a background of talking, questions and answers, and friendly laughter that must have lasted most of the night.

Still, everyone was up early for a breakfast of boiled sweet potatoes followed by the Morning Bible Hour. We thrilled at their intensity in memorizing the new verses, learning the new choruses and listening to the Bible lesson.

Although their enthusiasm carried over as we began the reading and writing classes, it was an unrelenting struggle. They giggled their embarrassment when they couldn't remember whether those marks meant "ba" or "ma." Or when the chalk wouldn't go the right direction on the small writing boards held in their laps. And in their giggling, they sighed and many gave up. These strange abilities seemed far beyond them.

After the classes Russell enlisted their help with the names of the books of the Bible. Rather than transliterate them so that "Genesis" became *Enesis* and "Exodus" *Esudu*, he had the God-given vision of translating the meaning. "Genesis" then became *Fagfasigadun* or "The Beginnings" and "Exodus" was *Fagalinan* or "The Going Out." Later we learned that the meaning of a name is important to the Tawbuid, so eventually Russell carried this innovation to include almost all the names in the Bible, as most of them express an idea. We were rewarded by their obvious enjoyment as they began learning the significance of the names in the Bible stories.

Then they began telling us their real names, overcoming the inherent fear that those who know your true name have power over you. As we thanked God for this increased trust and confidence in us, we prayed that it would be so strong that they would invite us to live right in their own village. This house-on-the-hilltop where they gathered when we came to teach them was good, but being a part of their normal lives would be even better.

At prayer time during the Bible Hour each day, four of the men took turns praying, and as we bowed with them, we worshipped our God who had brought such spiritual depth into their lives. The women didn't pray publicly, but when the baby, who had had the open sore on her back, was whimpering and kicking to be nursed, the mother, Dawa's wife, held her tightly and quietly bowed her head, making the infant wait before putting the little one to her breast!

Another evidence of response to God's Word was the questions they asked. The most pressing of the moment was, "Is it good if a man leaves his wife and takes another?"

Dawa's wife whispered to me, "They are asking about Balinguy's younger brother. You know he was given Balinguy's old wife who had no children. And now he wants to abandon her and find someone younger."

Personally I felt it was unfair that he was saddled with the old wife, gentle as she was, for he was about eighteen and she seemed very old at fifty. I would have liked to give him permission to find someone more suitable, someone his own age.

But the Scriptures were clear on that point and we could only hold up what they taught. Soon we would be duplicating First Corinthians 7:10-11 on one of the handout memory sheets done in giant primer type. Even if no one was yet able to read, the words would be faithfully memorized and obeyed, "And now I say, and even our Lord says to the married couples, Wife, do not leave your husband... And husband, do not leave your wife." Little did we realize that making no exceptions would set the pattern, begun during our very first teaching session before furlough, of permanent marriages for all Tawbuid believers. Separation would never even be considered an option.

In those first ten days of teaching after our furlough, the conviction began to grow that we should settle permanently here in Oriental Mindoro, ministering to these eager, responsive Tawbuid. Plans for moving our belongings from Ligaya to Pinamalayan began to form in our minds.

We left the hills to prepare more materials for our next ten-day session, praying the believers would not become too dependent on our presence. Traveling home from that initial visit, we were escorted by the Tawbuid who carried my pack for the four-hour hike. Russell purposely shouldered his own so they would know that being a teacher or leader does not exempt one from work.

During the hour ride to Pinamalayan, we vividly experienced the meaning of our isolation in the hills. As the jeepney was jumping from one rut to another, we were trying to balance our packs on top of the sacks of copra, converse amicably with the other passengers and yet not be bounced off the bench seats. Seeing our packs and muddy clothes, they began to ask us where we had been and what our work was. This was always a welcome opportunity to tell them of the Lord.

Suddenly one man raised his voice above the rest, "Who is President Kennedy's *Bise*?" He pronounced it "Bee-say."

Bise? Bise? And then Russell caught his meaning. "Oh, his vice-president. It's Johnson." But as Russell looked at him for a response, the man nodded his head, and said nothing more. Strange. We couldn't imagine why he was asking us that question.

It wasn't until we reached Pinamalayan that we heard the shocking news which prompted his question. It was November 1963, and President Kennedy had been shot! Assassinated! And already buried! We had been secluded in the hills and hadn't even known about it. And now Kennedy's *Bise*, Kennedy's Vice-President, was our President. It gave us a hollow feeling of isolation and loneliness, to have been so cut off from the outside world that we didn't even know what was happening in our own country.

But we hardly had time for loneliness. Rick, now

in fifth grade, and Becky in third came home for Christmas vacation, delighting us with their contentment at school and their joy of oneness with us.

On our second visit to the hills all four of us shared the hilltop-house with the Tawbuid. Becky enjoyed baby-sitting in their rattan hammocks, swinging whichever infant was awake. And she had nine to choose from! Rick was so eager to learn Tawbuid that he began a vocabulary word list which he later transferred to a miniature file. The visit was kept lively and challenging for all of us, not only by the children's fun with more than twenty Tawbuid-speaking playmates, but also by the perceptive questions of the adults, the reports of their activities while we were gone, and the sharing of their problems.

They told us that after our last visit they had decided to continue to meet every morning and every evening even though we were not there. They prayed, sang, recited memorized verses and even tried to retell one of the Bible stories for each meeting.

We were glad now that we had begun our teaching by simply telling Bible stories, the lives of men and women of the Scriptures. Because our Tawbuid had been so limited, we had not gone into long explanations or applications of the truths, but concentrated on making the stories clear and accurate. They had listened carefully, trying to remember each detail, and especially each name, which to them indicated that the event had actually happened. As the truth of each story gripped them, it increased their understanding of who God was, how he worked and how men should behave.

So, as one of the men would tell the story, his

attentive audience would helpfully supply any missing details! Applications were not given, for enough sweat was produced just trying to remember and tell the story. But the truths were understood, and their faith kept growing.

So did their problems. Intruders from the outside were not only trying to take their laboriously-cleared land, but also stealing their growing crops. What could be done?

Russell told them that planted trees help establish a claim to the land, and later he actually took a load of seedlings to them. He showed them how to put their thumb prints on a petition to request that the land be reserved for their use. "But it probably won't do much good," he remarked to me.

Other questions surfaced, too. "What are God's Words to new mothers," many asked us. "Are our own customs good? Is it good for visitors to be kept away from the mother and the newborn? Is it good for her to sit up for five days and nights after the birth?"

We not only wanted to show them what God's Word teaches, but also to help them in practical matters of life and health. This meant we had to carefully sort out our own customs as westerners, as Americans, and as Christians. To us, for example, both of these childbirth practices seemed to be good protection against infections. But it was not our way of doing things. So we also had to consider their customs as Tawbuid and their customs as spirit worshippers, not in the light of our practices but in the light of the Scriptures. We encouraged them to keep their own Tawbuid ways if they were not contrary to God's Words. We knew that as they responded to God, He would lead them to do what pleased Him.

Many of their customs they kept, or modified slightly, like allowing visitors to new mothers on the first day. They were constantly evaluating all they did in the light of new lessons from God's Words. Some practices they did change, like planning to take the New Teaching to the interior Tawbuid. Normally they would never go to another village unless there was a pressing need, like a wife for their son. Even then they were so suspicious they would not enter the homes, but would simply squat at the edge of the clearing, calling out their mission until they were joined by someone from the group of houses. Cooked food was rarely given or received as it might have been cursed or poisoned, which is the same word in Tawbuid. A trip by the believers into the interior would be one instance of God's courage replacing old fears.

At the same time, they were considerate of the beliefs of those they wanted to reach. Wisely they told us, "Those people in the interior are really afraid of paper, so the Wordless Book would not be good for them. They would be so terrified that they would never listen." They thought tape recordings or records could be used instead, and would also help them remember the stories and the teaching.

"If we could just read those papers," suggested Tiban, "we would be able to remember everything!" And as the others brightened at this suggestion our hearts soared in praise to our prayer-answering God. Now they would really want to learn!

The five delightful weeks with Rick and Becky were ended, and as they returned to Baguio it hurt to put away the tetherball, the beach towels, the ice-cream freezer, and their hill-hiking clothes. On Saturday, with heavy steps because we missed our children, we arrived at the hilltop-house. Sunshine broke through the clouds as Tiban announced that we would all be moving right into their very own newly-constructed village on Monday!

What a noisy, happy, scrambling crowd we were with chickens, pigs, children, baskets, rice sacks, and hobbling old grannies. Big kids were carrying little kids. Daddies shouldering big loads were guiding small sons. Mothers, helping tiny daughters, were carrying from headbands well-loaded baskets with baby tucked in on top. A joyous disorganized affair, slipping and sliding down, down, down the muddy slope, washing our feet clean in the rock-choked Banos River at the bottom. Crossing it we went up, up, up, with the last bit an impossible straight ascent on the side of a miry cliff. Then suddenly we were on the top of the world!

The winding path of the Banos River stretched far below us. Here on the hilltop we stood gazing at the first new, trim *Funbalugu Bale*, or "God's House." Standing solidly on tall firm posts, it had reddish bark walls, a thick palm-leaf roof and a sturdy bamboo floor. The front door had real ladder steps instead of the usual single pole. The back door stepped down into the leader's home, and the significance of elevating God's floor above his own did not escape us.

The *Funbalugu Bale* was our home while we were there. But no one else was allowed to eat in it, sleep in it or come in with muddy feet! It was jealously guarded to see that it was properly respected. And around it the people were building their new homes.

Six of them so far.

Even though leaders in the interior continued to threaten, sending curses down the river, three more families joined the believers as new listeners. One Sunday more than seventy Tawbuid attended the three meetings, though at the daily services there were usually about sixty, including the children. Tiban said two more groups wanted to listen but they had colds, so were not yet coming.

What was causing such response? They came when they learned that we knew their language, but apart from God's supernatural work there was more natural reason for them to be afraid and stay away! No sacrifices were made in the village to placate the evil spirits, so those who were not trusting in God's power and His Words were afraid to live there.

In an interlude between two visits to the Banos River, we went to Occidental Mindoro, and again saw that power of fear in which the evil spirits hold the Tawbuid. Arriving at Pangalkagan about midday, we climbed up into their bamboo and thatch house, and Binsulna seemed genuinely glad to see us. As we shooed away the chickens and settled ourselves on the cluttered floor, she told us that her mother, Mangena, in the house behind hers was seriously ill.

So we went around back into the tiny shack where she was lying on her bark sleeping mat, breathing with great difficulty under her blanket of sacking. Fear of death was prominent in the eyes of her son-in-law as he took the tiny can of fish we had given for the sick woman, and later as he offered us a piece of pork. We were saddened by Mangena's physical condition and the pig so obviously sacrificed for her.

But both Binsulna and her husband Karias listened carefully as I told them of the group of Eastern Tawbuid across the mountains who wanted us to live with them and teach them God's Word daily. And they nodded appreciatively when I described the little bark-walled *Funbalugu Bale*. When Binsulna heard that these Tawbuid tried to obey everything the Bible told them to do, she said, "We want to have you teach us God's commands, too, and we will obey everything He tells us." She had told us that before, but still they followed their old customs of evil spirit worship. All we could do was to teach them God's Word, and pray that they would choose God's way.

Perched on a small log that extended from the now-dead cooking fire, I began with a brief lesson on prayer. I told them, if they really believed in Him, to pray as they got up in the morning asking God to help them throughout the day. They could thank Him for their food before each meal. They could ask for His protection on the trail, for His help as they work in their fields, and for His care over the children left at home. I reminded them to pray for peaceful hearts before they went to sleep each night, since darkness brings many fears. How desperately I wanted them to commit themselves to the Lord and trust in Him.

Just as I finished, Baraku came into the house. Binsulna immediately turned to me, "Teach the newly-arrived-one all that you have just taught us." And so the review lesson began for Baraku, who soon might be their leader. Makisig, who continued to show little interest, was ill and growing weaker each day. After four days we reluctantly left them, pledging to visit them when we could.

Returning to Eastern Mindoro we were thankful that the rainy season had not yet begun. The Banos River was low, so we didn't have to fight the swift current. We did have to be alert, however, to keep our balance on the slippery moss-covered stones just under the surface of the water.

We were with five Tawbuid who had come out of the hills the day before to ensure that they would be at the end of the *karetela* track when we arrived early that morning. After the river travel, the ascent to the village began on a huge slippery log. Suddenly I saw Bumblebee climb onto the log ahead of me, reach out to take my very willing hand, and help me up its entire slope.

Continuing up the hill, avoiding the newly-sprouting rice, over more logs, and up slippery steps cut in the mud, I was kept steady by Bumblebee's strong grip.

In half an hour we reached the hilltop, and relaxed on the clean split-bamboo floor of the *Funbalugu Bale*. Showered with my profuse thanks, Bumblebee went on to his own house.

A few minutes later one of the believers stuck his head in the door (maybe his feet were muddy!) with sad news, "Did you know that Bumblebee's baby boy died yesterday while he was out meeting you?"

Shocked, I could hardly reply. "Why, no. No, we hadn't yet heard. Whatever happened?" The baby couldn't have been more than a year old.

As he described the symptoms, we were sure it was pneumonia. If only we had been there, we might have been able to help. Several weeks before, a baby girl with similar trouble had responded well to our medication. But we knew God did not make mistakes, even in timing. He was allowing them to be tested.

No one was there when the death occurred to tell these new believers how to conduct a funeral service, and it must have been very sad for Bumblebee's wife, as he was gone. Later we learned that they had gathered and sung from memory, "Don't fear, don't be afraid" and other hymns that they knew. Then, after taking the little bark-cloth-wrapped body out into the jungle, they returned to the *Funbalugu Bale* to sing the same hymns again, to pray and to recite their memorized Scripture. A vivid contrast to their old custom of sacrifices, spirit chanting and fleeing from their homes, all prompted by fear of the ghost.

Slowly and thoughtfully we went over to the home to comfort and encourage the parents and family, and to explain to them that their little boy was now "safe in the arms of Jesus" as Fanny Crosby has so aptly expressed it. We prayed that this deep sorrow would not turn them away from their new-found faith. The mother had already suffered severely at the hands of her evil brother, Balinguy, when she decided to follow the Lord.

The very same week that his baby died, Bumblebee decided he would like to be part of the first group to be baptized. We rejoiced in the steadiness of his trust in God. His baptism was a public declaration even to those in the interior, including Balinguy, that he had left the old customs of spirit worship and was obeying God's Words. And his wife, though not yet feeling bold enough to be baptized, was right beside him in her faith.

When we returned to Pinamalayan, Russell immediately began work on a new booklet, "When We Bury," to help them as they faced future deaths, even though no one could yet read. A few were trying to learn, and we were preparing materials and praying. Hymn sheets and verse sheets in large primer type had been mimeographed, and the preliminary translation of the first chapter of Mark had been completed.

Then on our visit to the hills just as rice harvest began, another sad incident reinforced their growing desire to read.

That evening our ten-day STBS began with the Creation Story, and continued in Genesis for nineteen sessions. Some of these were review, but we could now teach in greater detail with application of Scripture truths because we had more vocabulary and the people had more Bible knowledge.

After the meeting, a newly-arrived couple brought their thin two-year-old boy to us. A small swelling was noticable on his neck, and his mother told us he would not eat and cried when he was moved. The parents wanted medicine, but although we asked a number of questions we couldn't seem to determine any other symptoms. All we could do was pray.

Sunday morning after the second service, he died. We felt sad and defeated, grieving with the parents and the four-year-old brother. For the funeral service Russell used the new booklet, "When we Bury" that contained appropriate hymns and verses of Scripture. As they carried the little body out of the church, I prayed for this family who had almost no teaching from God's Word.

Quietly the leader's wife told me that the child's illness began when he fell from a rattan hammock that the children, trying to please him, had been swinging vigorously. *Could his neck have been broken?* I wondered sadly.

As we all visited with the parents afterwards in the *Funbalugu Bale*, trying to ease their sorrow, several of the men began to look through the new booklet Russell had used. Some of the song titles they could recognize, but no one could actually read the pages which told what God was saying to console those who were sorrowing. On this occasion it was obvious that their determination to master reading was given another nudge.

Then a few weeks later we made a startling discovery which not only encouraged us but also gave them an additional incentive to learn.

Chapter 10

LEARNING

"**T**aglagi can read!"

I had just come back from the stream with a full pan of clean wet laundry, and was starting to climb the ladder steps of the *Funbalugu Bale* when Russell came to the doorway, reaching out his hands for the heavy pan.

"I need the clothespins, Hon." I was breathing heavily from the hill climb.

As he went over to get them from our corner of the church, he called back over his shoulder those startling words, "Taglagi can read!"

Too amazed to speak, I quickly looked up, waiting for him to turn around. I expected his twinkling eyes to meet mine betraying his usual teasing. It just couldn't be true. As far as I knew, Taglagi, in his early teens, had not even been seriously studying.

Taking the clothespins, I searched his earnest face, "He can read? Really read?" I asked incredulously.

As Russell picked up the pan of laundry and followed me out to the rattan line strung between the church and the house next door, I asked, "Were you going over the First Primer with him?"

"No. It wasn't the reading primer at all," he replied. "I was just sitting there in the church, studying my Bible lesson for tonight, and some of the young people came in.

"Taglagi with that shy grin of his edged over towards me and picked up one of my sheets of typed notes. I heard him begin sounding out the syllables. 'Fun...ba...lu...gu. Fun-ba-lu-gu, oh! *Funbalugu!*' Then 'na..a..wat. na-a-wat, oh! *naawat. Funbalugu naawat!*' He'd really caught on! He worked through half a page for me with real understanding, making sense out of it. Honestly, Hon, he's as pleased as I am!"

I couldn't believe it! Shaking out Russell's dark blue short pants, I began to hang them up. "I wonder how long he's been able to do that? Maybe he practices on the song sheets and verse sheets we've handed out. Clever boy!" I concluded.

When the last piece of laundry was finally blowing in the soft breeze, we returned to the church to find Dawa's wife waiting to see us.

"Would it be good for you to stick this back onto my husband's shirt?" she asked, handing me a button.

Understanding her meaning, I took it saying, "Oh, yes, I will stick it back on for you." I didn't know any other word for sew. Hunting for the buttonhole in the well-worn garment, I wondered where the shirt had come from. Her husband had been too sick with TB to work for any of the lowland farmers, but maybe someone else had given it to him.

Finding my needle and thread, I was just beginning my handwork when Tiban came in. Realizing what was going on, he broke out in a big grin and showed me the holes in his old dark green T-shirt. "Would it be good," he began the typical way, "if you *infaut* these holes?"

"Oh, yes, I can *infaut* those for you," I said, smiling happily. For though my thread wouldn't match, I was sure he wouldn't mind. And I had just learned the word for mend — the same word that is used to describe an overgrown trail!

Others wandered in, commenting on the swiftly-moving needle, perhaps wishing they had a shirt, even one that needed mending. I was musing how many of their fears had been overcome by their faith in an all-powerful God, so that they were beginning to accept some changes from the outside such as a piece or two of clothing. But their new acquisitions seemed to require constant upkeep.

Later that evening I mentioned to Russell, "What would you think of me teaching the women to sew? I'm sure they'd enjoy it. Maybe I should do it in self-defense!" I laughed.

"Sounds like a good idea to me," he agreed. "But right now with Taglagi's inspiration, maybe we should concentrate on the reading classes."

When Tiban's chicken-guidance test brought his whole village to hear us, we didn't even know how to say book or page, paper or pencil, chalk or board, reading or writing, in Tawbuid. Even though these were new concepts to the people, they were not at a loss for words!

The first time we had showed them our Bible we told them, "These are God's Words and they tell us all about Him and everything He wants us to do. All of our teaching is from this."

"It is God's joined leaves," they said, for to them each page was a leaf.

Then as Russell began reading classes, he wrote syllables on the blackboard, and amid giggling and whispering we could hear, "He is design-making." They were using the term for cutting decorations into bamboo tubes with a jungle knife. And when he pointed to each syllable and read it, someone remarked, "He is counting the design." Counting baby chicks or rattan strips was the same word.

In those beginning months all "designs" looked alike to them. We had felt a great accomplishment if someone learned to recognize that "ba" did not look like "ma", even if the sound it represented was not remembered at all!

When we returned from furlough we found they had "learned" every page of the primer, and could "read" all the syllables and words with complete accuracy whether the booklet was upside-down or right-side up, whether it was open or shut! But very few could remember the right sound when we pointed to a particular syllable in a column, or a word in the middle of a page.

But now that we had moved right into their village where each family had its own home, the new bark-walled *Funbalugu Bale* became a buzzing hive of activity as the men and women studied at the same time on opposite sides of the church. Each morning after the 7 am Worship and Bible Study Hour, we divided for classes in reading and writing and leading worship services.

Besides the primer, we had mimeographed 38 different Bible verse sheets. During each visit we handed out one verse sheet each day to each family. On Sundays we gave out a new song sheet from the 23 we had duplicated, all in the large primer type.

No one, of course, could read, but we thought the verse pages and songs would be a good incentive for learning that skill. One encouraging factor was that by now they were all holding their papers right side up! And now we had learned that Taglagi could read. With new enthusiasm we plunged into our ten-day STBS.

On the second day it was the women's turn to have reading first. So the fourteen men sat on the bamboo floor in their compact circle and received instructions on how to use the song book, a "joined leaves" edition of the individual song "leaves." They were learning to lead the daily worship service. Although they could not read, they learned the page number of each song, and so could locate them in the booklet.

The seventeen women in their loose and wobbly circle, with babies and children constantly climbing in and out of laps, opened their orange-covered Tawbuid First Primer. A few knew some of the syllables already, and others could recognize a.few simple expressions like "Where is father?" and "There is father." But everyone began on the same page, and we "read" around. The women's shy, softly-spoken words couldn't be heard on the other side of the "circle": too many little voices in between! But in spite of it all, they diligently worked for an hour, and were sorry when the books had to be handed over to the men. These in their turn complained that the children were getting the pages dirty!

And now the women's writing class began. On green slates of painted masonite they tackled the laborious task of making their fingers push the chalk in the right direction. The tiny children and babies thought this was a delightful period of the day, as they played with, or ate, the chalk and marked on the slates! One new arrival was copying the letters in complete reverse. Others, making the letters correctly, began at the right hand side and went to the left. There weren't enough slates to go around, so sometimes two women had to sit opposite each other and both write on the same slate. I noticed on one shared slate that one was writing right side up and the other was writing upside down!

Each got the instruction she needed, and all seemed to be having a wonderful time, with a tiny bit of progress each day. By the end of the week two of the women could write simple primer sentences from memory, while others were still trying to form a correct "a". The men however, could even write their names, and Taglagi's letters looked beautifully neat and clear.

More thrilling than their actual progress was the reason behind their desire to read. In the worship hour they were learning the first verse of a new song, "Trust and Obey," our wedding song and life motto. Some couldn't even remember the words from one meeting to the next.

"If we could just read, we would never forget," one sagely observed, and we took up the theme. But what they didn't say, though we well knew, was that production of materials must keep up with advancement in reading. It would prove to be quite a race!

A second primer was nearly ready for those who would soon finish the first one. And the Gospel of Mark was now at verse 19 of chapter two. Translation progress seemed so slow, but it represented many hours of study, thought, typing, checking, retyping, and rechecking. And even then some parts still had to be marked as tentative.

As interest and diligence ran high, we were able to cover ten of the eighteen pages of the first primer during those ten days. After each class we noticed that the ones who learned more quickly seemed to automatically pair up with the slower learners, helping, encouraging and drilling them so they could keep up in class.

Returning to Pinamalayan with a light heart, we were not prepared for the letter that awaited us.

Becky had had an accident. Climbing up the fourteen-foot rope in the high-ceilinged car-port, she was nearly at the top when the rope suddenly came loose. As her letter told it, "I fell down a long way. I got hurt as I fell on my back and on my head and on my seat. I had to go to the hospital for an x-ray. It was the Baguio General. I had to stay overnight and until Friday afternoon. When I was at the hospital Miss Nicoll [their dearly-loved teacher] stayed with me. Green Eyes my [stuffed] dog also came to keep me company. While I was at the hospital I said Bible verses and sang hymns to my nurse. I am very well but my back aches a little."

Rick commented somberly, "And all that time I was playing baseball!" Thoughtful, caring Rick. Always looking out for Becky from the first day she joined him at school. And now in the present crisis he hadn't been able to play a part! We felt the same way. The x-rays showed no damage and two days later she was her old bouncy self, hiking with the rest of the children to the water-buffalo pasture. But as we read the letters we wept. While praising God for the house-parents and Miss Nicoll, so loved and so loving, and for those guardian angels who take care of little tomboys, we wanted to be the ones to rush to her side, to comfort her, help her and love her. It hurt to be so far away from our children.

But God encouraged us through our next hill visit. When we arrived we found the people in our absence had learned those last eight pages of the first primer! And the five best readers knew the pages perfectly.

So we began to introduce the destination names on buses and jeepnies, "Calapan, "Pinamalayan," "Bongabon," "Mansalay." And to teach the women, like the men, to become more familiar with numbers and how to write their own names.

Although they had been telling us their given names, there were no family names among the Tawbuid. Realizing that full names would be needed as they had increasingly more contact with the outside world, Russell decided to help them find family names.

"Would it be good to use the given name of your paternal grandfather for your surname?" Russell asked the believers. "However," he added sagaciously, "if that one was an evil person, would it be good to choose instead the given name of your maternal grandfather?" And so each family acquired a meaningful surname which accurately portrayed the family relationships.

Back at our base house in Pinamalayan we made a song book and a verse book for each family by sewing the individual "leaves" together inside bright green and orange tagboard covers. We also completed a third primer.

While Russell was mimeographing math worksheets for the men, I was out at one of the small Chinese shops, buying tiny spools of red, white and black thread and packages of needles with the very largest eyes.

Back up in the hills again, I began my new sewing class. The women sat in their characteristic circle, each with a needle and thread and two small pieces of cloth. Much giggling accompanied each attempt to push the thread into the needle. When this had been accomplished, with admiring smiles from the others who were still making vain attempts, the next hurdle was the knot at the thread's end. Finally the unruly bit of limp thread was knotted, and the stitching started.

I was learning, too. At first they followed my example carefully, holding the two pieces of cloth together and pushing the needle through one way, and then back. But soon they were giving it the Tawbuid flavor, drawn from their experience in weaving rattan baskets. The far end of the two pieces of cloth was held by their toes, while the left hand held the near ends. The right hand then stabbed the material and pulled the needle through.

Their crowning achievement was making rag dolls, using my pattern and their own soft newly-pounded bark cloth, stuffing them with rice straw. At the end of the week each one kept her needle and many bought the little three-cent spools of thread. Mission accomplished!

While this exciting activity occupied the women, Russell was giving the men instructions in simple math. When he asked, "How much is four plus four," one of the teenagers immediately answered, "Six!" How amazed he was to count four fingers on one hand and four on the other and find it actually was eight!

They not only learned from us, but also from believers in other tribes, like the visit Tiban and his nephew Kulas made with us to the Buhid where Bob and Joy Hanselman work and the first joint Tawbuid-Buhid evangelistic trek which followed.

The Buhid and Tawbuid had several things in common. The base house in Pinamalayan was shared by their missionaries, with the Hanselmans living on the ground floor while we were on the upper floor. And the two languages are more similar than those of any of the other tribes.

On that visit Tiban and Kulas were entertained in a Buhid home where one of the men was bilingual, while we stayed with Bob and Joy. This was the first time the Tawbuid had seen a missionaries' house in the hills separate from the church.

There were other firsts also. During the Sunday services the next day they saw tribal women praying publicly. And as the coconut shell was passed for the morning offering, they were full of questions. "Why is money being put into the *taya*?" "Who takes care of it?" "What will be done with it?" The next time we were with the Tawbuid in their services, we noticed that a coconut shell was produced and passed for the weekly collection!

They learned not only from the worship service on Sunday, but also how God can supply on Monday. The needed guide for the trip across the mountains just "happened" to be at the Buhid village and planned to return home that very Monday.

In just six days from the time they left, the six men were back at Hanselmans' Buhid tribal home, with sore feet, aching muscles and a good report.

Gospel Recordings records had been played in the

Buhid homes where they stayed along the way, and the two Buhid believers had talked earnestly to the families about the Lord.

On the third day they had left Buhid territory, and arrived at Makisig's village of Pangalkagan. We had prayed that he would accept a phonograph and a set of the new Tawbuid records, hoping it would help and encourage his people to trust in Christ. In the past they had always refused the phonograph, but the records then had only been in Tagalog.

Again Makisig was reluctant. But the others in his group were so anxious to have it, that he finally allowed them to take it in exchange for five large sweet potatoes. This made it their own, not just borrowed. Russell felt that it was only Makisig's reluctant spirit that kept the group from showing more outward enthusiasm for the message.

After the Tawbuid returned home, they had a renewed desire to teach in the interior as they had seen the Buhid doing. For those who still feared paper, the phonograph was used. For those who had listened to the explanation of the Wordless Book, the believers could have used other illustrated materials. But all the teaching posters we had seen were built around Tagalog words and phrases, making them useless to the Tawbuid. We saw the answer to this need just when we ourselves needed encouragement the most.

Our vacation in cool mile-high Baguio City with Rick and Becky and my sister Ann was very special that year. For the Baguio Chefoo school was closing, and the children had to go all the way to Malaysia for their next year of schooling. It would be almost five months before we would see them again.

The sunny mornings, unusual for that season, were ideal as Russell, Rick and Becky spent hours at the water-buffalo pasture picking wild raspberries. Just before noon Ann and I would come with the lunch. Then as the afternoon fog and drizzle began we would all hurry home to fill the kitchen with the tantalizing aroma of berry pies (thanks to Ann) and berry jam (thanks to Russell and the children).

Russell and I tried not to think of the distance they were going from us, but just to enjoy being together. Eating popcorn and roasting marshmallows in front of the big fireplace. Playing games. Working on stamp collections. Reading, knitting, and talking. And we told them about our new baby to be born during their next vacation at home. "Five months is such a long time to wait to see him," Becky sighed.

When we returned to Manila where the four girls and two boys would be boarding the ship with their beloved teacher Jenny Boyden, everyone was in a bubble of excitement. Jenny was such fun that there were no tears, no frets, just grandiose excitement as they oh-ed and ah-ed over the luxurious accomodations, even down on F deck.

But after they left there was that sad empty longing. On our way to the mission home from the docks, Ann suggested that we go by the OMF Publishers, for she wanted to pick up some tracts and books. When we walked in the store, our OMF manager called us aside.

"Say, there's something here all of you tribal workers will be interested in seeing!" he commented enthusiastically. When he brought out the proofs of the special new Mangyan poster, "The Gulf Bridged", we immediately brightened.

"They've drawn tribal people!" I said, thrilled. This two-page teaching aid was being produced in bold bright colors, depicting the gulf made by sin between God and man, and showing the cross of Christ as the bridge. There were no printed words to confuse the barely literate tribal "evangelists." It was just what was needed to make it easier for the believers to explain God's great plan of salvation to those interior listeners.

Seeing that poster helped to dry our inward tears and take us back to Mindoro if not with joyful enthusiasm, at least with warm encouragement.

When we arrived in the hills a week later we found the place buzzing with activity. A number of new faces encouraged us and the growing piles of soft fluffy rattan scrapings by every house intrigued us. Beside each pile someone was industriously splitting the double arm-lengths of round rattan, cleaning them and tying them into bundles of a hundred, ready for selling.

The purpose became clear on Monday when the men carried out ten thousand lengths of split rattan and returned with a pig!

"Maybe they're going to raise pigs," I suggested to Russell. But that wasn't what they had in mind! The next morning we were wakened by the jarring final squeal of the pig followed by the rythmic pounding of unhusked rice. And slowly it began to dawn on us, "They must be preparing a feast!"

As far as we knew this was the first feast that Tiban's village had prepared since believing. After accepting Christ they had no reason for killing an animal, which was done in the past only to placate the evil spirits. These new believers were now trusting, worshipping and obeying God alone.

Then an awful thought could not help but grip us. We had just heard about Dawa who had been dying of TB. Two weeks ago in his depressed state he had followed the normal Tawbuid custom and hung himself to end the suffering quickly. Were they thinking of his death? They just couldn't be going back to follow the evil spirits by sacrifice... could they?

But as we watched them, there were no chants, no ceremonies, no fear, no sadness. Laughing and shouting, they began to take pieces of uncooked pork around to each family, including ours. And almost everyone brought us a gift of fragrant newly-husked rice. The men were chopping firewood, and the women were busily cooking, all in their own homes. Later we were brought more gifts, this time cooked pork. They were going to be sure we did not lack in this special celebration feast to welcome us back from our long vacation! God was teaching them the joy of feasting and fellowshipping as believers. It was just the sunshine we needed to brighten our day with the children so far away.

And the fear we had seen in the West was absent. Dawa's sweet widow was diligently teaching her older daughter to read, and helping her memorize Scripture. We lifted our hearts to God in thanksgiving for His great working, and later wrote to our prayer partners, "Ask God for a good husband for the widow, to help her in the heavy chopping, clearing and burning of the fields for planting." We knew there were no single believers her age.

Safa and Dalandan
church elders 1975 –
Standing left to right:
Bulus, Gunye, Tigansi,
Faguguanun,
Dagadafug,
Squatting: Uan,
Kadaguman, Taglagi

Safa village church

Kalafe leading church service. He is finding the place in the book of Mark – see blackboard

Fetching the book from its rack

Barbara Reed with Mangena 1959

Russell Reed with Tawbuid at Banos River, Easter 1965

Tawbuid tribal house

Burning off a field before planting

Folks were wandering in and out of their homes, filled and satisfied, and gathering in small groups visiting, teasing and laughing. Finding Tiban and Kulas intently watching an arm-wrestling match, we approached them, asking, "Who are the new arrivals? I don't think we've seen them before."

"They're from the Malio area," Tiban told us. "When they heard about the teachers who knew our language they wanted to come and see you."

We marveled at such an intense interest that they would travel four hours over rugged jungle trails just to see us. With burning curiosity we asked the men, "But how did they ever hear about us in the first place?"

Tiban waited until the victor triumphantly overcame his opponent by forcing him to relax his wrist. Then with his engaging grin he turned to answer our question.

Chapter 11

SHARING

"**W**e were the ones," Tiban said, his chin gently tipped toward his nephew, Kulas. "The two of us and Maninduk. We made that first trip over to the Malio area."

Amazed, Russell asked, "When did you go?"

"Do you remember when you first came with the *Duena* to teach us? When we all lived together in the house-down-by-the-river?"

"Oh, yes!" I laughed, recalling those first three visits before our furlough. "We didn't even know the word for 'God' in Tawbuid! And we used so many expressions from the other side of the mountains that you had to ask the meaning of words in almost every sentence!"

"But we still learned!" he grinned. "Well, each time you came to teach us we talked of going to Malio afterwards to tell our relatives about the New Teaching."

Russell and I had no idea in those early days that they had even thought of sharing the Good News, for we knew that fear keeps the Tawbuid close to home. It was thrilling enough that they themselves had wanted to listen.

"So we visited them," Tiban continued. "Some were angry, but some wanted to hear more. Then when you left the phonograph and the new Tawbuid records, we took them with us, too. They would listen to those all day if we would stay!" he smiled with pleasure.

So that was why they were always asking us for more needles! And why the records, so regularly returned to us for replacement, had no sound left on them at all!

"We tried to tell them the Bible stories too," Kulas added, grinning apologetically, as if thinking of his poor memory. "After several visits there were many who wanted to memorize the Bible verses. And we even taught them some of the songs!" he concluded, shyly triumphant.

Trying to suppress a smile, I thought of those budding evangelists teaching hymns! No Tawbuid had been able to learn our Western tunes, though they had memorized all the songs and Scripture verses word perfect!

"One of their greatest desires was to see you," Tiban added. "That's why we've had visitors come now and then from Malio when you're here. They want to see these white teachers who can speak our language."

Instantly my mind was jarred and I recalled that amazing day three months before. Rick and Becky, still in the Philippines and home for vacation, were playing tetherball in our big yard. Russell was at his desk writing word slips for the dictionary file while I was busy answering letters. From the top of a stack of mail that had accumulated while we had been in the hills, I picked up and began to re-read the warm and encouraging note from one of our prayer partners. Slipping a clean sheet of paper into the typewriter while assembling my thoughts to answer the under-standing questions, I suddenly heard shouts in the street below. "Mangyan! Mangyan!"

I knew it couldn't be Tawbuid. Although they might have the courage to hike out to the closest lowland settlement, they would never be brave enough to climb into a jeepney, pay their fare, come to town and locate our house.

As I went down the broad stairs to the big front door, I could hear a buzz of murmuring and shuffling on the porch outside. Opening the door, I was totally unprepared for what I saw.

A group of tribal people were huddled together on the low wide cement porch railing like birds seeking protection. These were complete strangers, cautious-ly waiting for me to make the first move.

"Are they Tawbuid?" Rick asked, coming to the porch steps.

"Oh, I think so," I told him, guided by their characteristic baskets and bark-cloth attire.

"*Sakboi!*" I greeted them cheerily. "Come in! Come in!"

But no one moved. Instinctively I stepped back into the house. "Honey, come on down. There're some Tawbuid here," I called up the stairs. "At least I think they're Tawbuid!" I added lamely.

"*Daginan am?*" Russell greeted them gently when he reached the porch. "Where did you come from?" Furtive glances passed back and forth. Realizing they would be afraid to come inside, Russell quietly took a seat on the doorstep and waited.

"*Go... am...*" one began hesitantly. "Are...you... Are you the ones? Are you the teachers who know our language?"

"*Ken*!" Russell replied. "Yes. We are the teachers who know your language."

And then the incredible, "Would you come to our place and teach us, too? Teach us like you are teaching Tiban's village on the Banos River."

"*Daginan am*?" Russell repeated his earlier question. "Where are you from?"

"From the Malio River. It's a branch of the Talun. We are a village of sixteen men," was the answer.

Russell interpreted to me, "The Talun is Tawbuid for the Pola River. So they live north of Pinamalayan while Tiban's village is south. The two groups must be quite a distance apart."

Imagine! Another whole village wants to be taught. Sixteen families, in a new area. I wanted to rush right back to that paper waiting in my typewriter and quickly tell our prayer partner that God was doing unheard of things in answer to prayer!

How thankful I was again for the six isolated years in Western Mindoro that had given us a working knowledge of Tawbuid. We could go tomorrow if they wanted us to. Except that we were scheduled in two days to attend our annual missionary conference in Manila and afterwards see the children off for their last term of school in Baguio. Suddenly I realized that if this delegation had come two days later, we would not have been here.

After chatting with them for a while, arrangements were made for Russell to meet them in four weeks. On the appointed day he took a jeepney to Sabang, but returned to Pinamalayan discouraged and wondering. No one had been there to meet him. After waiting several hours, he hiked up the Pola River, but found no one. Had they been frightened by a bad omen? Had they forgotten or become mixed up on the day? We heard nothing more from them. All we could do was write to our prayer partners and pray.

And now, more than three months later, as we talked with Tiban and Kulas at this special feast, we heard these welcome words, "They are asking if you can come to their place and teach them. They are ready for you now!"

"Ready?" I wondered what that meant.

A new date was set. This time they did come to Sabang to meet Russell and when he returned home three days later, I learned the details of his visit. For two hours they had hiked up the Safa River, a branch of the Pola, but before they had gone as far as the cut-off to Malio, they had climbed a steep slope to a clearing at the top. He could hardly believe what he saw. Ready for immediate use was their newly-constructed *Funbalugu Bale* sitting high and alone above the rushing Safa River. Gathered in the church were not the sixteen he had expected, but thirty men and teenage fellows, mostly from Malio!

Everyone lived in the church that weekend, listening intently to the stories of Creation, the First Couple and the First Sin, followed by the birth, life, atoning death and resurrection of Christ.

"But Hon," he sadly told me, "they're all afraid to bring their wives and teenaged daughters!"

"Afraid? Of what?"

"They told me," he continued, "that one old man in the area is looking for another wife. Do you remember that old grandfather who visited us in the Banos about two months ago?"

How could I forget? I had thought the little

paralyzed ten-year-old he was carrying must be his granddaughter. But he had told us before he left, "If you could have made her well, I would have married her."

Russell continued speaking about him, "He's had about seven wives, it seems, and he leaves them, or they leave him, for one reason or another. And no one wants him to take their wives or daughters!"

"How can we ever reach the women then?" I asked gloomily. But I wrote to our prayer partners, and a month later when I took my first trip into Safa, I saw God's answers.

This trip was different from that into the Banos. Our bursting-at-the-seams jeepney went north from Pinamalayan rather than south. After covering the four miles on the main road, it turned west onto an old lumber road heading toward the hills. The next eight dirt-road, pot-holed miles took nearly an hour. As we forded the last small stream and headed into the lowland village of Sabang, we were relieved to see two Tawbuid waiting for us under the awning of the miniature store.

For almost three hours as they carried our loads, we crossed and re-crossed the small, low Safa River. During more than an hour of that time we waded up the center of the stream where the banks on both sides were impassable jungle.

Resting at the foot of the hill on which the *Funbalugu Bale* was perched, Russell wanted to know, "How're you doing, Hon? Feeling ok?"

"I'm all right, but tired and hungry." In two more months, the doctor said, I would have to stop my hill trekking until after the baby was born.

The ascent from the river had been made easier

by the thoughtfulness of the Safa listeners. All underbrush had been cleared from the trail. Steps had been cut in the muddy hillside. And in some very slippery places a long banister had been made by stringing a large round rattan vine from one tree to the next along the side of the trail. The climb took about 25 minutes, though the return trip down would take less than fifteen!

After washing off some of the mud in the little stream near the top and mounting the ladder-stairs to the *Funbalugu Bale*, we were each handed a plate of steaming hot rice which banished our weariness. Looking out the doorway, Russell noticed that three little houses now surrounded the church. And people! There were men *and* women. Husbands *and* wives. Children of all ages! Seventy of us crowded into the little *Funbalugu Bale* for that first exciting meeting.

Our lessons were from the life of Christ. His power over evil spirits, over lack of food, over sin, over nature, and over sickness. We knew now that it was not His love for them that first led the Tawbuid to trust Him, but his unsurpassed power and goodness. In their fear-dominated lives they felt the need of a dependable and powerful God. They concentrated on every word we said, and if some couldn't understand our Tawbuid, others would rephrase it for them.

We noticed that the verses and songs they already knew from Tiban and Kulas' visits had been learned with some minor word errors, though the meanings were intact. But by the end of our visit, they were reciting them word perfect.

We even started a reading class using syllable and short-word flash cards, wondering if this would interest them. They were so enthused that they asked us to bring eighteen First Primers with us next time, one for each family! Their eagerness to pay the small cost of the books showed how keen they were to learn.

Between classes they told us that many of them were from the nearby village of Malio, although others in that village did not want to listen at all. The larger part of the group, however, had come from Dalandan, trekking four hours from the jungle interior. The Dalandan group had first heard about the New Teaching from the listeners in Malio after the visits of Tiban and Kulas. They were so interested that some had even made that long trip to the Banos to see us, like the couple whose little boy had died after falling out of the swing.

Tree-Branch, the old shaman leader of Dalandan, informed Russell, "We left thirty people behind in our village, even though they all want to come out and listen. But this *Funbalugu Bale* is too small for everyone. And the three houses we built around it for our people are very tiny."

Before we left at the end of that glorious weekend, the Safa and Dalandan men were making plans to enlarge the church, so that when we returned on the promised fourth Saturday everyone could attend!

The following week we went south again to the Banos River. As we began the first river crossing on our way to Tiban's village, what a sight greeted us! A broad one-lane road had been bulldozed by the lumber company. Quickly and easily we walked up its wide tracks where trees, rocks and small hills had been pushed aside, and the number of river crossings had been reduced to a bare minimum. I felt thankful for an easier hike, three and a half hours instead of five, but Russell was apprehensive. Any unscrupulous outsider would find it easy now to settle on Tawbuid land, steal their food, and frighten or intimidate them. He was anxious that the registration of their land would soon be finalized.

Arriving at the Banos village, we heard a disturbing report that some of the Safa listeners were angry at them. A few of the words in the songs and verses taught by Tiban and Kulas were not exactly the same as we had taught at Safa. In their evil spirit chants the words must be exact to be effective, and evidently the Safa listeners felt that had to be true also when worshipping Funbalugu. We explained that the meaning and thought, not the words, were important, and that we were still striving for the best way to express these ideas in Tawbuid. Would this misunderstanding drive away the Safa listeners?

This reemphasized the importance of a thorough knowledge of the Scriptures. As we discussed this with the believers, we told them about the "Studying Place" for God's Word that would be started for all six Mindoro tribes. They were enthused. To think that for twelve weeks believers could study God's words every day, all day long!

"But the teaching is all in Tagalog," we had to tell them, "so that all who attend can understand, even if they don't know each other's languages." Hiding his embarrassed laughter behind his hand, Tiban remarked, "We don't know Tagalog." Oh, he could arrange for his men to work for a lowland farmer and follow simple instructions about the field work. But that was about all. And the others knew even less.

A strong desire to attend might make them

willing for the perseverance and hard study required to learn Tagalog. Perhaps helping with the beginnings of the Mangyan Bible School would give them the needed zeal.

"Would it be good," Russell began, "if some of you went with me to Ayan Bekeg for seven days to help build this studying place? One house is needed for a teaching place and others for the teachers' and students' sleeping places. Also the land must be cleared and crops planted."

"Crops planted?" someone asked.

"Yes, for their food, and for others who come to later sessions," Russell explained. "And at the end of the work-week everyone will study God's Words together for two days before the builders return to their homes and the ones studying begin their classes. Even if you don't know much Tagalog, I will be there to explain in Tawbuid."

"Where is Ayan Bekeg?" Tiban wanted to know.

"It is in Alangan territory, up in the mountains above the city of Calapan. If you went out to the highway and boarded a bus just at sunrise, you would arrive at the Ayan Bekeg trail when the sun is up there," Russell explained with his arm stretched out toward a ten o'clock position. "And if you began the hike right away, you would reach that Alangan village just about there," he concluded, stretching his hand almost straight up. More smiling behind embarrassed hands. Only Tiban and Kulas had ever been so far from home. But if that was what they should do...

Russell returned from his next visit to the Banos with the three men who had decided to go: Tiban, Squint, and Yudgulian, a new member in the group.

His wife was another sister of evil Balinguy, the third in that family to come to the Lord. My sister Ann arrived from the south that afternoon with two Hanunoo believers who would be attending the school, while downstairs in the Hanselman's home thirteen Buhid believers and thirteen children had arrived. All would head for Ayan Bekeg the next day, escorted by Russell.

I was excited to think of the fellowship the isolated Tawbuid believers would have with those from the other Mindoro tribes, even though they would not be part of the twenty who would remain for the three months of study.

Ann stayed with me for several days to use our mimeograph. I was writing the script for the new "Gulf Bridged" poster, working on the revision of the third Reader, and typing the stencils of Russell's newly-translated Matthew 1 and 2 that would be handed out at Christmas time.

Russell returned from Ayan Bekeg just before the much-anticipated arrival of Rick and Becky on their seven-week Christmas vacation from Malaysia. Our two joyous weeks together in Pinamalayan were climaxed by an early family Christmas on December 15, 1964. Then Becky, Rick and I packed our suitcases for Manila so I would arrive, as the doctor advised, a month before the baby was due. Meanwhile Russell was filling his pack with lessons and illustrations to explain to the Safa listeners the meaning of their first Christmas.

Following his Safa visit he would hike into the Banos to join Tiban's group as they crossed the river for Christmas worship services with the Tadyawan believers. *How fitting*, I thought. For it was these Tadyawan who first brought the gospel to the Tawbuid, giving them Christmas.

I left Pinamalayan reluctantly. Another parting with so little time together as a family! But during the two long months of intermittant separations, we saw many evidences of God's special care.

A deep, unused brick fishpond in the Manila mission home patio was one source of joy. Rick and Becky, enthusiastically cleaning and then filling it, were rewarded with many hours of swimming-pool fun. In the house Becky was delighted to help make the Christmas fruitcakes, while Rick was ambitiously repainting the borrowed baby basket. I dreaded Christmas Day without Russell, but it was actually relaxing and enjoyable, even though we all missed him.

Russell joined us in Manila before the baby's birth, which took place just two days before Rick and Becky's flight back to Chefoo school in Malaysia. While they visited me in the hospital, the nurse unexpectedly brought baby Robby into the room, leaving him with us for almost an hour!

Fondly we watched the children holding him and playing with him, trying to decide the color of his very dark eyes and whether he really looked like Becky as the nurse said he did. Then Rick, figuring out on which side his own hair was parted, had brushed Robby's black fuzz to resemble his own. Inwardly I thanked God for this precious family time.

After putting Rick and Becky on the plane the next day, Russell returned to the hospital to cheer my lonely mother-heart.

"I wish you could have seen their faces just before

they boarded the PanAm jet," Russell told me with a grin, "when I gave them each one of those 15-minute-old snaps of Robby that I had taken."

Feeling warmed and comforted I asked, "Did you have any trouble getting them ready to go?"

Russell sighed. "Helping them finish their packing made me feel about as lonely and helpless as when I was by myself in Pinamalayan!" Then he added more cheerfully, "As soon as I get you back to the mission home, I'd like to take a couple of close-ups of Robby and send Rick and Becky each an enlargement!"

When Robby and I did return to the mission home, the floor of our room was covered with neat little piles of dried fruit, dried meat, condensed milk, bouillon cubes, sugar, tea, medicines, mosquito repellent, sleeping bag, and ground sheet. Immediately I recognized Russell's preparation for the proposed trip with Theo Herren up the Mongpong River and down the Lumintao in Western Mindoro.

Returning to Manila from that trek several weeks later, he called it the most rugged hike he had ever taken. "Even at the end," he remarked, "we had three days of hard walking, swimming and climbing just to get out of the river gorge. And then over the mountain pass to Bongabon and home again to an empty house in Pinamalayan.

"But we did meet about sixteen Tawbuid," he said, brightening. "Including two interior leaders. While they were guiding us down to the river, I was able to talk to them about *Funbalugu*. One was so interested that he kept stopping just to ask me more questions, which really bothered his companion."

We returned from Manila to Pinamalayan in March 1965, and while Robby was still tiny, Russell continued to go to the hills alone. He came back from each trip with some little token of delight that God had given him. One morning just before the service had started, a mother, father and small son sitting at the front of the church began examining each other's hands. Deciding that their little boy's were the cleanest, they gave him the precious song book to hold while they were singing!

Desk work and care of Robby kept me from loneliness while Russell was gone. In the colorful cartoon-type booklets of "The Life of Joseph" and "The Life of Paul" I pasted a Tawbuid translation over the Tagalog script. On the large primer typewriter I cut stencils for Russell's new "When we Marry" booklet, for the latest chapter of Mark (the fifth), and for the newly-translated Matthew 28 to be distributed to every family at Easter time.

Returning from another visit to Safa Russell told me that the Dalandan listeners had really lightened his day.

"The *Funbalugu Bale* at our place is now finished," they had proudly announced to him, "and we have chosen our church elders. Would it be good for you to come to our village and teach all of us so we will know what God's word tells us to believe?"

Suppressing a smile at their premature elections, he had replied that he had wanted to go for some time, but that the typhoons had prevented him.

"Every Sunday and every Hot Day we meet," they continued.

"Hot Day?" he had asked, mystified.

"Oh, that's our prayer meeting day in the middle of the week," they enlightened him. "By the time we have all finished praying, the morning is already very hot as we go to our fields."

"You know, Hon," Russell added, "They are the farthest from civilization, seven hours hike from the end of the jeep road, and the most earnest in their new-found faith. And they, like the Safa listeners, heard the gospel without us even being aware of it!"

"We're just like spectators at God's great show!" I remarked.

Easter would be Robby's first trip to the hills. His life at the Banos River would be very different from the rugged, almost outdoor life that baby Becky and toddler Ricky had experienced in the hills in the West. And we wouldn't even have to live in the *Funbalugu Bale* any more. We would now have a tiny, but well-built, windproof home of our own. Rolls of bark walling were all ready to put on when Russell visited there three weeks before.

One of the blessings of the Easter celebration was the baptismal service when seven more Banos believers publicly declared their faith in Christ. This time Bumblebee's wife was included, and Yudgulian and his wife. Both women were sisters of evil Balinguy. But his younger brother was still following charms, so he was not baptized although his elderly unwanted wife was. Dawa's widow and her mother, along with her cousin Faguguanun, a very promising young man, made up the seven.

Nine women and seven men were now officially in the Banos church. But the blessings of the day were not over. Discussing how their offering money, set aside each week, should be used, the believers decided to share it with Homay, a Buhid church leader, for his Bible School expenses in the June term. Not only did they give the five pesos needed for his transportation, but also an additional five pesos to help with his food expenses! This represented collecting, scraping and selling two thousand rattan strips, more than ten days work for one man!

Then they asked Russell, "Would it be good if you bought for us, with *Funbalugu's* money, a small notebook for listing our expenses, a blackboard for our *Funbalugu Bale*, and a clock?"

"A clock?" Russell asked, astounded. What an interesting first acquirement from the outside!

"Yes, a clock," they answered stoutly. "If we could just know on cloudy afternoons when it is five o'clock, then we could begin our meeting and have enough light to read our hymn books and God's Words before it gets dark at six."

Russell smiled. Not a bad idea at all! And they wouldn't even have to adjust for summer and winter, as the days so close to the equator are almost the same length all year.

On his way around Mindoro to visit Pangalkagan again, Russell took the gift to Homay in his Buhid village. He returned from that Western Tawbuid trip with mixed feelings. Joy that a tiny light was still burning there, especially from Nardo who had helped make the Gospel Recordings. But sorrow that there was no one to minister to Makisig's village. Deeply burdened, we prayed for someone to share God's Word with those Tawbuid in the West.

Summer came and Rick and Becky were home again, enjoying their six-month-old brother in our spacious Pinamalayan house and in our cute little home in the hills. But at the end of their vacation we faced the most difficult period of our twelve-year missionary life.

Chapter 12

OBEYING

Rick and Becky were going to the States to continue their schooling, and our furlough was not due for two more years. We had prayed and agonized over the decision, but finally agreed that they would go together to the OMF Home in Wheaton, Illinois for our Junior-high and High school missionary children. Perhaps in each others' company the pain of parting from us and the inevitable hurts of life would be lessened.

Seeing them go that hot August day in 1965 was almost unbearable, though we knew they were in the Lord's special care. A stewardess would personally escort them, and dearly-loved Grandma and Grandpa Flory would be waiting for them at the Los Angeles airport. From California they would revel in the two-thousand-mile sightseeing trip with Grandpa and Grandma to join the other OMF children in Wheaton. But would they be happy, truly loved and cared for? Was this the best for our precious children? I returned to Mindoro full of doubts and apprehension.

Then God spoke to me. We could have lost Rick when he fell from the little bed-on-the-wall at the Agricultural School, and nine-month-old Becky could have died when she had diarrhea. But we still had them. Alive. And well. They had enjoyed their young life, even with its painful moments. And we had loved every minute we had with them, experiencing God's enabling in each one of those heart-tearing separations. "Can you not trust me now for all of their future?" He was asking me. And I was trying to obediently say "Yes, Lord." Surely, He would reward them for this sacrifice they were making for Him.

That first trip into Safa with eight-month-old Robby had more special encouragements from the Lord than any other single trip. God knew our aching hearts needed evidences of His special love, for I was still battling, "Is it worth it?"

It was just noon when we arrived at the hilltop clearing, thrilled that nine houses now surrounded the new, enlarged *Funbalugu Bale*, our home for the week. Although I was exhilarated to be in the hills again, Russell had deep misgivings. Unlike the Banos where we had our own tiny tribal home, we would be living in the church. Everyone did try to keep the floor clean, because it belonged to *Funbalugu*. When mud was tracked in, blood dripped from leech bites, or babies made messes, a flurry of activity with water gourds and leaves quickly cleaned the surface. But Russell could still see germs lurking everywhere.

A brisk breeze welcomed, cooled and relaxed us. We both had wondered if the listeners from Dalandan would join the Safa group as usual. Just last month after a sudden death they had all fled from their village to avoid the dreaded ghost. Some seemed willing to return so Russell had encouraged them to obediently trust the Lord and go back. And now *all* of them had come to Safa, making a congregation of 117 people!

In the daily morning worship Russell read from the latest translated chapter of Mark which they "followed" on their mimeographed sheets. He also taught the "When We Bury" booklet to prepare them for facing the fears caused by death.

During their prayer time, he introduced the use of cards with a village name at the top, and people listed below who needed prayer. Some place names were from the Hanunoo area where Ann worked, and where we, with several Tawbuid, hoped to visit after Christmas.

Morning classes included the story of Joseph, reading, writing and the study of the huge calendar we had brought for the *Funbalugu Bale*. "We don't follow the moon when it is new, or when it is full," Russell explained. "We only follow this paper." Unbelievable!

In writing class Russell introduced four medical terms, *Karatas, Karios, Kasigung, and Galagnat* (Diarrhea, malarial chills, headache or malaise, and fever). He thought if they wrote them, they would learn them, a necessity for his latest innovation.

We had medicines for these illnesses, but if we were not there, the people had nothing. Excitement erupted as Russell showed them the four small bottles for every family, each one filled and carefully labeled with the illness and the dosage. These would be safely stored on the high shelf above each fire hearth, ready when needed.

In the afternoon classes we told the missionary story, *Udsun Taylur*, using large flash-cards. Old China's culture with chopsticks and pigtails was entertaining, and Hudson Taylor's trust for daily needs and obedience in leaving home to tell others was thought provoking. Would any of the Tawbuid ever be called to such obedience?

During the week Butuan proudly showed us two sturdy hardwood posts from the jungle and the location of the new house they wanted to build for us. I thought how delightfully easy it would be to keep Robby clean in a home of our own!

About three days after we had taught First Corinthians 7:10-11, "A husband must not divorce his wife," Butuan told us that Chopped-Cheek had left his wife and wanted to marry a widow in the group. Butuan had urged him to obey the new memory verse and Chopped-Cheek seemed to listen. This use of God's Word thrilled us, and we prayed that others would solve their problems the same way.

I thought of our last Banos trip when we had counseled Tiban and his wife, who were losing their mutual love and respect. As a last straw, each had dreamed a name for their new baby girl and neither would give in. Russell had often said, "As the leader goes, so the village goes." Surely this marriage would not break up! Like Chopped-Cheek they did listen, and in their obedience God brought them back together permanently.

On our last morning at Safa we told them we would be back on the fifth Saturday, showing them the date on their new calendar. We also pointed out the date of their fast-approaching second Christmas, but I was not eager to face that special day, for it would be our first Christmas without Rick and Becky.

Their descriptive weekly letters from Wheaton now told of ice skating, tobogganing, and shoveling snow. Rick had a morning paper route (brrr, it's cold) and was learning to play the trumpet. Becky was busy with Pioneer Girls, after school sports and her clarinet. Already a special Christmas package had arrived, which included a cute, gray jumping donkey for little brother Robby. We wrote, sent packages and prayed constantly for God's joy and blessing in their lives. But was that enough? The joyful believers in the hills were the ones who lifted our spirits.

Six days before Christmas everyone in Tiban's Banos village put their sweet potatoes, rice and bananas in their big head-band-baskets, and gathered together their children and their chickens, as well as two of the village goats. Before the sun was hot, they began the difficult trek through the jungle and across the hills to Safa River. The men, realizing how hard the trip would be for the small children and mothers with babies, had built a halfway house on the long trail. Taking time to forage for food along the way, they arrived three days later.

Everyone had saved rice from the harvest except the Dalandan listeners who had been afraid to adopt its cultivation. Each village brought a small pig and the Banos folk, to whom we had introduced the raising of goats, provided a young billy for the feast as well as a nanny for the Safa listeners to begin their herd.

The split-bamboo floor of the Safa chapel had been especially propped up to support the congregation of 167, which included the babies. Everyone had a place to stay with relatives or close friends, while we enjoyed the little home they had built for us, complete with its own fire hearth on the floor of the front porch.

During those five days the Christmas story was taught with special attention to its application in the lives of the believers. On Christmas Day everyone gathered in the church for a feast of all the rice and meat one could eat! Recreation was provided by a tetherball, with bare feet churning up a real pig wallow around the base of the bamboo pole.

Each family received a blue-covered copy of the Christmas story translated from Luke. Even the younger family members who could read were given their own copies. We also made calendars with a brightly-colored Bible picture at the top and a Tawbuid Scripture verse on each month's tear-off page. Hanging from every convenient projection, they gave the church a festive air. After the Christmas meetings they would decorate every palm-leaf or bark-walled home throughout 1966. We were sure that this first joy-packed inter-church fellowship, was as great an encouragement to the Tawbuid to press on for the Lord as it was to us.

Before we left, we proposed a week-long visit to three Hanunoo churches. Each village enthusiastically agreed to choose two men to make the trip with us, the first time anyone from Safa and Dalandan had ever been so far from home.

For months the Tawbuid had been praying for the Hanunoo whose names and villages were on the prayer cards. The day before this trip, two believers from Dalandan and two from Safa trekked across the hills to spend the night with the Banos believers. Early the next morning, joined by Tiban and Bumblebee, the men hiked the four hours out to the road to meet our bus as we came from Pinamalayan. Together we continued the six-hour trip south to

Mansalay, the Hanunoo missionaries' coastal base town where Ann awaited us.

After spending the night there, we all walked down to the sea just as the sun was rising. Six wary Tawbuid gingerly climbed into their first motor-*bangka*. Even with the reassurance of our presence and of the long outriggers that kept the canoe-shaped craft upright, they hung onto the gunwales for dear life while we bobbed and churned for over an hour down the coast.

As we disembarked, much to their relief, we were warmly greeted by several Hanunoo brethren. While the Tawbuid made valiant attempts to reply in Tagalog to their friendly hosts, one of the Hanunoo volunteered to carry Robby in his pack seat, and another picked up our 25-pound load which included all we would need for this week of hill travel and living.

It was an hour's hike nearly straight up the hill to the Hanunoo village of Tarubong where the Mangyan Bible School (MBS), this term serving the needs of the southern tribes, was now in session. We arrived just at recess, and the six Tawbuid were able to watch the volleyball game and later try their skill at hitting the elusive ball!

After a refreshing swim in the nearby river, the men all returned for the "Question and Answer" class. The teaching was entirely in Tagalog, for those attending came from different Mindoro tribes, but the thrill of attending the classes was not at all diminished for the six men. When we set the date for this trip, we had not realized that MBS would be in session at Tarubong. But God was using it now to capture their interest.

During the five-day visit to the three Hanunoo churches, the Tawbuid saw Sunday schools for the first time and were challenged by the believers' Sunday afternoon outreaches. In spite of the very real language barrier and the strange, dry taste of green boiled cooking bananas, the Hanunoo's staple food, the fellowship was warm and meaningful. Returning home they were loaded down with the gift of banana suckers for planting and a billy goat for the Safa nanny.

Several weeks later Russell made an eleven-day trek to the west, returning with the news that he had met two new groups of Tawbuid and renewed contact with several others. "The response was really varied," he told me with some amusement. "One frightened listener asked us, 'Why have you come here? Why are you in our area?' And when I quietly explained to him that I'd come to tell him about the Good Creator *Funbalugu* and His Son Jesus, he quickly shot back, 'Well, now you have told us, please go!'

"And then there were two other men," he continued, "that we had met earlier. They were a bit afraid, but they listened thoughtfully to the entire explanation of the Two Roads poster! I kept thinking that every contact means a less fearful listener the next time."

Even here on the Eastern side of the island fear was not entirely eliminated among the believers. In Safa where baptism was unfamiliar, some hesitated to make this public declaration to all still in heathendom that the old way of sacrifice and chants to the evil spirits was ended. After a week of baptism classes, seven couples asked to be baptized.

In our American way, we planned a private questioning session with these fourteen. But we didn't reckon with the Tawbuid system!

After the morning service Russell announced, "Those who have asked to be baptized can stay so we can talk about it." But no one left. Everyone just quieted down.

"Just the ones wanting to be baptized should stay," he explained further. But no one moved. Then we began to reflect. No matter who was having a discussion, everyone gathered around. Nothing was done in secret. We hadn't even found a word for "private" in Tawbuid.

So with the candidates sitting in their regular areas on the floor surrounded by their families, Russell began asking each one about his faith in Christ. Good comments came from the audience about various ones, but it wasn't until we considered Chopped-Cheek and his wife that we realized how little we knew about Tawbuid ways.

"You can't baptize him or his wife," someone boldly stated.

"Why not?" another defended him. "He didn't leave his wife and marry the widow when Butuan reminded him of God's commands."

"That's true," put in a third, "but he and his wife have not been living in the same house."

"Oh, they are now!" the first speaker asserted. "But there is something else. If they really are believing, they must obey *all* of *Funbalugu*'s commands. But they are disobeying, for they are sleeping with a log between them!"

Nods and murmurs showed that others were also aware of this situation. These believers expected absolute obedience in everything! That couple's baptism had to be postponed.

In spite of daily rain since our arrival, baptism day dawned clear and bright. After the regular morning worship, we sang a hymn, prayed, and then began the twenty-minute slide downhill to the river. Around the pool at the end of the trail, everyone either stood on the gravel or perched on the huge boulders to watch their first baptismal service. Afterwards the newly-baptized believers stood together at the water's edge, singing with all of us, as a vow,

> "Our desire is to obey Jesus, forever and forever.
> We will follow Jesus' words, forever and forever.
> Even when we are alone, we will truly obey,
> Forever and forever."

Returning up the sun-dried trail, we did not realize the amazing response their courage would inspire.

On our next Safa visit, several Dalandan believers were eager to be baptized. When Russell asked the whole group who was ready, eighteen married couples and a single young man responded! Nine of them were from Safa, including Chopped-Cheek and his wife who had now renewed their marriage, and 28 were from Dalandan. All 37 publicly declared their defiance of the evil spirits and their trust in Christ alone! That same month in tiny Banos village ten more were baptized, including two young fellows and two teenage girls.

Suddenly there were 75 baptized believers, which with one or two exceptions was the entire adult population of the three villages. Obedience to all of God's Words was the goal of each one, making them diligent in learning to read, and keeping us busy preparing reading and Bible lessons, including a series on church organization, as well as pushing ahead with Bible translation.

As each chapter of Mark was checked with Russell's translation helper, it was mimeographed and distributed. Ambitiously reading and studying each verse, the other believers sometimes discovered errors or found better ways to express the passage. Russell had finished through chapter ten, and had roughly translated the last six chapters which needed hours of checking before even getting to the mimeograph stage.

Isolated verses pertinent to current problems were also translated and inserted in each family's thickening Verse Book. Soon the little blue plastic-covered treasury became known as the "Thick Book."

"Thy Word have I hid in my heart, that I might not sin against thee" from Psalm 119 seemed a particularly appropriate verse. It was faithfully memorized and recited often, as were all the verses in the Thick Book. I even set the Tawbuid words to the music of the children's chorus, so it was recited and sung, much to my pleasure.

Many weeks later, probably waiting for the needed courage, one of the believers lingered after the morning service and nonchalantly began a conversation, "Now, just how does that verse go? Thy Word have I hid in my heart...."

I was sure he knew the verse and didn't need help from me, but I filled in, "that I might not sin against thee."

After a session of throat clearing and feet examination, he asked, "What does this verse really mean? What message is it carrying?"

"Oh," I brightened, realizing now that he wanted to be sure he understood it. "We learn God's words. We memorize them. We just keep on remembering them, so that we won't do what is wrong. We won't sin against *Funbalugu*."

He nodded his head sagely, and I was sure he had known what the verse meant. Then he said, quietly, "This... this verse, when we say, 'I hide something in my heart' it really carries the message that 'I have done something very bad, very evil, and I am never going to tell anyone about it!'"

I was horror struck. What had we been teaching these believers? What had they learned from this verse? Quickly I sought a remedy. As Russell and I later got our heads together we came up with the simple, "I will always remember your words so that I will not sin against you." Years later we learned the true Tawbuid idiom when we heard one believer mention to his companion, "I've stored up the leader's words in my ear!"

Stimulated by the daily study of God's Word in their churches, many Tawbuid were developing a desire, reinforced by the Ayan Bekeg work-week and the Hanunoo visit, to attend the Mangyan Bible School. Reports from MBS were encouraging, for church leaders and believers were already using their knowledge to teach others in their own tribes. But among the Tadyawan, Buhid and Tawbuid the potential leaders knew so little Tagalog that they were unable to attend this school. We began to pray for a way to teach them more Tagalog.

At our annual OMF missionary conference a

preparatory Bible school was proposed — to teach Tagalog, introduce Tagalog Bible terms and names, and carry out a simplified Bible school program. Later the dates and place were set for the first three-week session: June 15 to July 8 1966, in Tarubong. The Hanunoo could speak Tagalog and were enthusiastic about being the hosts.

Joyfully we shared these plans with the believers. Enthusiasm ran high. Now we faced the problem of how to prepare them in reading and writing Tagalog, and in learning some Tagalog Bible terms.

All of us were deeply moved and encouraged when the Buhid from Apnagan Village sent a gift to help the Tawbuid with their transportation expenses. These believers lived near the tiny village where Marie Barham began the Buhid work that Russell and Dr B had visited when we were first in Calapan thirteen years before. Marie saw little response in her lifetime, but after the Buhid at Batangan River had welcomed Bob and Joy Hanselman and had turned to Christ, Apnagan had responded.

Besides this enthusiasm for the Preparatory Bible School plans, other good news thrilled us. The once-shaman leader of Dalandan, baptized the previous month, had taken a bold step of faith, deciding that he and his village would plant rice this year. Fear of reprisals from the evil spirits for bringing an outsiders' crop into the hills had prevented its cultivation in the past. But now they were trusting Christ, clinging to the verse from the Thick Book, "When I am afraid I will trust in thee."

Keeping our scattered family happy in across-the-seas oneness was our ideal. Little brother Robby, for example, when asked, "Where's Becky?" or "Where's Rick?" would get the appropriate picture and give it a sweet smile and a big hug!

Rick and Becky's comments about the new baby coming in July were fascinating. Rick wrote "I like the name Ruth Virginia, but Randall George... Just Randy George, Mom!" And Becky's plea was, "It has to be a girl so things will be even!"

Knowing how they would miss us at such a special family time, it gladdened our hearts to learn that when the baby would be born, they would be having a glorious summer with Grandma and Grandpa Flory in California.

While Russell continued to teach and to check his latest chapter of Mark in the hills, I was in Pinamalayan translating the Life of William Carey. After the baby was born, I would teach it with large flashcards as I had Hudson Taylor.

The dates were meshing beautifully. While Robby and I were in Manila to await the baby's birth, Russell would be escorting the men to the Preparatory Bible School and staying on to help them. Then suddenly, with only a brief radio warning, violent typhoon Irma arrived, lashing out against Mindoro.

That day in Pinamalayan had begun with a quiet, steady rain. But in the early afternoon the wind came up, and for four hours it raged from the north so furiously that rain poured in through our *closed* windows. The infinite number of tiny panes of translucent sea shells are rainproof enough in an ordinary storm, but not with typhoon gales. As water poured in we mopped the flooded floors and moved the furniture. Mopped and moved. Mopped and moved.

Just as it began to get dark there was the briefest lull before the wind began from the east and rain poured through our front windows. The electricity had been turned off at the plant to prevent a short from hot wires falling and crossing. So we lit the kerosene lanterns. By the time the wind veered to the south the rain had become lighter, so we didn't have to work quite so fast as we mopped and moved furniture near those windows. About midnight we fell exhausted into bed.

In the morning we woke to an eerie silence. Opening our rain-soaked windows we looked at the nightmare of destruction in our yard. All the bananas were broken off about four feet above the ground. The jackfruit and frangipani trees were down, and the leaves were gone from the cacao trees. The clothes lines were fallen and twisted, the fence was flattened and the lawn was covered with six inches of water. Quietly we praised the Lord for a sturdy wooden house with a rain-proof corrugated iron roof!

In the hills it was far worse. Russell returned from a brief trip to Safa with the sad news that Mr One-Eye was fighting for his life. When the high winds had suddenly begun on Tuesday he was in his fields, and before he could return the top of a broken tree had pinned him to the ground. No one could look for him when he didn't come home that night, for the storm was violent. On Wednesday they found him and carried him home, wounded, cold and unconscious.

Four days later when Russell arrived he still could not eat or drink, and was hardly conscious. Russell gave him some medicine, and then prayed with this newly-baptized couple and their two tiny children before returning to Pinamalayan.

No reports had come of damage at Dalandan. We earnestly prayed that they would not think their newly-planted rice was in any way responsible for this storm!

At Banos village destruction was even worse. Russell returned from his visit there commenting, "You would never even recognize the place. They must have been in the direct path of the storm!"

"Was anyone hurt?" I wanted to know.

"No, though some of the men who were working in their new fields about three hours away weren't able to get home for a couple of days because of swollen rivers. But that wasn't the worse part." He sighed. "The church was blown flat. And so were a couple of other houses. And you should see our house. The roof is completely gone!"

"Is our stuff still there?" I could see it all soaked and moulding.

"You know these believers! Our big tins and household stuff are all in their own homes, dry and well kept! But the big hill is threatening to landslide, so the families in the five houses there have moved out. And there's not an upright banana tree anyplace."

In the end it was the loss of banana trees that cancelled the Preparatory Bible School. Among the Hanunoo, where the school was to be held, every banana tree was down, so there would be no green cooking bananas available to feed the 18-20 men who planned to come. We turned to God, trusting Him to bring order out of the chaos, disappointment and hunger facing the believers all over Mindoro.

In Safa there was a bright rainbow. We were not in the hills when One-Eye died, but were told later how the men had conducted the funeral service, and care and comfort had been given to his widow and two small children. Not only was his house not abandoned, but it was enlarged, so there was no thought of fleeing. His newly-planted rice was being cared for and food was being harvested from his other fields. Trusting Christ was not only stabilizing them emotionally, but also raising their standard of living. Their homes as well as their crops were no longer deserted in fear.

During the next few months our rejoicing increased, as did the size of our family. To welcome us at the end of the jeep road and get their first glimpse of four-month-old baby Randy, were 23 Tawbuid! Our five loads, including the two little boys, were passed from one to another as we hiked together up the Safa River. Randy slept comfortably in his plastic baby seat while Robby sat high, facing forward, in his new carrier.

Going back into the hills as a family of four was a happy occasion, even though we longed that it be the six of us. But we delighted in reminding each other of God's unexpected and creative ways of making life fun for His children even while separated.

Foremost in our minds was the occasion in July. Randy's birth certificate read, "Randall George Reed, born at 11:58 o'clock am on Monday the Eleventh day of July 1966." Rick and Becky, while spending the summer at Grandma and Grandpa's house, had received the news by cable at 10:00 am, July 11th, two hours before Randy's birth-time in the Philippines! Thanks to the international date line, this was their day of fun. Telephoning friends and relatives just after ten o'clock, they made their big announcement: "Hey, did you know? Today at 11:58

our little brother Randy is going to be born! He will weigh eight pounds and twelve ounces, and will be 22 1/2 inches long! He will have dark hair and blue eyes. Isn't that cool?" Followed by giggling, laughter, and "What did you say? Tell me that again!"

On this hill visit we celebrated the Tawbuid Thanksgiving, always the last Sunday in October, when the harvest was finished. The special joy was the first two Christian marriages. God had provided Mrs One-Eye with a new husband, a young baptized believer who had recently lost his wife. And Kalafe, the young man who had been baptized with all the married couples in Safa, was marrying a young Dalandan believer.

Another first was the nomination of church officers whose names would be prayed over for two weeks before elections took place. This was the first step in the formal organization of the Safa Church.

Before we left Safa, we joyfully completed travel plans to the much-delayed Preparatory Bible School. Four days later two men from Safa and two from Dalandan along with four from the Banos met Russell at the bus road. Joined by seven Tadyawan believers and their missionary, they all went south to the Buhid village at Batangan River where the school was now to be held.

We had prayed that this session for the Buhid, Tadyawan and Tawbuid would spur them on in their study of Tagalog and be a challenge to them spiritually. After Russell left, I began to realize that it would actually show them how hopelessly little Tagalog they knew and how overwhelmingly much was required. Would they really try to master this unknown language? Or would they decide it was simply beyond them?

Chapter 13

CARING

Returning from the Preparatory Bible School, the eight men eagerly began that long uphill climb toward Tagalog mastery, and were even bringing the other believers along with them!

The DZAS radio kept at the church was turned on each morning at six am as the believers intently followed the Tagalog Bible lesson. In groups and alone they faithfully studied the Tagalog Sunday School book. We constantly heard conversations sprinkled with Tagalog words and phrases, often accompanied by embarrassed giggles or choruses of laughter.

Spiritual challenge from meeting other elders and attending the Buhid church was also apparent. In the three Tawbuid churches that were fast becoming self-governing, all the men took turns as before, but now one elder was in charge of each meeting. Often he would give a few words of encouragement or a brief exhortation from the passage read that day.

Offerings were faithfully recorded. After caring for the church and the missionary house, the rest of the money was given to others: to DZAS, to the Pinama-layan town church, or to an elder from another tribe for Bible School expenses. Church problems were brought before the elders, and believers were wisely and gently counseled, as answers were sought from God's Word.

At the Christmas feast and services held that year in Banos Village, we listened with awe as Kulas from that village, Kalafe from Safa and Sibnai from Dalandan each gave brief messages on one aspect of the Savior's birth. And we rejoiced as gentle, understanding church elder Dagadafug, whose wife had died from a cobra bite, married Dawa's widow.

An annual problem surfaced at that celebration. The visiting believers could not carry all they needed to feed their families for five days, and no host village had a supply of food adequate for 170 people. It wasn't a matter of unwillingness, for love and caring were constantly evident. Just a few months before, the Safa and Dalandan believers had travelled the rugged trail to Banos village to help build the new church and missionary house to replace those destroyed by Typhoon Irma.

The elders of all three churches met to pray and discuss the food problem, and God gave them a plan. Early in the year all the believers would help enlarge the fields and plant extra crops at the site of the next Christmas gathering.

Back in Pinamalayan, we pushed ahead with preparations for our next teaching visits, as well as for Easter. The three villages would meet separately for that celebration, with the services conducted entirely by the believers. The stencils had to be typed for mimeographing the newly-translated Resurrection story from John 20-21. The sets of hand-sized flash card pictures of the Easter story needed to be put in order. Each set would be the "sermon notes" for the men who were to preach. They would turn up each card, and tell the events they depicted. We were typing up brief notes for each card that they could study beforehand, for no one could read well enough to use the notes as he spoke.

We also began outlining Sunday School lessons from Genesis, for in Safa a class had been started for the children.

By the end of that week, New Year's Eve, we fell into an exhausted sleep, glad that our boys were too young to know about welcoming in the New Year. About midnight we suddenly became aware of motorcycles roaring up and down the streets. This was the first year there had been any in town, and all the drivers must have felt that the sound of a revved up, mufflerless motor was a suitable welcome to the New Year!

When we first came to Pinamalayan, the only transportation around town had been the high, difficult-to-board, horse-drawn *karetela*. Then several years later we rode in pedicabs, side-cars attached to bicycles, which gradually began to have small motors added. Now those motorized bicycles were being replaced by "Hondas," as every make of motorcycle was called. But at midnight we would have preferred the horses!

The quiet of the hills was a welcome relief. During our twelve days in the Banos, the believers were intrigued with the maps we introduced for our study of Paul's journeys from Acts. Anything new was always an attraction. What a change from their old ways in which anything new brought terror!

About a week after that visit, we went to Safa where a different role began to emerge for us.

Although we were still their teachers, we became part of the congregation. The elected elders from both Safa and Dalandan took complete charge of church affairs. At the end of the lessons on baptism which they had requested us to teach, the Safa and Dalandan candidates were examined and later baptized by the elders from their own churches.

Back at the *Funbalugu Bale* afterwards, the elders conducted the Lord's Supper. Russell was asked to begin the meeting, however, for they were not sure of all the words in the newly-translated First Corinthians 11 booklet which they wanted read during the service. Then as the roasted sweet potato was broken and passed to all, and the water was poured into each of the believers' miniature bamboo cups, the elders quietly reminded us to think of the Savior's death.

The growth and maturity of these young believers in Christ continued to amaze us, as they instantly obeyed everything they knew from God's Word. Then an incident occurred the next day which made us realize how much they had to learn, and how desperately they needed all of His Word in their own language.

Before the sun was even up, one of the believers called at our door, "*Sama! Sama! Takamoyung!* Friend! Friend! Teacher!"

Very sleepily Russell opened the door. "*Ken, Sena, nataw?*" he called gently into the gray dawn. "Yes, friend, what is it?"

"*Sama*, Baltugangan's wife gave birth in the night." It was the anxious voice of Dawa's widow, now Mrs Dagadafug.

"Yes, my friend," Russell answered, relieved that this Dalandan elder's new baby had arrived safely even though they were far from home. They and all their village were in Safa to listen to our teaching from God's Word. "Was it a boy or a girl?"

"A girl," was the answer. Then with obvious apprehension, "But the mother is not rocking the newborn in her arms!"

By this time I was beside Russell at the door, and while he tried to think of what to say to that comment, I whispered to him urgently, "Hon, maybe something's wrong. That baby wasn't due for another month at least. Maybe even two."

"Why does she not rock the little one?" Russell's soft voice asked.

"She doesn't want it," was the startling reply.

Doesn't want it? Was it dead? *No*, I thought, *I'm sure they would have said if it were.* I was thrown into confusion. The Tawbuid love their children. They are exemplary parents. And Baltugangan and his wife were a lovely couple. "Maybe we should go and see," I suggested to Russell.

Russell stayed with the boys who were still asleep, while I quickly slipped into a dress and went across the village to the home where Baltugangan and his wife were staying.

Approaching the tiny palm-leaf-covered hut I called, "*Sama! Sena!* Here I am. I have just arrived."

Baltugangan came to the door with his ever-friendly grin. "*Nataw, Sena?*" he asked. "What do you want, my friend?"

"Is it good if I see the mother and the baby?" I asked.

Confusion replaced his grin. He cleared his throat, then mumbled, "It doesn't really matter..."

The house was toasty warm but smoky. Linday

was sitting on the floor near the fire, leaning against the homemade back rest that every new mother uses. For five days after the birth she is not allowed to lie flat, but sits up whether awake or asleep.

Squatting beside her I asked, "How is it with you, dear friend?" But she only mumbled and turned away. And then I saw the babe, and felt sick.

About six feet from the mother on a stiff piece of bark was this tiny premature form, naked, uncovered, with the uncut cord and after-birth beside it. Impulsively I moved nearer, and touched the wee one. Some kind of yellowish goo had been smeared above her eyes and all over her head. But she was warm! Breathing! Alive! I thought how good for the baby that the fire was burning so brightly, keeping the house almost too warm. But if her life was to be saved, I knew that something must be done right away. I wished Russell were there.

I hardly knew where to start. "What's that all over her head?" I asked Linday.

She didn't seem to understand what I meant, but her husband, after clearing his throat several times, spoke for her. "Sweet potato," was his mystifying answer.

"What's it for?" I persisted, looking at Linday.

With eyes of a hunted animal, she looked at her husband. No one would answer. So I tried another approach. "What is wrong? Why don't you hold her?"

"It is not our custom," Baltugangan answered. "She won't live."

I know she won't live, I thought in despair. *It's amazing she's still alive now.* I wanted to say, Oh, Baltugangan, aren't you, as church elder, the one who encourages your people to listen to God's Words and obey them? What are you doing to this baby God has given you? But I controlled my feelings and softly asked, "Why won't she live?" I wanted to understand and help.

With uncertainty in his eyes, Baltugangan took a deep breath, glanced in the direction of the newborn, and began, "This came two months before the normal time. It is not truly a person. It is just part of the after-birth. It will not live."

I felt sick. But as I sat in stunned silence, I tried to put myself in their shoes. That was the problem! They didn't wear shoes! Their culture, background and training were so different from mine. How could I really understand them?

But I could try to walk their trails. They were taught love, respect and obedience. They always showed great care for everyone in their family, clan and village. Why such unconcern for this precious little one?

I probed my mind for any hint of how they felt. Then I realized that through the years they had learned a premature baby does not live long. Often it cannot nurse. It dies before it is able to recognize its mother or father. Rather than watch it sicken and die, causing grief to the family and fear of the ghost to the whole village, it is merely considered non-human. To remove it from sight would be a relief to the heart-broken mother and a solution for the confused father.

Feeling completely inadequate, I gently told the parents, "God wants you to love and to care for this tiny one He has given you. Just like He loves you."

Baltugangan's eyes opened in surprise, confusion registering on his face. "You mean," he managed to stammer, "God wants us to love this thing?" Then after a pause, "Should we hold it... and nurse it?"

"Yes, and we will help you." Putting feet to my words, and telling him I wouldn't be gone long, I dashed across the village, up our stairs and into the house.

Still panting I burst out, "Oh, Honey! You just can't imagine!" And I described to him the pathetic scene, adding, "I had nothing to even cover the baby. It's just good the house was so warm. What can we do?"

"I'd say it needs a hot water bottle, and something to cover it. How about using a cardboard box for a crib? That'd keep the warmth in."

Our blackened teakettle was already over the open fire, so using one of our drinking water bottles, we filled it with hot water and pinned a small towel firmly around it. With this as well as several soft cloths for blankets and a cardboard carton, we were ready to return. Several of the believers were standing by our porch, observing what was going on. Asking one of them to watch our sleeping boys, we rushed back to the little palm-leaf home.

Oh, the joy and praise that filled my heart as we entered. The cord had been cut, and the baby was being lovingly cleaned. With words of encouragement and prayer for this brave family who had been strengthened by God to defy old customs, we helped tuck the baby into the new warm bed. As we left, we gave instructions about refilling the strange hot-water bottle.

Returning to the house we could hear our two-year-old calling, "Mommie! Mommie! Robby all finished! All finished bed! Mommie!" So I bounded inside and began untucking mosquito nets, getting the boys dressed, and putting on the breakfast oatmeal, all the time praying for Baltugangan and Linday and the new baby.

"*Sena, Sama,*" the insistent call came from the front porch. Going out I saw Dagadafug's wife sitting at the top of our steps. "She is holding the baby and nursing her now!" she excitedly told us.

"Tell me," I asked her, "why did they smear sweet potato on the baby's head?"

She looked down at the round pole stairs and began to pull at the rattan strips which tied them. Finally, finding the courage to answer, she looked up uncertainly, "You see, the grandfathers taught us that such a one is not a real person. And we are to put it out in the jungle..." She swallowed, uncertain how to say it, "and... and the animals..." She didn't finish. She didn't need to. Now I saw the horrible picture. The sweet potato was an attraction so the life would be ended quickly. I shuddered.

Blinking back the tears for all those wee babies before Christ was known, I thought of this first tiny life God had rescued from death. I bowed in worship to such a great God, giving faith and courage to this young couple who had come to know Him only the year before. And who, although they were trying to obey all they had heard, had much to learn of His loving, caring ways.

On our next trip into the Banos, the river was very deep and swift. Four of the believers came out to meet us, and by the fourth crossing we all joined hands, splashing hip-deep through the torrent. The Tawbuid laughed and shouted encouragements, I squealed at the cold water, and the boys acted as though they had never been on such a happy holiday. I was glad that the solid, sturdy Tawbuid men were carrying Robby and Randy and our loads. We hit one especially swift crossing and, as I lost my footing, my slippery wet hand let loose of Squint's sturdy grip. Down I went, to be swept away by the current, but he instantly reached out and grabbed my wrist.

Amid all the splashing and laughter, he got quite a good-natured ribbing from the others for losing his hold on me. But I knew I had let loose of him and he had saved my life!

That week we had classes in Tagalog and long-hand writing, but we spent most of the time teaching a leaders' class for all the men. They were delighted with the novelty of the colored flash-card pictures for "sermon notes," and challenged by the newly-translated Easter story from John, which they diligently practiced reading.

On Saturday at our usual afternoon meeting, Tiban looked around the church, asking, "Where is Squint?" No one knew. "He hasn't come home yet," was all they could say.

Sunday he still had not appeared. We were worried, for he was not too well, and the river trip had been tiring. On Monday Tiban came back from the interior fields with the news, "He's left his jungle knife on top of his seed rice in his field shed."

Why the sudden fear in everyone's eyes? After the meeting we asked Tiban. He told us, "If he does not return for the knife, it means he has ended his life."

My mind would not accept that. He was a dedicated believer, one of the first to be baptized here in Banos Village. He was a loving father to his five children. A faithful husband. A rock of Gibralter for me in those difficult river crossings. I owed my life to him.

But the jungle knife remained unclaimed. Talking to his wife and to Tiban, we learned he had been depressed. He had been angry with Tiban for his arrangement of the men's field work, and the morning he disappeared, had had an argument with his wife.

During those tense days, I was disturbed. Had he been depressed because they teased him in the river? Why hadn't I told him how much I appreciated his help? Would it have made a difference?

Finally, his body was found hanging in the jungle. The believers visited and sympathized with his bereaved family, even helping clear his fields for planting. Discussing the events, we learned two reasons for suicide: to end a terminal illness quickly or to spite someone who has made you angry.

The shock upset us. We had seen Christ's power deliver the Tawbuid believers from fear, from hatred and from anger. This incident made us realize the power of Satan as he seeks to snare the believers and ruin the work God has done.

After Easter we were in Safa village, enduring an unusually intense heat wave. Dripping with perspiration, we taught Tagalog classes, feeling inadequate with our slim knowledge. Introducing church studies was no easier, as we tried to explain clearly in Tawbuid the Statement of Faith and Church Customs (the constitution). Our furlough was due in a few months, and we wanted the churches to be firmly established by then.

We weren't the only ones working hard in the heat. Even though this was a busy month with clearing of land for planting, all the men and boys from Safa and Dalandan had spent four full days at Safa's new village site, constructing the large church and the small missionary house.

Evening coolness the last day of that week was a welcome relief to everyone. We spread our double sleeping bag on the floor with baby Randy's on one side and Robby's on the other. Turning out the kerosene storm lantern, we crawled under the mosquito net between the sleeping boys.

It seemed like we had been asleep only minutes when loud shouts startled us awake. Peering through the cracks in our bark wall, we saw a huge fire over the hill behind our house. More shouting and exploding bamboo accompanied the flames. We thought it was just a flare-up of an earlier fire for field clearing.

The believers, however, were pouring out of their houses, bounding up the hill. Going out on our porch, Russell called out into the darkness, "*Nataw*? What is it?" We could sense the panic.

"Suklinyan's house is on fire!" one of the men shouted back over his shoulder. We knew he was hurrying to help pull down the burning house so the flames would not shoot skyward and spread ignited debris to other homes. It was their only method of fire fighting.

"Is everyone safe? Has anyone been hurt?" Russell called out, fearing the worst.

"Everyone got out in time," the hurrying figure replied, turning our fear into sorrow and sympathy for what they must have lost.

Returning from the scene, they told us that while

everyone was asleep, a smoldering log had rolled off the fire-hearth onto the floor. Everything was so dry that the floor quickly ignited, spreading the flame to the grass walls and the roof. By the time Suklinyan and his wife and their two Dalandan guests had awakened, it was too late to save any of the seed rice so carefully stored in the house.

At our morning service the next day Russell asked what had been lost. A number of items were mentioned such as medicines, pencils, Bible portions and study books, but the seed rice and ubi yam tubers for planting were emphasized. It was suggested that those who wanted to help could bring their gift to the afternoon service, and as a result every family gave a share of their own meager supply of seed rice and ubi tubers so that Suklinyan could plant next month. We promised to bring him another set of the miniature medicine bottles as well as new copies of the hymn book, the Thick Book, the chapter of Mark and the various study materials.

Out again in the lowlands, Russell took another trip to the West, returning with the news that Makisig had warmly welcomed him, gladly accepted a new phonograph and records, and asked him when he could come and teach them! While we were rejoicing in God's work in their hearts, we were saddened that we were going on furlough and would be unable even to visit him. "Who, Lord, can go teach these Western Tawbuid?" was the question constantly on our hearts.

"I've got good news, too," I told Russell. "Just look at this reply from Evalinda. She'll be here in just three weeks to start Tagalog classes at Safa. What a help it'll be for the believers to have a teacher whose language is Tagalog."

"That means we won't have time for the trip we planned into the Banos, if we are going to move into our new house at Safa before she gets here." Russell paused thoughtfully and then continued, "Look. Why don't I go to the Banos this weekend by myself and teach, and tell them about Evalinda's coming to Safa. And then we can go to Safa on Monday or Tuesday to teach and get the new house ready for her visit." Neither of us had any idea that he spoke with God's very special guidance.

He left for the Banos, and was back the same evening with a distressing report. As he had unlocked the bark door of our little hill home, he had felt weak with astonishment, for everything we owned was gone! The trunk had been torn open at the end. The wall medicine cabinet had the bottom ripped off. The huge tin lard pails were lying open and empty on the floor. The thief had crawled in where the bark wall meets the grass roof and had taken his loot out the same way. The Tawbuid children had actually seen some outsiders taking their chickens, but were much too afraid to stop them.

All Russell could do was turn right around and come back to Pinamalayan, for he didn't even have a bar of soap for bathing! That evening as he was packing for an early morning return, he remarked, "It's a good thing we didn't all go up to be surprised by that empty house! We couldn't have returned like I did."

At the beginning of the next week when we arrived at Safa, the planting had been finished, with the innovative Dalandan believers making small fields at Safa so they would have food when they came for our teaching!

That week the big move was made to the new village site. Almost all the families had completed their new homes or were just putting on the finishing touches. We were delighted to exchange our seven-by-seven-foot doll house for a more spacious home, all their own idea, design and construction.

For Evalinda they built a little four-by-eight-foot room at one end of our house. At the other end was the entry porch with our floor-level cooking fire. The main room in between was about eight by ten feet, with a wide shelf across the center at head-height. This held our sleeping bags and mosquito nets when we were eating or studying, and our study materials when we were sleeping.

At our first service in the new *Funbalugu Bale*, four men from Safa asked prayer for a village they had visited which was friendly, though apprehensive of their message. The Dalandan church leaders told of an interior Tawbuid so interested that he was willing to listen to Gospel Recording records. Russell jotted down the names so he could make prayer cards for the churches. At the end of the service the new *Funbalugu Bale* was dedicated followed by the observance of the Lord's Supper. We returned to Pinamalayan promising to be back on the second Friday accompanied by Evalinda.

Three active weeks with enthusiastic Evalinda began the minute we arrived back in Safa. Still feeling soggy and tired, I glanced out the door to see her breaking up the hard, stubborn soil with a long jungle knife.

"This is one of the driest dry seasons we've had," I

told her. "What are you doing so ambitiously?"

Pushing back her thick, black hair, she wiped her damp forehead. "Well, I'm making four little seed plots for the new vegetables I'm going to introduce." During her stay, almost every family planted some of her seedlings in their fields, and were carefully following her watering instructions, a strange custom to them.

To the delight of the believers she produced a ukulele and taught them several Filipino folk songs. But her main work was a full morning of Tagalog study every day for the men.

Near the end of the first week Dagadafug came to class with fever and red eyes, and we knew the dreaded measles epidemic that had already run its course in the Banos had now hit Safa. A week later more than half the class was down, many with severe cases. Why had this tragedy struck just when they were advancing in Tagalog which was imperative for acceptance into MBS? Even the daily worship attendance dropped to one-third, for so many mothers and children were ill.

Then Robby began a high fever which lasted five harrowing days before he finally broke out, lowering his temperature. I desperately wanted to take him home to his own little bed with clean, cool sheets, but he was far too ill to travel. Randy had a brief intermittent fever, breaking out the day after Robby.

At each meeting new reports told of other children or parents becoming ill. As we, too, shared Robby's and Randy's progress, we sensed a special bond of caring love.

That week Randy had his first birthday and

Evalinda her 21st. Sweet dumplings on top of stewed dried apples had to suffice for a cake, though Randy didn't feel like eating anyway!

The measles epidemic in Safa brought five deaths, including Pig-Tooth and his wife, leaving their orphaned son. How we praised God that they had finally decided to put their faith in Christ the year before. As the believers slowly overcame their shock and sorrow with their faith strengthened, we were encouraged.

The Banos believers had a different kind of testing. Food, always in short supply, was being stolen from their fields by intruders from the low-lands. Some bolder trespassers were actually moving onto their land and taking over. A good rice harvest heartened the believers, but then a number of outsiders invited themselves to help bring it in, collecting the traditional one-fourth of their harvest-ings. Too afraid of violence to refuse these "helpers" or check on the amount they carried away, the believers lost a large part of their crop.

They had thought of moving farther into the interior, but knew it would be more difficult for us to visit and teach. We wrote to our prayer partners, and the Lord led the believers to resettle on some land Tiban had at Fandung Creek, between Safa and Dalandan villages. Instead of protecting their Banos land from intruders, God was guiding them to a more advantageous area. The move would be difficult, for it was a long tramp over jungle-covered hills, but fellowship among the three churches would be easier, a welcome thought in the light of our coming furlough.

At the Thanksgiving feast we learned of the temptation that had faced Tree-Branch, the former shaman who was the leader of Dalandan village. An old shaman from the interior visited him, bringing a fat white pig and a very logical request. "Since you no longer use your spirit paraphernalia or recite your chants and songs of power, why don't you give them all to me, teaching me your old practices? And I'll pay you with this white pig!"

The temptation was overwhelming. A highly-valued white pig, so different from their small black ones, was within his grasp. His people had begun a goat herd, with the help of the Safa believers, but pigs were still more highly desired. And now that he was a believer, he had no use for the old spirit ways. Why not sell his knowledge? But our prayer-answering God gave him wisdom from above.

"*Sama*," Tree-Branch began gently, "It does not please our *Funbalugu* to use the chants or the spirit paraphernalia. We must not worship or appease the old spirits. That is evil. We are to worship and trust Him only. I cannot give you those things."

Then, taking a deep breath, he put forward his proposal. "For these past two years we have planted rice, for we no longer fear the curses of the evil ones. Our *Funbalugu* is stronger. And we had a good harvest. If you will give me that pig, I will pay you with a supply of rice." Uncertain thoughts must have raced through Tree-Branch's mind. Would the shaman be angry? Would he curse their village?

To this interior shaman the gift of unobtainable rice was very welcome. The taboo against planting does not extend to eating this highly-desired food. So he happily accepted both Tree-Branch's testimony and his proposed payment. God was honored and we were thrilled!

Long before furlough we had asked God to help us prepare the believers for our year's absence. As Russell made his last trip to the hills, his pack was filled with God's answers. Besides the last two chapters of Mark which would complete that book so each family had a copy, he was taking more verse sheets to expand everyone's Thick Book. The new Tawbuid hymn, "I've Found a Friend" had already been pasted into their green-covered hymn books. A bundle of brightly-colored 1968 Tawbuid calendars and copies of the new pink-covered booklets of the Christmas Story from Luke were also taken for each family.

And last was a small hand-operated battery-amplified tape recorder which had been sent to us just three weeks before. Russell had recorded the continuous fourteen-minute reels with Tawbuid Scripture, Bible stories and teaching. These could be used for the believers' own instruction as they met in our absence, for others who might visit their village, or for those they met in the interior while on evangelistic trips.

God was guiding our family, too. Rick and Becky had again spent the summer in California with their beloved Grandma and Grandpa Flory. In the fall they had entered school there, ready for our arrival. We flew home to America just before Christmas 1967 with the joyous anticipation of being together as a family of six for the very first time.

But all of us were concerned for the Tawbuid believers. Would they stand firm in our absence? Would their vision of attending Bible School fade? For now they had no one there to help and encourage them.

Chapter 14

STUDYING

It was a bright April day in sunny Southern California, four months into our year of furlough. Rick and Becky had biked to their nearby Junior High School as usual that morning, and Robby and Randy were making mountains and roads in their spacious outdoor sandbox. Russell was organizing his Tawbuid materials for attending the Summer Institute of Linguistics in June, and I was singing joyously as I cleared up the morning's breakfast clutter.

Mom and Dad are so special, I thought for the umpteenth time. *Their love is always giving and sacrificing, especially for us three missionary daughters.* They had loaned Russell and me their almost new home, while they had moved to a tiny rented apartment. How I loved them, and my native Southern California! How I loved my family! *All six of us together, like it should be*, I thought reasonably. *Normal. Right.*

Just then I heard the mailman and quickly went out to collect our letters. My sister Ann had written from Mindoro, so I hurried back to the kitchen for a knife to slit open those resistant airforms and began reading, "First of all let me tell you about the Tawbuid and MBS..."

"Oh, Honey," I called to Russell who was deeply engrossed at the desk in the next room. "Here's a letter from Ann about the Tawbuid and MBS. Sounds like they haven't lost their vision of going to Bible school at all!"

"You mean they were able to go this year?" he asked incredulously.

"I dunno. I haven't read it yet," I said, approaching the desk. "Here's what she says, 'Jeremias,' that's one of Ann's Hanunoo young men, 'Jeremias took two Hanunoo students to MBS, which is now permanently located in the hills above Calapan. He was accompanied by eight Tawbuid. Three from Safa, two from Dalandan, and three from Banos. But unfortunately Dave felt none of the Tawbuid were really ready for school...'"

"I wonder how they'll ever be ready. Tagalog comes so slowly," Russell said thoughtfully.

I nodded and went on, "'Apparently they thought they would learn to read better and to write at MBS! They really must be hungry for teaching.'"

Suddenly I thought to myself, *Our kids need us and the Tawbuid need us. Oh, Lord, I simply can't leave Rick and Becky again. I just can't!*

Swallowing hard I read on, "'Jeremias would like to visit them and I have encouraged him. He is so humble and loves everybody. The Tawbuid weren't at all discouraged. Dave gave them hints how they could study and help one another to get ready for next year.'"

"Next year? I don't think they'll make it," Russell commented. "But when Theo and Maria join us they'll be able to help. They know Tagalog so well."

"'Don't *you* be discouraged now,'" I continued to

read, "'though I'm sure you must be disappointed.'"

I sighed. *Lord, I see their need. Part of me is willing to return and part of me just isn't!* I thought of His special promises to those who leave all to follow Him, knowing I must return. All through that joy-filled year at home, I didn't once think of the rest of that verse from Mark 10. "With persecutions."

When we were ready to go back, Rick, now in high school, and Becky, in the eighth grade, returned to Wheaton, and Satan began his warfare. All my life he has been shooting those same fiery darts, the latest being as I write this! "Did you do right by your children? How could you leave them for others to care for? Are they really happy? Is this God's best for them?" And each time I would have to raise that Shield of Faith and simply say, "Lord, you know. You answer. Strengthen my shaky faith."

We arrived back in Manila on Robby's fourth birthday, January 19, 1969, and later that week were on a big Mindoro bus speeding south from Calapan to Pinamalayan. I looked across the wide restful lowland fields to the distant purple ranges and felt a welcome calm, God's reassurance that this was exactly the place He wanted me. Those jungle- and grass-covered mountains were filled with neglected tribal people. He was asking us to be a part of His plan for them. I knew He would specially care for Rick and Becky and would continue to comfort all of us in our separation.

A few days after our arrival, we answered a loud knocking on our front door and found a delegation of grinning, bright-eyed Tawbuid believers. Though they rarely made trips to town, they wanted to be sure we had really arrived!

Russell visited the three churches about a week later, returning with a glowing report. He had enjoyed the fellowship in Safa, and then, with several believers, he climbed the rugged four-hour trail from Safa to Tiban's new village of Fandung, located between Safa and Dalandan. In their neat little chapel they were having a Tagalog service!

"They were singing from a Tagalog hymn book. They read from the Tagalog Sunday School book and a Tagalog copy of Mark, and even prayed in Tagalog. Rather impressive!"

"Well, bless their hearts," I said warmly, "They're really taking this Tagalog mastery seriously!"

"That afternoon we went on to Dalandan. You should see their church, it's even got a bell!" Russell said.

"A church bell? You're teasing! Where'd they ever get a bell?" I asked.

"It's really one lug off a caterpiller tractor tread," he confessed with a grin. "I suppose they just found it in the jungle from an abandoned logging operation. They ring it with an old transmission gear."

"How clever! Does it really chime?" I asked.

"Sure. Sounds like a real bell!" Then he continued, "When we first got to Dalandan, Baltugangan had just arrived from a trip to the interior. He said he hadn't been very well received, but some had listened to God's words. Oh, Hon, some sad news. His little premature baby evidently became a happy, active two-year-old, but she died of pneumonia just last month."

"Oh, I'm so sorry! Those poor parents!" I said sadly. I had envisaged this child growing to adulthood, a glowing example to all the unbelieving Tawbuid of God's caring love.

"And yet, it hasn't shaken their faith," he said. "It's amazing what God is doing. Even though the elders in the three churches have had no training, they've led the people so that all the believers continue to meet and study God's Word every morning and every evening."

"How did the nominations go?" I asked. One reason for his trip was to help them with new elections of church leaders.

"The believers have chosen truly devoted men," he answered appreciatively. "But that isn't all. Every church has sent substantial gifts to Gospel Recordings, or to the Pinamalayan town church for its building, or to the DZAS Christian radio station, and one even sent a gift to MBS for their general running expenses."

"With their tiny incomes that must have used all of their *'Funbalugu's* money'," I calculated.

"No, it didn't. And this is the best part. Every church has been sending money regularly to MBS to be saved for food and books of the Tawbuid men who one day will be attending! Kalafe from Safa and Baltugangan from Dalandan have even asked me to buy them Tagalog Bibles."

"Where'll they ever get the money?" I asked.

"Everyone's busy scraping rattan, and all they use the money for is the Lord's offering or His work," he answered. "I figure it'll take 1,400 strips to pay for a Bible."

"That'd be about seven days' work for one person! They're sure people of single vision!" I said admiringly.

On our first after-furlough visit to Safa we found our little home had a new floor, a new roof and a bigger fire hearth. Cumbersome, slow travel with two small boys prompted us to make Safa our headquarters in the hills. Believers from Fandung and Dalandan would come to study while we were there, and if some couldn't attend, their returning elders would share what they had learned.

Each day the believers led the meetings as usual and Russell took the morning Bible Study. Afterwards he sat on the tiny porch of our house checking the first draft of John 1 with his translation helper. Two-year-old Randy played near him in the house or was with me on the bamboo floor of the church. There I taught the men Tagalog for about three hours, while sometimes sneaking a look out the church door. All the children including four-year-old Robby were taking turns going down the steep smooth slope on a palm-trunk sled. I chuckled as they paid their fare with a leaf, for the Tawbuid term for paper money is "leaf."

Each evening one of the men gave a brief message in Tawbuid from that morning's Tagalog class. If MBS study was to benefit the whole church, the men must be able to teach in Tawbuid the truths they would study in Tagalog. But attending Bible school in April seemed an impossible goal. The best students could read, often haltingly, both Tagalog and Tawbuid, and their writing was still painfully laborious.

That week the leaders of all three churches decided to have a joint feast and conference at Easter like they had at Christmas. But their main discussion centered around a completely new concept.

Missionaries in each tribe were simultaneously

presenting the idea of a Mangyan tribal church association to the believers. Russell introduced the subject, "There's going to be a gathering at the Bible School of several men from each tribe."

He had wanted to say a *representative* from each tribe. But he was stuck. Tongue-tied. For the Tawbuid have no concept, and therefore no word for "representative." Elders and leaders among the Tawbuid lead, they don't represent, and yet every follower has the opportunity to express his opinion. We hoped they would understand the new idea when they saw it function.

He then explained, "These men will tell what God has been doing in their churches and among their people, talk about their problems, listen to ideas for solutions and be of one mind together for help and encouragement, especially if some believers face opposition."

Silence greeted this curious proposal. Then, warily, "Who will go?"

"Everyone will help choose one person from among all the believers," Russell told the men. "A second person needs to be chosen to go with him. If the first person becomes ill and can't attend the meetings, the second will be there to take his place."

"We can't understand Tagalog," some said in a typical Tawbuid understatement. What they really meant was, "We won't know what to do, or what to say, or how to act at such a meeting."

When the choice was made, Bumblebee from Fandung and Kalafe from Safa reluctantly agreed to go, with Baltugangan from Dalandan as a backup. The leaders then decided that each church should contribute to the transportation costs.

Russell surprised me after the meeting with, "How'd you like to escort Kalafe and Bumblebee to the Leaders' Council?"

"Me? I'd love it!" *Bless his heart!* I thought. For I knew that managing a house and two little boys was not his cup of tea!

After an hour's hike from the jeep road, I had my first delightful glimpse of the Mangyan Bible School. With walls of vertical round bamboo, the buildings looked like huge golden pipe organs artistically arranged on the hillside. I thought every sound from that place must be music to the Lord.

The music to my ears was not just the harmony of the diverse yet wholly dedicated church elders from the six different tribes, but also the surprising news Dave gave me after he had interviewed prospective student, Kalafe.

"Did you hear that we have no definite registrations for the beginners' term next month?" he asked me. "And yet for the following term, fifteen are already accepted!"

"How strange... Why hasn't anyone registered?" I asked.

"Well, we don't know," Dave answered. "But the staff decided if Kalafe and three or four other Tawbuid would like to come, we can take them all. We'll just gear the studies to their level of Tagalog, and to their reading and writing ability."

Why, of course! It wasn't strange at all! God was answering our prayers. It was His miracle for the Tawbuid!

"And by the way," Dave continued, "did you know the Tawbuid churches have already sent over a hundred pesos to pay for the food and books of their men when they are able to come?" Calculating quickly, I realized that represented seven months' wages!

I was overwhelmed. Perhaps four men, I thought, would be able to go. For they not only needed seven pesos for a Tagalog Bible, but they also had to leave their fields and families and face the demand of constant study.

On our next hill visit, amid a fury of activity of collecting, measuring, splitting and scraping rattan, we were told, "Four men from Safa are going to study at the Bible School."

"Four men will go to MBS!" We were thrilled.

"And two from Fandung and two from Dalandan," they added.

"Eight!" Our joy knew no bounds!

Three were Safa church leaders, Kalafe, Suklinyan and young Faguguanun, along with teenaged Taglagi, the first Tawbuid to learn to read. From Dalandan were two church elders, Baltugangan and Gunye. And then Bumblebee, the Fandung elder, and young, bright Uan. The innovative, caring believers in each village had already volunteered to finish clearing the men's fields, and plant and weed them while they were gone. So their wives were free to accompany them!

On the appointed traveling day eight men, six wives, two babies and a babysitter (so the wives could work in the fields!) with baskets, bundles and sacks came shyly out of the hills. All were wide eyed at the crowds of people, the mysterious languages and the fast buses.

The men had never sat on a bench or at a desk,

had handled few books and papers, and had never taken notes nor written an exam. Later when Russell visited them briefly, he found them diligent and cheerful, eager to stay the full two months in spite of the strangeness.

As the men determinedly studied, the believers in their home villages were facing problems. Rats and dry weather meant that many of the fields had to be replanted, including those of the Bible School students, and there was little extra seed rice. An outsider was surveying the Safa village site, planning to claim it for pasture land. Four elderly members in interior Dalandan were threatening to return to the old customs, for they objected to the introduction of the Tagalog language into their village.

Word also came that Theo was to be appointed OMF Tribal Superintendent when he and Maria returned to Mindoro. All the tribes would gain, but losing them as co-workers was a deep disappointment to us and to the believers. And the Western Tawbuid were still unreached.

Russell had returned from another trip to Pangalkagan discouraged that everyone who had enthusiastically welcomed him on his last visit, probably because opposing Makasig was dead, had now moved away. Encouragement came from Rodrigo Embate, however, a young widower who had accepted Christ in Ligaya while we lived there and was now a Christian worker who periodically visited in the hills. The Tawbuid in neighboring Pusug, the village we had wanted to reach, had welcomed him. Even though his teaching was in the unfamiliar Tagalog language, they were "listening."

These burdens were lightened when the Bible

School men were welcomed home with their fresh, enthusiastic contribution to the churches. In the daily morning and evening meetings, one of the men briefly reviewed the previous day's passage, read the next consecutive Scripture portion, and gave a short explanation or challenge. Then he chose one or two appropriate verses from the Thick Book, and a closing hymn to add to the meaning of the Scripture. During the prayer time the two cards taken from the folder were not merely read, but up-to-date information was added, some of it from MBS.

As they gave the Sunday and Wednesday morning messages, quiet boldness was replacing their characteristic shyness. One even attacked an ever-present church problem by saying before his sermon, "Now I want all of you to be quiet and to keep your children quiet and make them obey you. For if I have to speak very loudly, I probably will get hoarse!"

They spent hours searching their chosen passage for teaching about God, or instructions of an example to follow, a command to obey, a sin to avoid, a promise to believe, or a prayer to use. Writing in their notebooks was the next laborious step, along with selecting illustrations from Scripture or from life. Literally by the sweat of their brow they gave their painstakingly-prepared sermons to the spiritual benefit of all, including themselves.

After four months at home, the eight men left again for MBS, including brave young Gunye whose wife and first-born baby had died just the month before. The men would repeat the beginners' course again this term, as suggested by the Bible School staff, to consolidate their gains in Tagalog.

For their Thanksgiving feast the believers decided that everyone should meet together, like they did at Christmas and Easter. This established the custom of gathering in one village for each of the three yearly feasts. Dalandan, four hours jungle hike beyond Safa, would host this celebration, and we would be able to go! For the believers had surprised us with word of a new house waiting there for us.

At Dalandan Russell would be giving each church one of his new "Every Morning, Every Evening" reading guides. It indicated short consecutive portions to be read each day from Mark or the first seven chapters of John that we had translated and distributed. Questions for the congregation were given with each selection. He also had new pages for everyone's Thick Book, which now had at least one verse from every book of the Bible in biblical order. "Sword Drills" had become the rage, challenging all the believers to learn the names of the Bible books in order, so they could quickly flip the pages to the announced verse.

At midnight, the day before we were to leave, we were awakened by *"Sama! Sama! Takamoyung!"*

"Yes, my friend," Russell answered, pushing open our warped bark door.

"Our brother is being visited again by the evil spirit! Come! Come quickly!" said the insistent voice in the darkness. "He is attacking Butuan with his fists and he says he will not stop until Butuan proclaims himself the supreme leader of the area and promises to defend the people against all the interior shaman!" As he accompanied the believers to the house, Russell realized that the Possessed One was trying to humiliate Butuan. For no Tawbuid would be willing to take such a rash stand against the powerful evil shaman.

The confrontation that night was disturbingly indecisive. The next day, with all of the Safa believers including the Possessed One, we hiked the exhausting jungle and mountain trail to reach our new home. On the way several of the men looking for Butuan were relieved to find he had not hung himself as Tawbuid custom in that situation might demand.

In Dalandan the leaders of all the churches met and decided if the spirit came again they would ring the church bell, and then gather at the house where the Possessed One was staying while the rest of the believers prayed. During the meeting that evening, Chopped-Cheek, his brother, rushed over to the church calling for the elders. The spirit had come. Russell stopped his message, told everyone to pray and went with the men.

He told me afterwards that as the rhythmic bouncing and demands of the spirit increased, he had spoken plainly, reminding the Possessed One that we do not worship or obey the spirits, we worship and obey only *Funbalugu*. And *Funbalugu* will not help us against the evil spirits if we are having any dealings with them. Then he commanded in the name of Jesus Christ that the spirit leave and not return.

But the next night the spirit returned. As Russell asked about ill feeling between the Possessed One and Butuan, he learned that the Possessed One was dissatisfied with the division of the land. Butuan had taken a large, desirable piece while he had been given a small, hilly interior plot. When he was finally promised another piece of land, and told at the same time that he would have to go live in the far interior if the evil spirit continued to come back, the spirit left him and never returned.

Was he truly possessed? The believers felt so. Or was he using a culturally accepted method of attacking an enemy and getting his own way? We never did know. But we praised God for His healing and keeping power as there was never a recurrance.

Christmas brought a different kind of testing. After three days of unexpected heavy rains, we and the Safa believers were finally able to slip and slide our way to Dalandan. The next day Russell came down with shaking chills and high fever, and even a dose of malaria medicine had no effect. What should we do?

Although he was prostrate, Russell felt that Robby and I should take the hour hike to Fandung for the Christmas celebration with the other Dalandan families, leaving Randy to "take care of Daddy" until we all returned in the afternoon.

During that hour, made easier by the clear bright day, I kept wondering if Russell was all right. Would the fever go up? Would he be able to care for Randy? Should I have left him?

I was cheered by the new trail the believers had arduously cut for us, eliminating much of the river travel over large boulders, and comforted at the first meeting by their prayers for Russell. Afterwards the copies I had brought of the newly-translated Christmas story from Luke were given out and read.

Following the feast, we had our final meeting, crowned with a special wedding. Gunye, whose wife had died just before the last session of Bible School, was married to a bright young Christian from Safa.

Back in Dalandan, I nursed Russell through three more days of high fever before he was able to distribute his newly-translated First Timothy 3:1-13 and teach the qualifications and responsibilities of church leaders.

That spring Gunye's new wife not only accompanied him to MBS but became our first Tawbuid woman student! Originally Gunye was scheduled to wait until the October session and Baltugangan was to go in April. But because Gunye's bride would be able to study, while Baltugangan's wife had children needing her care, Russell asked Baltugangan, "Would it be good if you exchanged dates with Gunye? For only in April can a new student, like his wife, begin."

"*Ken, Sama!* It would be good!" he answered. "Because I have some work I want to do now."

"What work is that? In your fields?" Russell asked.

"No," he said, "I want to visit the interior villages in our area, and teach them from God's Word."

"But didn't you try that before, and were not welcomed?" Russell reminded him.

"Oh, several years ago one group chased me away, hitting my back with the blunt edge of a *bolo*. But they were just showing me that my teaching wasn't wanted there," he explained. "There may be some who will listen now."

Besides Gunye, Kalafe and his wife and little boy returned to MBS. And two from Safa entered for the first time, Butuan and Durfu, each with his wife and two children. But the two youngest men, Taglagi and Uan, did not go back, for they were to become part of a new exciting project.

As soon as this session of MBS was finished, my sister

Ann used the school facilities for her first eight-week session to train tribal believers as teachers for children's schools. The two months' study would equip them to teach the first six-week term of first grade.

The idea of these schools had first occurred to Russell during our furlough. Children would learn to read and write without the trauma their parents were now experiencing, and if Tagalog were also taught, those who later wanted to attend MBS would be equipped. Preparing the four-year curriculum, in which one grade would be taught each year with the cycle repeated every four years, would be a new and demanding venture. But Ann, a trained and experienced elementary teacher, accepted the challenge.

The five would-be teachers, some with wives, arrived. They ranged from the G-string-clad and mini-saronged Tadyawan and Tawbuid who carried rattan head-band baskets, to the well-dressed and meticulously groomed Buhid. An additional man from each participating tribe also came to learn how to build the school house and desks.

Ann couldn't tell these men how to use rattan, cogon grass, bamboo and other forest products so they would come out with a building. But she did indicate the size and height of the structure which was to be built on the ground, not on stilts, the location of the windows and door, and the pattern of the desks. In a few days these three men seemed as satisfied with the instructions as she was with the sample desk they had made, so they went home to begin work.

Her teachers-to-be learned many strange and wonderful things! To play games like hop-scotch, jump rope, and cat-and-mouse; to use rhythm band instruments; to color, cut (a real art for these scissorless people) and paste pictures on classroom charts. Practice teaching the daily children's lessons followed, and in eight weeks her willing learners, with no previous formal education, became teachers!

Rick and Becky's 1970 summer visit from the States brought all four children joyously together again. Rick backpacked with Russell around the island, visiting the Tawbuid both at Pangalkagan and Pusug. Fun-loving Becky kept us all happy in spite of the pouring rain, which we hoped was not affecting the hikers. Randy looked out one morning at our newly-flooded yard and shouted, "Look, everybody, look! Our big puddle is clear up to the top!"

And so were most of the rivers that Russell and Rick had to cross, they informed us when they returned. "But Pusug is a real encouragement," Russell told us. "Probably ten men and fifteen women are already believing. But how can they feed on God's word? They can't read, and there's no one there now, for Rodrigo's mission has assigned him to city work near San Jose."

As we discussed the situation, Russell came up with a suggestion. "What if a couple of the Pusug men came over here for the all-Mangyan tribal conference that's being planned for next spring at the Bible School?"

"What a good idea!" I told him. "I'm sure that'd encourage them to see so many other believers."

When all six of us hiked to Safa, Becky counted each crossing of the Safa River, surprising us with a total of 44! During that week Butuan, chin-pointing to a newly-cleared area close to our little home, asked us, "Would that be a good place for our new house?"

"Oh, yes!" I said, thinking how I'd enjoy them as neighbors.

We returned to the hills from seeing Rick and Becky off to the States to be cheered up by the opening day of the Safa children's school, where first grade would be taught this year. New teacher Taglagi slowly raised the Philippine Flag on its bamboo pole as the 21 children sang the National Anthem in Tagalog. The neat schoolhouse with its woven bamboo walls and grass roof, set in the new jungle clearing just outside the village, filled my heart with praise while my eyes filled with tears.

Then, to our amazement, we learned that the spacious, new house built close to our old one was not Butuan's, but was for us! More than twice the size of the old one, it had walls of hand-hewn boards, a high bark roof, and an abundance of light and airy windows. A half-height bark wall divided the main part into a front room where we would study and eat, and a bedroom where the four of us would be able to stretch out comfortably side by side. Our only piece of furniture, the big Tawbuid rattan hammock, would hang there during the day.

But their ingenious love-surprise to us was a real kitchen! As I stepped down into it from the end of the front room, I was amazed. Across the far wall was a waist-high clay-filled fire table with cooking-pot hooks dangling above it. Along the left wall was a neat bamboo counter for fixing vegetables or doing the dishes, while on the right was a perfect "dip and pour" corner for bathing. What luxurious living we would now enjoy!

We wanted all the believers to be able to study and mature like those who attended MBS. So we planned another Short-Term Bible School just before Christmas in Dalandan.

Classes began with my doctrine study, using "One Hundred Questions Answered from the Bible." Russell's Bible Survey of James through Revelation followed, with a daily hand-out sheet for each book giving the author, date, recipient, main theme, general outline and verses to remember. The colored folders for each set of papers would be expanded at later STBS's.

In my exposition class on First John, I was actually checking the rough draft of my translation, writing down any ideas and suggestions I heard as we discussed each verse. I found that group checking would only work in small groups, for often I didn't have time to write down one comment before another suggestion demanded my attention. Then the missionary story of Ti-Fam from Haiti with large flash-card illustrations ended the morning's studies.

Then with *bolos* and *sabi*-baskets, everyone headed for their fields. No noon meal was cooked, for the Tawbuid eat only two meals a day, snacking in between on bananas, papaya or sugar cane.

The evening devotions were led by Russell, spiced with new choruses that Baltugangan, Gunye and his wife had brought back from MBS. The greatest benefit from their training we could not see, for it came when they did the teaching in our absence.

That Christmas, as Russell talked with the believers, he found their vision for the unreached areas, encouraged at MBS, included the Western Tawbuid. He told them of his latest visit to Pusug, when village leader Tumas had urged Russell to go with him to an interested group in the interior. As Russell was explaining the Two-Roads poster, Tumas kept urging the listeners, "You must make your choice. Do you want to go to hell with the evil spirits, or to heaven? Choose right now! You have to decide! Which way do you want to go?"

The believers at the Christmas feast were impressed. Then Russell asked them, "How can Tumas' people study God's Words? They can't read, and most of what they were taught was in Tagalog, so they understood very little." Then he made his proposal, "You know this coming dry season there is to be a four-day Mangyan Believers Conference at the Bible School. Would it be good if we went to the West to bring back a couple of those Pusug listeners to that conference?" They heartily agreed, and two months later Suklinyan accompanied Russell on the trip.

A week before conference Russell and Suklinyan, with the Western Tawbuid listeners Tumas and Markus, arrived at our hill-home in Safa. All the believers were elated that they had come. Then two days later Tumas and Markus wanted to go home, saying they were worried about their families and their crops. Perhaps the dialect difference was disturbing them, and waiting was boring them. Discerning Suklinyan saved the day by taking them to help in his field clearing, while others showed them how to prepare scraped rattan to sell on their way to the conference.

Meeting believers from the other five Mindoro tribes was exhilarating for all the Tawbuid who attended the conference, whether Eastern or Western, even with the difficulty of communication in Tagalog.

Gunye, Mansangi and Russell escorted Tumas and Markus back to the West. Before they left, Russell and I had discussed how we could possibly give effective teaching to both Eastern and Western Tawbuid, and yet continue the desperately-needed translation of God's Word. We felt it just could not be done.

Chapter 15

TRAVELING

"Would it be good," Suklinyan asked the gathered leaders of the three Eastern Tawbuid churches, "for two or three of us to go to the West right away? Tumas and Markus are eager to learn more of God's Words." Russell, quietly observing as he sat in the circle of elders and deacons, was impressed by the earnestness of the group as they assumed this new responsibility.

"We need to go," Baltugangan agreed. "But what about our fields? If the rains had stopped when they should have, we wouldn't be so far behind on burning and clearing them."

"Besides that," said Butuan, counting on his fingers, "there are nine families who just left for Bible School. We need to clear and plant their fields, too."

Finally they decided the trip should be made when the planting was finished. Rice could be furnished by all the believers while transportation costs would come from *Funbalugu*'s money. Two church elders, Baltugangan from Dalandan and Suklinyan from Safa, volunteered to go.

Two months later in May 1971, when every Tawbuid field had been dotted with the surface imprint of the planting sticks, Baltugangan and Suklinyan were ready to go with Russell across the island on their first teaching trip to Pusug.

For us the timing could not have been more perfect. In Manila we had just said goodbye to Robby who, in high spirits, had left for his first school experience in the new Chefoo School in Baguio City. Missing him was minimized because we didn't have to return to our quiet lonely house in Pinamalayan. I was to care for the Manila mission home for several weeks, and was delighted to be at the hub of Manila activities. Five-year-old Randy, happily enjoying each guest, kept track of everyone's room number even when they changed daily. And Russell was reveling in his favorite sport, trekking, with Baltugangan and Suklinyan.

With rice and dried fish, their Tawbuid Scriptures of Mark and of the newly-completed Gospel of John, and the teaching materials Russell had helped the men prepare, they hiked across the mountains in the south, learning the least expensive way to go west. After four days battling typhoon-swollen streams and deep mud trails, with three nights sleeping around Tawbuid campfires, they arrived in Pusug.

Eight adults, largely the relatives of village leader Tumas, gathered in his house, eager to listen. Conscious that his presence might intimidate the Eastern church elders, Russell visited the surrounding areas, freeing the men to use their initiative and ability in their daily teaching. The listeners increased to thirteen, all eager to know God's words and to learn to read. But in his wanderings Russell had found no other villages, not even Pangalkagan, that would welcome teaching.

With thirteen listeners asking for more teaching

as well as for baptism, the Eastern believers began to plan immediately for a second visit. But field work was demanding, food was scarce, the typhoon season was unrelenting and Baltugangan and Suklinyan, as well as six other men and their families, would be leaving for another three-month term at MBS.

Although the next trip would have to wait until after the harvest, they decided to send four men: two for Pusug and two for Pangalkagan where, they prayed, the people would be willing to listen.

Back in Pinamalayan, our loneliness for our three absent children was well expressed by Randy when he suggested, "Let's make our house into a mission home, Daddy, so lots of people can come stay with us!"

The weekly letters from Rick and Becky, however, made us feel close to them. Rick gave us a delightful day-by-day report of the week that summer when all the missionary kids traveled across the States from Wheaton to the new OMF teenagers' home on the eight-acre "Ranch" in Pleasant Hill, Oregon, and mentioned his plan to enter Willamette University in the fall. But I wept as I thought of his High School graduation that we had not been able to attend.

We were excited when Becky told of the six-week Spanish Club trip she would be taking to South America, made possible by Grandpa Reed. But again I wept that I could not be there to help her get ready or welcome her home. Satan's fiery darts of doubt came thick and fast, for we desperately wanted to be part of their lives during such important years.

These unsettling thoughts were hard on my supply of correction fluid as I typed the stencils for

the first chapters of Genesis in Tawbuid. Randy on
the floor beside me, busily pressing the tiny circles on
his ingenious cardboard box typewriter, suddenly
remarked, "Oh! I typed that wrong! Quick, where's
my mistake glue?"

I laughed, and relaxed. "Thank you Lord, for our
precious children. But as we work for You, we so long
for them. Draw them close to yourself. Help them in
the difficult places. Give them many people to love
them."

Between the lashings of seven successive storms
during that typhoon season, we saw the believers in
the hills plod through the mud planting corn, weeding
rice, clearing sweet potato fields. And yet they took
time each month to study at our ten-day STBS's and
to continue their witness to nearby areas. At MBS
mid-term the wives came home to help with the
harvest, which was finished by the time the men
returned.

As soon as they arrived Suklinyan approached
Russell. "Would it be good," he began, "to have
chapters two and three of Daniel translated into
Tawbuid?"

"Is that what you'd like me to do?" Russell asked.

"Yes," he answered. "Then we could teach what
we studied at the Bible School."

The Gospel of John was completed and in the
believers' hands. Genesis was being distributed chapter by chapter, while Luke had just been started. Now
Daniel would be added to the list.

The MBS men, many of them church leaders,
shared their new knowledge in the daily services and
at the outreaches, still doing all their own field work

when home. According to Tawbuid custom leaders are not paid, and church leaders came under this same tradition.

In mid November, five months after the first teaching visit, two church leaders and two other believers set off with Russell for the west. Baltugangan and Nuganbagu would teach the thirteen listeners at Pusug. Suklinyan and Kulas would go to Pangalkgan, praying for a good reception. Both of the newly-chosen companions were men of sturdy faith, but not students. Their training would come through practical experience rather than through MBS.

As Ann, Randy and I waited in Safa for their return, I helped the remaining MBS men improve their reading and writing skills, especially in Tagalog. Ann instructed the elementary school teachers who by this time were ready for the second term of second grade. She had chosen Safa with its large adequate school as the best place for the two-week class, since four of the seven teachers were from the Tawbuid tribe. Four teachers were needed this year because Dalandan and Fandung villages each had their own schools, and in Safa there were two classes, readers and non-readers. Gifted Uan would teach the latter group, for all of the pupils in his last year's school read well. The other three teachers in Ann's class were from the Buhid and Tadyawan tribes.

When the five men returned from their two-week Western visit, they reported a warm reception in Pusug. After the Sunday services, Baltugangan, Nuganbagu and Russell had battled their way to Pangalkagan through six miles of deep mud. At first their reception had been cool, and village leader Baraku seemed frightened, but as the teaching progressed he became more friendly. Attendance had been good, and the listeners had asked thoughtful questions about the spirits, shaman, and marital problems. At the end of the week, the teachers were asked, "When can you return and teach again?" Encouraged, the men felt that some in Pangalkagan might already be believing.

Just after Christmas that year the Dalandan elders faced their first major church problem. A very young married woman with an elderly, ailing husband who had given her no children, had become pregnant by her husband's teenaged son. They had repented and been disciplined, and now her elderly husband came to our house.

"What do we do about the one that will be born?" he asked.

"Do about it?" I didn't understand.

"Yes," he explained, "Should we nurse it and care for it?"

Immediately I thought of Baltugangan and his premature baby that would have been rejected. Here was another instance of tribal custom dictating the death of the innocent newborn.

"Oh, yes!" I told him. "God wants you to care for the baby, and to love and nurse it like it was your own!"

Satisfied, he left, ready to obey this strange new order of things in which loving care was the key word.

While the men were at MBS for another term, enthusiasm was increasing for a third teaching visit to help construct the church at Pusug and to reap the imminent spiritual harvest in Pangalkagan. During the dry season three months later, the two who were "helpers" on the last trip took two other believers and made the trip again, accompanied by Russell, though he felt by this time he was not really needed.

Amazed to find the Pusug church already built, Nuganbagu, Dagadafug, and Russell decided to go immediately to Pangalkagan, while Kulas and quiet Yudgulian, who would later prove his gift as a soul winner, would teach the baptism lessons at Pusug. With light feet and in good humor they eagerly hiked the four-hour trail, anticipating a rewarding week. But they found the village completely deserted.

Finally locating one of the families, they learned the tragic news. Right after the men's last teaching visit in November, all 29 of that small village's inhabitants had become ill, and within two weeks seven had died! The symptoms were swollen neck, fever, and chest pain. Those who died were spitting blood, and those who survived had a persistent cough for months.

It reminded Russell of our experience more than ten years before when five in that same village had suddenly died after being forced to take part in a spirit feast prepared by an evil shaman from the interior. Satan had gained another victory, because the remaining families were now afraid to listen to God's words. It brought a curse. But at Pusug, fourteen listeners made a public declaration of their faith by being baptized.

Returning back across the mountains, Pusug village leader Tumas and another young believer accompanied the teachers to attend the 1972 Mang-yan Believers Conference at MBS.

Afterwards Butuan and Baltugangan returned to

Pusug with the two men to help with the first steps of organizing their church: choosing church deacons and observing the Lord's Supper. They went without Russell, proving their ability to find their way (after one false start), and to teach on their own.

The Eastern believers were unwilling to abandon unresponsive Pangalkagan, so the trip two months later included plans to teach that village as well as Pusug. After Butuan, Baltugangan, and Faguguanun had gone, Russell and I hiked to Dalandan. Just the two of us. For Randy had joined Robby at Chefoo school in Baguio City. I was glad to leave our Pinamalayan house, now as quiet as a mortuary, and take my aching heart to the hills where we always found comfort and understanding.

We stopped first in Safa to enjoy the weekend under our new galvanized roof. When two other families in the village installed metal roofs on their houses, we decided it was time to replace our bark roof, bringing to an end our chewing-gum-mending program for plugging up the recurring beetle holes.

In Dalandan we held another STBS, with a survey of five minor prophets, a study of the newly-translated book of Jonah, a class in message preparation using Genesis, and an attempt at music instruction, which was great fun.

Music is not a cultivated art of the Tawbuid, at least not as we understand music! Their native "songs" are more like chants, with rhyme and rhythm, but very little tune. Since we were unsure about putting Christian words to them, we merely translated our hymns and then tackled the impossible task of teaching our Western tunes. The children, helped by their school classes, learned quickly but the adults had a difficult, though thoroughly enjoyable, time trying! One advantage of knowing Western tunes was their usefulness at the annual Mangyan Believers Conferences.

In the other classes everyone in the village sat on the bamboo floor of the church with their books spread around them, eagerly looking up the passages being studied, responding to the questions, and some even taking notes!

Just as the last Sunday evening service was closing, Baltugangan arrived from the West. The church became unusually quiet as he told of hiking to Pangalkagan only to find that the entire group was moving to the interior because their land was being taken over by the Prison Colony.

In Pusug good attendance and intense interest in God's Words had continued throughout the week of study. Baltugangan asked prayer for a new couple who was now listening, and for two other families living near the church who were not yet interested.

"One old man we met told us, 'No, I don't want to listen. And don't pray for me either!' But we prayed anyway," Baltugangan told the congregation.

Back in Safa we learned that the believers on their own initiative had decided to put a galvanized roof on their church, not just so they wouldn't get wet from the typically leaky bark or grass roofs, but so their precious books of God's Words would be protected. The cost would be heavy, but would be worth it, for they met there every morning and evening. The elders, deciding that the money should not come from the church offerings, estimated that twenty pesos per family should cover the expense.

As they were telling us that they had already

collected over 430 pesos, Bulus, father of five who was just recovering from spinal tuberculosis, painfully made his way over to join the group. Smiling shyly, he apologetically told us that he had given only fifteen pesos.

Immediately one of the elders explained, "Yes, we decided it would be only fifteen pesos for those who couldn't walk."

I thought, *How characteristically thoughtful of the elders, and they stated it so gently!* For Bulus was the only one in that category! Although his muscles were now supporting him for short distances, he couldn't go into the forest and haul out rattan, the source of most of their cash.

Believers from Dalandan and Fandung were also helping with the roof expense, in typical Tawbuid togetherness. But even after all the money was in hand, those 3 x 12 foot sheets of roofing must be bought in Pinamalayan, loaded onto a jeepney, and taken to the end of the road. From there the men must carry these heavy sheets for two hours up the Safa River trail to the village.

In the lowlands our house again rang with the boys' shouts and laughter, so that it was sometimes delightfully difficult to concentrate on the stencils of Daniel I was typing, or on the translation of Luke and revision of Mark that occupied Russell. As I worked, I thought with thankfulness how the Lord had specially cared for our Mission children during the past month of flooding and landslides in Baguio City. Some houses were crushed, one very close to the school. Their trip down to the lowlands had also been without incident, even though parts of the road and some bridges had been destroyed.

With the boys at home we missed Rick and Becky more than ever. We wrote them that Robby didn't like his "baby name," opting for Bob, and that Randy wanted to be called by his middle name, George, "just like Grandpa Flory."

Rick was now in the United States Navy's Basic Electricity and Electronics School near Francisco. Becky in her last year of high school was inquiring into colleges for next year. In a recent heart-warming letter she had said that our family was closer, for all the miles that separated us, than the families of many of her girl friends who lived at home and were pouring out their problems to her.

Two developments at this time would have frightened men of weaker faith from making another teaching trip to the West. Powerful interior leaders were angry at several believers who knew their interior trails, probably fearing their power would be diminished when the gospel reached their area. Then martial law was declared by the President due to increased communist activity. But still they planned a sixth teaching trip after Thanksgiving.

Before they left, quiet Yudgulian brought his frightened brother, a shaman, to Safa. Because he had been listening to the New Teaching, his life had been threatened by his villagers who did not want to lose their means of controlling the spirit world. With him came his two wives and their children as well as another family. These five adults with their seven children enthusiastically began studying God's Word and learning to read.

Kulas, going to the West for the third time, took

Mansangi and Turungana for their first visit. Russell gave them letters of authorization stating the purpose of their trip, "to teach others of their own tribal group," should they be stopped by the authorities while travelling through the lowlands.

Two weeks later, on a wet and windy evening, the three weary, famished travelers arrived at our door in Pinamalayan. As I began supper, I caught snatches of their conversation.

They had only been two nights on the trail going over to Pusug, but their return was a different and terrifying story, for they hadn't known that typhoon Undong was about to hit the island. On the first day after leaving Pusug, they reached the lowlands and hiked along the mud-choked road to the Lumintao River. Heavy rain made it impossible to kindle a fire, so they huddled together in the cold, wet darkness, trying to sleep without supper. At dawn the rain lightened, so they cooked their kettle full of rice twice, eating it all!

Constant rain and strong winds, combined with the deep mud and flooded rivers, meant extremely slow travel. After three days of slogging, they arrived at the flooded Hayakyan River to find they were unable to cross it. Laboriously picking their way up cliffs, over boulders and through thick shoulder-high grass, they climbed to the mountain pass, taking two days instead of the normal six hours. Then they descended quickly following the smaller Eastern rivers to the main road where they took a bus, arriving at our house just before dark.

As we all gathered around the table where they hesitantly applied the still unfamiliar spoons and forks to their plates of steaming rice and bowls of fish and vegetables, the rigors of the trail were forgotten and they shared with us the joy of teaching others. Since none of these three men were students, but simply lovers of God's Word, they had based their teaching on Baltugangan's and Suklinyan's initial series of lessons, used on that first teaching visit one-and-a-half years before. Two of the Pusug men, they told us, could now read well, so those two had helped the others who were struggling with the new words in the third primer. But when the hymn books were used, every one seemed to be able to read!

"Oh, by the way, Kaliung has died," Kulas told us.

"Kaliung?" I asked, searching my memory.

"Yes, the older of Tumas' two wives. Now he is like all the others with just one wife," he explained.

Although tribal custom dictates one wife, leaders and shaman have enough power to flout the custom and take two, allowed by the government in minority groups. One we heard of even had five! The believers knew that God's Word commanded singular marriages. But to abandon a second wife and her children did not seem right, so Yudgulian's brother and his two wives were welcomed into the Safa church, just as Tumas and his two wives had been a part of the Pusug church.

"Several folks who used to live at Pangalkagan passed through Pusug while we were there," Kulas added. "They have all moved farther inland to Diulang since losing their land."

"It would be good if we could send teachers to Diulang," said Mansangi wistfully, "for there are nine who want to be taught. But Baraku, their leader, is unwilling."

One more teaching visit was made by four

Eastern believers, three of them MBS men, before my most exciting experience of our soon-ending term, our back-packing trip across the island.

From the East coast Russell and I hiked up the gravel bed of the Bongabon River to the Siyangi River, which took us to the Alianan River. At its headwaters we emerged onto grass-covered mountain slopes, glad for the light cloud cover over a scorching sun. Reaching the 3,500 foot summit, we carefully picked our way for over an hour down the steep shale slopes of the Western side, coming to the Hayakyan River where we camped for our second night. Weaving back and forth across the Hayakyan, we finally reached the fair-weather road where we found a truck going north to Ligaya.

After two delightful days with our friends, the Santos family, we took the trail to Pusug. Halfway up that last long hill we met Yautin.

The first time Russell had met Yautin, he had two Tawbuid "six-shooters" on his hips, that is, two gourds for cursing enemies. We had been living in Ligaya then, trying to reach the Pangalkagan Tawbuid where he was visiting his uncle. Now as he came down the hill from Pusug, surprised to see us and offering to carry my pack, Russell reminded him of that first meeting when he was carrying the two *liwas*.

"Oh, I don't do that any more!" he said emphatically. We learned he was now a new believer in Christ! That very Sunday he was married, and on the next Eastern believers' teaching visit he and his wife were baptized.

In the new Pusug chapel, complete with pulpit and blackboard, we watched the believers read the

Word of God, having been taught only by the Eastern men. Their well-conducted daily services with a definite Eastern imprint were attended by thirty eager believers, 25 already baptized. Amazingly, another ten, five of whom were also baptized, were meeting four hours away in Balani village, and even twenty more wanted to listen in Alifut, but their leader opposed!

Five from Pusug, who been saving their money, returned East with us to attend the 1973 Mangyan Believers Conference with the two hundred others who gathered at MBS. Then after a visit to Safa, they were accompanied home by Eastern believers who again taught them for a week.

During our furlough God worked even more amazingly. On a cassette that Ann helped them record, the Eastern church leaders told us there were a hundred more listeners and that they had baptized forty new believers! To us it seemed impossible! But God was honoring their faithful teaching visits and answering the prayers of those at home.

We were thanking the Lord, too, for the ways He was leading our children. Becky had not only done exceptionally well in her first year at the University of Oregon, but was also engaged to King Wilson, as gentle and thoughtful as he was tall, at six foot four inches! And we would be attending Rick and Vicky's wedding just a few days before we returned with Bob and George to the Philippines in May 1974.

Then one night as I was tucking the boys into bed, Bob began to weep quietly. As I gently put my arm around him he whispered, "Oh, Mama, I don't want to go back to the Philippines. I like it here in America.

There isn't any library like we have at Trent School, and there aren't as many kids to play with. I like it here better."

"I know, Bob," I said, choking back tears. "Things are nice in America. But you know why we're going back, don't you."

"To teach the tribal people," he answered quietly.

"And you know what we want to do? We want to put as much of God's Word as possible into their own language. So the church leaders have lots to teach the people. Why, we're almost ready to mimeograph *Luke* for them now!"

"Oh, Mom," he said catching my enthusiasm. "Then pretty soon you can just put all the books together and have a nice cover that says HOLY BIBLE in the Tawbuid language."

"That's right! And I know if you're willing to go back to the Philippines so we can do the work the Lord has asked us to do, then when you get to heaven the Lord will give you a star in your crown, and He will thank you for being happy to go back. And besides, the Lord will give us nice surprises and special treats along the way. He always does. Look at our nice house in Pinamalayan, and the beautiful school you have in Baguio. He'll make us happy and see that we have lots of fun, if we do what He wants us to do."

The tears were all dry now, and after our prayer-time both Bob and George snuggled down, going right off to sleep. An answer to prayer for our sensitive nine year old.

Just four days after our flight to Manila, the boys climbed into the school's new deep red mini-bus, finding seats by their special friends. Laughing and talking, they weren't even thinking about the five-hour trip from Manila to the school and the separation involved. As the bus pulled out of the driveway, they hastily shouted their happy goodbyes, while we thanked God through our tears. Immediately I went out and bought a pair of red and white polka-dot thongs, which cheered me through their whole next school term!

On our first trip to Safa we were thrilled to see adult classes had been added to the regular Sunday Services. Their daily morning and evening devotions were well planned ahead with a reading schedule and questions written and typed by gifted Uan, a skill Ann had taught him. Their ability to run their own churches as well as doing much of the teaching meant we were free to spend more time on Bible translation.

Especially now they needed God's Word for strength and encourgement. A wicked outsider was still trying to take some of their land, demanding seed rice and hospitality, and even molesting several terrified women, in spite of our legal efforts to deter him.

Added to this, while we were in Safa, leading church elder Faguguanan's brand new house had burned to the ground just before he was to give his Sunday morning message. After the fire he spoke movingly on First John 2:15, "Love not the world, neither the things that are in the world. If any man love the world, the love of the Father is not in him."

The believers' eyes were fixed on the Lord and their commitment was still to the Western Tawbuid. They were already saving and planning for the next teaching trip in two months' time, when six men would go.

During these trying days, all four of our children brightened our days with their welcome letters. Becky's were full of their wedding plans for the fall. Tears came as I realized I would not be with her. But everyone at the Pleasant Hill church, as well as many Mission friends and all King's family would be making up the "hundred-fold" the Bible promised for those who give up "mother and father and brothers" like Becky had, for the sake of the gospel. Even though it was still months away, I wondered how I would get through September seventh, their wedding day.

In the meantime the six Eastern believers, after two weeks simultaneously teaching at Pusug and newly-responding Balani Village, stopped for the night at Pinamalayan before returning home.

While the air was filled with the fragrance of newly-harvested rice cooking, they folded the large plastics used for rain coverings and gathered up the thongs, necessary on the scorching hot dirt roads in the West. Shoving them into a cupboard to await the next teaching trip, Baltugangan turned to us with his ready grin, "Did you know that in the Balani church 31 are already baptized? And many others are listening?"

As he talked, Suklinyan began to dig into his flour sack "suitcase" and finally produced a tiny dog-eared notebook. Russell looked over his shoulder at the neatly-written list of names while Suklinyan explained, "At Pusug too, there are, let's see, 32 who are baptized now, and in both places I have orders for books."

Turning the pages and pointing at the various lists of names he continued, "These want Gospels of

Mark. These have ordered hymn books. And this list is for the Thick Book of Scripture verses. Besides that, everyone wants one of the heavy plastic book bags so their papers won't get wet or dirty. And some have already given me the money for their orders!"

Immediately I began to muse, *Amazing! They want to learn to read so they can study God's words even if what they read is in the difficult and sometimes confusing Eastern dialect. Oh, Lord,* I sighed, *do send us co-workers to translate the Bible in Western Tawbuid!*

September seventh 1974 came, and we were able to rejoice in Pinamalayan as Becky and King were rejoicing at their beautiful garden wedding halfway around the globe. Just at that time, Bob and George had school vacation. Bob baked the cake, and our friends came to share it with ice cream, coffee and juice, joining us in prayer for the newlyweds and in happy, laughing fellowship around the table. A cable from Salem, Oregon brought love and prayers for *us* on their special day, making our celebration complete.

When Bob and George returned to school, our loneliness was eased by another trip to the west, this time by bus and boat. We returned home to make a hundred reprints of the Tawbuid hymn book, for every new listener wanted to buy one. We learned their importance from an overheard conversation.

"Is he believing now?" one friend inquired.

"Well," the other replied, "He is singing God's chants." This seemed to imply one more step beyond "listening."

Russell accompanied four men later that month, delighting the Western believers with their first frizbee. "It doesn't keep rolling down the hill like a ball does!" they said with admiration. While he was gone, I attended the Thanksgiving feast at Dalandan and was able to finish checking two new hymns, "Fairest Lord Jesus" and "Great is Thy Faithfulness" as well as three more verses for "Trust and Obey."

Even though the men returned through Typhoon Yaning, their rejoicing knew no limits. Three villages had been taught simultaneously, Pusug, Balani and now Maltungtung! Twenty-eight listeners had made public declaration of their faith by baptism, and at Balani a chapel was being built and church officers had been elected!

Surrounded by rejoicing, Russell and I sat down for a serious discussion. How were these babes in Christ to be fed and cared for? Occasional teaching trips, exhausting the believers and their funds, were not enough now. Finally we came up with three ideas, but each presented a major problem.

Idea One. We could teach in the West for six months or a year as we had in the Eastern beginnings. But what about our translation work?

Idea Two. One leader from each of the three Western churches could attend the Beginners Course at MBS in the spring, returning to teach their people. But that would be too long to wait, and who would teach reading and writing?

Idea Three. Another missionary couple could become our co-workers, taking over the Western work. But even though a new couple were appointed, nearly two years of Tagalog study were needed before beginning tribal work, and then the tribal language would have to be learned.

There seemed to be no solution. But we forgot to reckon with Tawbuid ingenuity.

The morning church service at Safa had just ended. Kulus had quietly crept across the bamboo floor until he was sitting beside Durfu. A few days before, the elders of the three Eastern churches had discussed the care of the new Western believers, and had conceived the idea of sending a family to the West to live and make their fields for a year while teaching the new believers. And Durfu had volunteered to go.

Kulas began in his gentle voice, "*Sama*, is it good for you to take your wife to the West? Would it be good for another family to go instead? You have no relatives over there to help if there is trouble when you deliver the baby. Who will be your wife's companion when you go to the fields? How will she become strong again, for food is not as plentiful over there?"

Durfu turned his wide innocent eyes on the speaker, and with his shy smile, earnestly replied, "*Sama, lag katanya*. Don't say that, my friend. My wife is quite willing to go and it pleases *Funbalugu* for us to obey Him. He will take care of us."

I was thrilled! Ever since teaching the life of *Udsun Taylur* we had prayed that the Tawbuid would become missionaries. But we probably would not have chosen Durfu to be the first!

Only his congenial personality and disarming grin made it easy to excuse his late rising, his nodding sleepy head in church or his absence when work needed to be done. Laziness is not characteristic of the Tawbuid. But he had volunteered and had been warmly accepted. After all, he was one of the three graduates from the three-year MBS course, had been elected an elder of the Safa church, and would have the prayer help of all the believers.

While the churches began saving money for the transportation, and the believers set aside rice for their trip, the elders struggled with the question, "Should Durfu go to the older believers at Pusug, or to the very young babes in Christ at Balani and nearby Maltungtung?"

Durfu faced an even more basic issue: counting the cost. He was taking his wife, Martina, and their youngest child, trusting God not only for them, but also for their older children left behind with relatives to continue their schooling in Safa. Although Tawbuid children sometimes live with relatives as a helper or babysitter, no child had ever been left while the parents were gone so far for so long. We felt their heartache, for we not only missed our children but also realized the sacrifice the children made.

Even traveling had a cost. The terror of riding the big crowded wooden buses would be fresh in their minds from their trips to the Bible School. I had seen them tightly gripping the seat in front while the bus raced over unpaved pot-holed roads and around precarious curves. The rigors of jungle hiking with swollen rivers, knee-deep mud and unstaunchable bleeding leech bites also faced them, with the lowland counterpart of feet-blistering paths under a merciless sun.

As preparations went ahead for their January departure, three church leaders decided to go at once to the West to help the newest believers observe Christmas. They would miss their own Eastern celebration in Safa where a large temporary porch of bamboo poles had already been built along one side of the big church. For the special services the woven bamboo church wall would be untied and removed so those on the porch could fully participate.

Perhaps it was the thrill of eight more baptisms at the Christmas feast, or the marriages of three young couples who would now establish Christian homes. Whatever the reason, God led Falakan from Dalandan to solve the dilemma of which Western village should have the missionary, and to set Kulas' heart at rest concerning Durfu's loneliness.

"Would it be good if my family and I would go with Durfu's family to the West for the year?" Falakan asked the church elders. They agreed. God honored his faith, for when the rice offering was collected and the money counted, there was ample for both families.

Just before the missionaries were to leave in early January 1975, the three elders returned from the West. And with them were eleven Western believers who had come to escort Durfu and his family back across the mountains!

"It is good we are so many," they told their brethren at Safa, "for the Hayakyan River is waist deep now and very swift."

"But it is going down," another added optimistically.

"Would it be good," an Eastern elder asked, "if two of our families went instead of just one?"

With wide grins of acceptance they replied, "*Sabu, Sama!* Oh, yes, friends! That would be good!"

"*Sabu, Sama!*" injected another. "Then one family could live in Pusug and the other in Balani where those from Maltungtung also come for teaching."

Thirty brown calloused feet, with many weary, painful days ahead of them, splashed through that first river crossing on the trail from Safa village to the bus road in the lowlands. Just a few days earlier, seven key men and their families had returned to their studies at the Bible School. Daily the Eastern churches would pray for them and for the two missionary families serving in the West.

At the end of the first month, Russell visited the missionaries. In Pusug Falakan was teaching faithfully and even reported that one believer hoped to attend MBS in May! At Balani a very homesick Durfu had approached Russell hopefully, "Would it be good," he had asked, "if some other family would come and take our place?"

"Oh! that would be something the church elders would have to decide," Russell had told him sympathetically. He wanted Durfu to stay, not to please us but because God was leading him.

Durfu brightened considerably, however, when he took Russell to neighboring Maltungtung village. Russell remembered that during our trip three months before we had met a few Maltungtung "listeners" at Balani. But on this visit he worshipped in Maltungtung with 24 baptized believers who met every morning and evening in their own grass-roofed bamboo church, still green in its newness. Most had never before even held paper in their hands, but now all were eager to be able to read so they could learn *Funbalugu*'s songs and study His Words.

Two months later in mid-April, one of the hottest days of the year, five Western men suddenly appeared in Safa. Questioning eyes peered out of every house. Was it good news or bad? Were the missionary families well? The reason for the visit spread like wildfire from house to house.

"The men are here on their way to Bible School!"

"All five of them?"

"No, just three. The other two came along as companions."

The biggest news was announced in the service that evening, "Twenty-three more listeners from the three Western churches were baptized at the combined Easter Service!"

What a joy, I thought, *to visualize them singing, 'I have decided to follow Jesus, no turning back, no turning back.'*

"They are asking for more Tawbuid books and also for medicines," Linayu from Balani added, handing Russell a well-worn note. Prompted by that list Russell made his first delivery trip, taking simple medicines as well as the requested Scriptures. The easily-understood doctrine booklet, "One Hundred Questions Answered from the Bible," was in great demand, for both Falakan and Durfu were teaching from it.

On their return Russell reported to the Eastern churches, "You know how Durfu has been on the verge of returning home several times? Well, when I arrived for this visit he told me that he and Falakan had wanted to go home before the end of October for Thanksgiving. But he had heard that the rivers would still be very flooded.

"Then he said to me, 'I think it is really best if we wait and go home at Christmas. But you know how Falakan is. He gets so lonely!'" Everyone chuckled along with Russell.

On succeeding visits Russell returned with news of Baby Rakel's safe arrival, of the return of the students from the Bible School and of interest in another village, Buswangan. But their unsympathetic leader, Sintus, would not allow a church to be built in their village. Not only did the Eastern believers pray, but also in August four of the church leaders visited to encourage Durfu and Falakan.

The believers had also decided to visit powerful Eastern interior leader Sumsumagan, but their three attempts so far had failed. Hearing that his health was deteriorating, they were concerned for his soul and for those under him. If he would put his faith in Christ, his whole interior area would be open to the New Teaching.

During this year of Eastern missionary activity both in the East and the West, we were merely spectators of the miracle God was performing. For the first six months I was kept out of the hills by major surgery (though it gave me many precious days in cool Baguio near Bob and George). My long convalescence made us realize the wisdom of God in the Tawbuid plan to send Eastern families as missionaries to the West, for if we had tried to take that responsibility, we would not have been able to carry it out.

Russell worked long hours to finish First Corinthians, while I typed the stencils for the 24 chapters of Luke. Then in October, when the Tawbuid were celebrating their Thanksgiving, we attended a workshop for Bible translation consultants. Although Russell's translating combined with my consultant checking now took even longer hours, it produced more accurate, more readable Tawbuid Scriptures. And in our absence the Eastern believers continued to develop their spiritual gifts as they faithfully shouldered the entire burden of caring for the churches, both East and West.

Near the beginning of December Durfu and Falakan and their families returned home. I was amazed at my first sight of their "Faith Baby," Rakel. The fattest, healthiest Tawbuid baby I had ever seen! And their progress report of what the Lord had done was even more amazing. At the Western Thanksgiving Feast 22 more believers had been baptized, over half from newly-reached Buswangan village. And Sintus, the leader who had prohibited the building of a church, was one of them!

"If we had come home before Thanksgiving," confessed Durfu with his delightful grin, "we would not have seen this answer to your prayers. And besides that," he added, "we've brought good news. The houses are already finished for the three families who will be taking our place in Pusug, in Balani and in Maltungtung."

The three young families had already been chosen. Two of the men were Safa church leaders and MBS graduates — Suklinyan, whose child had died when he was at MBS, and Faguguanun, whose house had burned down just before he was to preach at the Sunday service. The third was Baltugangan, the

Dalandan elder who had almost finished his MBS studies, and who had also been matured by sorrow when his child died. Suklinyan and Baltugangan were the ones who had gone on that very first teaching visit to the West more than four years before.

"Would it be good," asked one thoughtful believer, "to send a fourth family, so someone could go to Buswangan?"

"And who would the fourth one be?" asked the ever-practical Kulas.

I was disturbed when later they chose Kulas, planning to send him to Balani, the largest of the four Western churches! He had spent hours, months, even years trying to master reading, but it just had not clicked. And the only time he had been to Bible school was to to help construct the buildings for the very first session at Ayan Bekeg. In front of the congregation he dripped with perspiration when trying to lead the meeting or speak. Only his dogged determination accompanied by his friendly smile and quiet chuckle carried him through the many embarrassing moments. And although he had gone several times to the West, he always had a companion to help with the teaching.

"Surely this is a mistake," I confided to Russell when I learned of the elders' choice. "Even sending him at all. But to the largest church?" Always hasty to react, I urged Russell to step in. But not Russell. He didn't do things that way. He was even careful never to ask "Why?" realizing that doubt would be thrown on their prayerfully-considered decisions.

Then I stopped to fully consider Kulas' qualifications. He was always there when anyone needed a helping hand, and his sturdy faith did not waver in any storm. Although he was not proficient in reading and writing, he loved the Lord and desired to serve Him. Hadn't he been the first to take the old box phonograph to Safa village and initiate their interest in listening to *Funbalugu*'s words? Wasn't he present every day when those words were read and studied in the morning and evening services? Hadn't he, along with the other believers, "stored up in his ear" the more-than-one-hundred Bible verses in the Thick Book and each one of the thirty songs in the hymn book? My initial objection began to soften, and finally to melt away in the warmth of my true regard for this humble man.

Just before Christmas the four families left their homes, their friends, their customary way of life, and some of their children, as Durfu and Falakan had done.

Baltugangan and his wife took their two youngest children, as well as their middle one for a babysitter, leaving the two older school children with relatives. They would go to Pusug where Falakan, also from Dalandan, had served.

Kulas surprised us when he decided to take his twelve-year-old son, Yumunsan, along with his youngest child. Yumunsan didn't need to stay in Safa for school, for he had completed the four-year course as a star pupil, but usually the babysitter is one of the younger children who can't work in the fields. Months later we would learn Kulas' reason.

Although leaving wasn't easy for any of the families, Faguguanun's was the most heart-rending. When they said goodbye to their three-year-old daughter, she was lying pale and feverish on her bark mat in her grandparents' house, too ill to run and splash with the others in the farewells at the first river crossing.

With the recent death of another small girl still fresh in everyone's mind, we all wondered, "Does their child have the same illness? Will God heal her, or take her to Heaven while they are gone?" Faguguanun and his wife did not know, but they bravely started their trip trusting God in their anguish. I was ashamed, thinking how often I had pitied myself after a separation from our strong and healthy children.

Another testing waited for this couple in the West, for they knew that no church nor home would be ready for them when they arrived in newly-reached Buswangan village.

Suklinyan from Safa would go to Maltungtung with its growing number of baptized believers, who also needed more help in reading and writing.

One sticky hot afternoon two months later our door bell in Pinamalayan began to ring persistently.

"What a bother," I thought with a tired sigh. We were busy unpacking after ten days of Scripture checking in Safa village, where we had delighted in seeing Faguguanun's little daughter energetically playing with the other children.

Opening the door, I was startled to see a thin, shaky Suklinyan, eyes filled with confusion and fear, accompanied by two exhausted Western Tawbuid believers.

"*Sakboi, Sama!*" I managed to say. "Come in, friends, come in!" As they climbed the stairs and stretched out on our sala floor, I gave them time to collect their thoughts while I went to the kitchen to get glasses of water.

"Whatever could be wrong with Suklinyan? What could have happened?" I whispered to Russsell as he headed for the *sala*. Only the month before we had been rejoicing over the good report Russell and eleven-year-old Bob had brought back from the West. In Balani they had seen Kulas' unique father-and-son team. His son was the literacy teacher, able to read the Bible and write on the blackboard proficiently, Kulas taught the Bible lessons. His sometimes halting presentations were not threatening or intimidating to those young Balani believers, so that all of them, including the two MBS students, had found courage to exercise their own gifts in that large church.

In Pusug, Baltugangan had been faithfully teaching, while in Buswangan the church and a house for Faguguanun were near completion and six new believers had been baptized at the Christmas feast. The leader of a neighbouring village said he would only listen if the Buswangan believers helped him pay his huge debt to an outsider. But their meager cash was already buying Scriptures, study books and a church blackboard, chalk and eraser, which Russell and Bob had delivered at their request.

Suklinyan, teaching a responsive group of very young believers at Maltungtung, was living in the nicest of all the missionary houses with a fence around his neat yard to keep the pigs and dogs away as his little girl played outside. But it could not ward off the attack which had reduced Suklinyan to the confused, pathetic young man who was now lying exhausted with his two friends on our *sala* floor.

After a hearty supper, Suklinyan's companions

began a disconnected account of his ordeal. Gradually we pieced the story together.

Two weeks before, he and two believers had attempted to visit Quezon, the powerful interior leader of Western Tawbuid and Alangan. Returning home discouraged after a difficult and fruitless trip, he became seriously ill with fever, vomiting and weakness, followed by amnesia, symptoms most commonly associated with potent spirit curses.

After the believers prayed, the fever and vomiting subsided, but the frightening amnesia remained. As new believers, they did not know what to do. In their old life they would have sacrificed and chanted to the spirits and returned the curses to the senders. Praying to God for guidance, they decided they should bring Suklinyan to the East. This difficult and expensive trip was to solicit the prayer help of his home church and perhaps visit the Christian doctor near Pinamalayan. His brave wife, with a faith as sturdy as her health, remained in Maltungtung with their little girl, confidently awaiting his return.

Arriving at Safa the next day, Suklinyan was warmly welcomed and lovingly cared for. As the believers prayed for his recovery, they also prayed for another pressing problem. "Lord, if it pleases you, turn away the land grabbers and help us to keep our land. But if not, just do your will."

Within a month a restored but weak Suklinyan returned to his waiting loved ones in Maltungtung. Later when we as a family visited the West during the boys' school vacation, taking along a box of the new enlarged hand-sewn edition of the Thick Book, we found him in excellent health. And he was cheered by our news that the Safa land decision had been handed down in favor of the Tawbuid.

Several weeks later, we sadly had to move from our Pinamalayan home of twelve happy years. Our new house, however, proved more suitable, newer, cleaner and was owned by a Christian. The crowning joy was renting for my sister Ann the cute little bungalow behind our new home, whose front lawn merged into our back lawn. She was just returning from three years at home and wanted to be more centrally located for overseeing the Mangyan Christian Elementary Schools (MCES) in Eastern Mindoro and beginning these schools in the West.

Months before, when the four missionary families had come back from the West with glowing reports of the four growing churches, they brought an unexpected request. The Western believers asked that children's school teachers be sent the following year instead of more church workers, for the churches were now able to function on their own.

Uan had decided to make a survey, and afterwards wrote to Ann, who was then still in the States, pleading with her to return. More than seventy children and young people of the believers in the West wanted to attend the schools, and she was needed to prepare the materials.

In March 1977, one month after Ann arrived, our tiny downstairs *sala* was crowded with the Tawbuid families who were going to the West to open the four schools. They came with their babies and baskets, their Tawbuid Scriptures and hymn books, their rice kettles and food for the trip, and some with a newly-purchased shirt or shift or rubber thongs. But most of all they came with faith in the Lord, for they had been told that food was scarce in the West.

After a good meal, the usual Tawbuid evening devotions, and some time to chat and get things organized, they all went upstairs to our larger wooden-floor *sala* to sleep for the night.

Nagiubay, who would teach in Pusug, chose the place under the library table, close to one of the smoking mosquito coils. This winsome eighteen-year-old, next to youngest son of Tree-Branch, the old Dalandan village leader, had finished the four years of school and then helped teach in the second four-year cycle.

Linagum, son of the village leader at Safa, and his wife Likwai settled on the mat by the big front window, with two-year-old Linda close to them and Dariyai, Likwai's fourteen-year-old sister, nearby. Dariyai, saved as a newborn infant by nurse Dode's care of the open sore on her back, would help when the new baby arrived. Linagum had finished the four years of school in Safa, though he had never taught. So he would have the school in Maltungtung, because it was closest to Balani where Gunye, the head teacher, would be.

On the opposite side of the room, Sikamawayan, Bumblebee's son and Fandung's capable teacher, and his wife Bayanyus settled down with two-month-old Ansun snuggled against his mother and seven-year-old Maria beside her. Two others were left with Grandma and Grandpa Bumblebee in Safa village. With Maria as babysitter, Bayanyus would be able to help her husband at the Buswangan school in the mornings and work in the sweet potato fields with the other women in the afternoon.

Gunye and his wife did not come with this group, for he was still at Bible School. In just a few weeks he and Baltugangan would finish, bringing to seven the number of Eastern Tawbuid graduates. Then he and Uan, the MCES Supervisor, would go to the West with Ann where Uan would be responsible for instructing the teachers.

In order to finish all the materials needed for the four new Western schools Ann would be literally burning the midnight oil, for the Pinamalayan electric plant had closed down.

At four o'clock the next morning I got up to put on the breakfast rice. By 5:15 Russell and the nine Tawbuid had boarded the south-bound bus for Bulalacao where they would take the trail across the southern end of Mindoro to the West. When Russell returned from that trip a week later, he was able to report that food was not as scarce as they had feared, though it was not in abundance.

At the Easter Feast that year we distributed First Corinthians in its sunny yellow plastic covers. The accompanying daily reading guide booklet with questions would be ready in a few weeks' time.

As long ago as February the First Corinthians stencils had been ready for the mimeograph, but we had waited for the restoration of the electricity. After two months, Russell finally decided to run the machine by hand. More than 10,200 cranks were needed to produce three hundred good copies!

During our two weeks in the hills Russell and his translation helper worked on the first chapters of Romans over in the church, while I checked Genesis with Sikiagum in our little tribal home.

When the churches began using First Corinthians in their daily devotional meetings, Acts was in the last stages of production. George and Bob were home for a long four-months vacation before flying to the States where they would enter sixth and seventh grades, and were a tremendous help in assembling the three hundred copies Russell had mimeographed, again by hand!

"How many times do you suppose we have to go around the table to put together all three hundred books?" George asked his brother.

"Well, only 22 stacks of pages fit on the table," Bob began thoughtfully. "That's 44 pages, and there are 110 pages altogether. So that's three times for each copy."

"Wow!" George exclaimed. "Nine hundred trips around the table. If we do it all ourselves, that's 450 trips each. I wonder how many miles that is?"

While we worked together, we shared the news from the West, received from our new co-workers, Larry and Anita DuBois, who were now living there and learning the Western Tawbuid language. Sikamawayan at Buswangan had been blessed not only with eager students, but ambitious parents who were reaching out to Pipe Village where seven were now believing.

Gunye's brown envelope of Bible school notes had finally reached him. Weeks before, he had sent word back with Ann that he was sure he had left it on the sleeping mat at our house. "I must have it," he told her. "It is all my sermons!"

At Balani some of the adults had asked Gunye for reading and writing classes. "If you will teach us in the afternoons," they told him, "we will work in your fields for you." So three days each week, after an exhausting five-hour morning with the children, he spent the afternoons teaching the adults.

Soon the other school teachers were doing the same. Only later did we learn that early in the first term of school, each teacher had chosen an understudy from those adults, training him as a future teacher for the children's school. God's special guidance in this innovation became evident even before the first term ended.

Linagum's baby had arrived strong and well just seven weeks after they set up house in Maltungtung, relieving some of his homesick tension. Then he heard that his father, the Safa village leader, had a large, painful growth on his back. Linagum, however, did not waver. He faithfully taught the children in the mornings, trained his understudy, and held classes for the adults in the afternoon.

As Linagum's father became weaker from the malignancy, his family asked if he, the only son, could return home at the end of that first school term. By the time Uan came with all of Ann's prepared materials to instruct the teachers for the second term of First Grade, Linagum and his family had already returned home.

But Uan found that Linagum and Gunye had done such a thorough job of training their understudies that those two Western believers, with no formal schooling and only one term of in-service observation, were able to teach. One would replace Linagum at Maltungtung and the other would take Gunye's school at Balani. This would free Gunye and his wife for supervizing these two new, rather shy teachers.

As we rejoiced in the way God was solving these problems, we wondered how He would work out Bob and George's flight home. Their tickets to the States routed them through Seoul, Korea, where they would have to change planes, and they had no escort. Although it was only nine months until our furlough when we would be with them again, the uncertainty of their plane connections in an unknown land made an upsetting and tearful parting.

We should have worried less and trusted more. For when they wrote us from the States, they told of an easy plane-change in Korea, with a very solicitous airline staff. And on the Seoul-Los Angeles flight, as they began talking to their seat mate, they found him to be James Hudson Taylor III, great-grandson of our Mission's founder, who would later become OMF's General Director!

Chapter 17

FELLOWSHIPPING

"**H**on! Looks like Uan's arrived!" Russell called down from his vantage point upstairs where he could see the front gate. He was at his desk drafting the last part of Romans in Tawbuid.

Pushing aside the Genesis questions I was writing, I headed for the front door. We knew Uan was coming to spend the night so he could get that pre-dawn southbound bus that connects with the motor-*bangka* to the West. He was scheduled to instruct supervisor Gunye and the four school teachers there for their last term of First Grade. Glancing at the three big plastic-wrapped boxes of materials along the wall that Ann had prepared for him, I wondered who he had brought as his companion and helper. Then, opening the door I was startled to see, not the expected two Tawbuid, but a dozen!

"Come in!" I said. Filing into our tiny downstairs *sala*, they were chatty and bright, excited about seeing the unknown West and celebrating Thanksgiving with their yet unknown Western brethren. As they piled their baskets, bundles and sacks in the corner, I thought, *How can they all afford to go?*

For Uan and his companion, transportation by bus, motor-*bangka* and weapons carrier would be paid from school funds. But his ten companions must have been saving their money and rice for months to be able to make the trip. Each fare could have bought a couple of dresses or shirts, a large new kettle or several jungle knives. But for them fellowship was more precious than ownership.

Over the years we had watched that fellowship between East and West develop slowly and naturally. The early teaching visits of the Eastern church elders followed by two years of Eastern missionary activity had produced at first a relationship of teacher to pupil, preacher to listener. But as the Western believers matured and the churches grew, the pattern gradually changed to one of equal fellowshipping with equal.

We saw that equality when Western men came to Bible School and stopped for a few days at Safa to share their problems and their joys. We saw it when Western believers began capably ministering in their own churches, and Eastern missionaries were needed only for the children's schools. We had seen it when two Western men had begun teaching in two of those schools. And now we were seeing it for one of their special feasts, as Eastern believers would receive hospitality in the West.

Later two more men came by who were going to hike across the southern trail because their money was limited. Fellowship was worth the three days of rugged river-bed and mountain travel, even when it involved the fearful aloneness of sleeping out along the way.

Although I wasn't in the West to see their rich fellowship, two weeks later their joy again filled our house. I had just settled into my comfortable rattan chair when there was loud pounding at the door, and

I called out in Tagalog, "Who's there?"

"*Ami wan!*" came the answer in Tawbuid. "Just us!" As I opened the door, in tumbled six happily-grinning travellers, tired, dirty, hungry and well-laden. Into the corner went three big baskets of chickens, besides all the usual bundles and bags, and one little white dog!

A wash under the pump, a big pot of rice with bean sprouts and fish, enthusiastic reports of their Western visit, then the welcome sleeping mats on the floor with mosquito coils smoking and tiny kerosene lamps burning low, and soon the company was soundly asleep.

Three days later just after lunch, Uan and the other believers appeared, just as buoyed up as the first arrivals had been. Leaving last term's Western school materials for Ann's cupboard, they hurried home to the hills, for it was still early afternoon.

As I thought of their happy Thanksgiving celebration, I realized how much we, too, had to be thankful for during the past month. In Safa as I had worked on the Acts study booklet with my translation helper, Sikiagum, I had wondered if her coming baby would wait until we were finished. Finally we completed checking the 360 daily reading selections and questions which would be used by the churches during our coming furlough year. The very next day Debi was born!

Ingki and Russell had been able to finish the first Romans check because her thoughtful brother had helped with her harvest. Even the rains had waited, pouring down and flooding the rivers just after we were safely back in the lowlands. Later we learned that even Bob and George's American Thanksgiving had been special because Becky and King had taken them three hundred miles south to Grandma and Grandpa Flory's for the long weekend.

But the beginning of December was sad. Not only did we miss our children, but also the telegram telling Russell of his mother's sudden death did not reach us for five days, increasing our terrible sorrow and loneliness. Then Bumblebee came from the hills and brought the startling news that Tigansi and Sikiagum's house had just burned to the ground.

When Tigansi came into town to apply for duplicates of his land tax receipts and identification papers lost in the fire, I thought of the first time I had seen him twelve years ago. He was the small son of Pig-tooth and his wife, who had been orphaned by the measles epidemic just a few months after his parents had decided to trust Christ. Now he himself was a dedicated believer and church leader.

Christmas 1977 brought joy as the Eastern school teachers returned from the West, reporting that Western believers had been trained to teach in each of the schools, now ready to begin grade two. And before the end of the month news came from Rick and Vicky, now in Hawaii, of the safe arrival of baby Catina. As we shared our happiness, the believers delightedly called us *Fufuina* and *Fufuama*, Grandma and Grandpa!

Concerned for their brethren in the West, with the Dubois family on furlough, several Eastern church leaders went over. In Biku's house at Pipe Village, near Buswangan, five new listeners were meeting for daily worship.

"But it would be good if all of us pray," the elders urged, "for Biku, just like Aime before him, is demanding that the believers in Buswangan help pay his large debt or he says he won't continue to believe." Then as requested by the Western believers, two Eastern families were chosen to help in that expanding ministry. Dagadafug and Sibnai became the thirteenth and fourteenth missionary families to go to the West.

Marriage ties also bound the two sides of the island. During that dry season Berting from Buswangan came to Safa to find a wife. Several days after presenting his request to the church elders, he was told of Lanikaw, daughter of Bumblebee. Berting knew the name, for her brother, Sikamawayan, had just finished his year as school teacher in Buswangan. Two months later at the 1978 Easter feast, a very shy Lanikaw and a quiet, thankful Berting became husband and wife.

That was not the first marriage between East and West. The previous year widower Rikardu, also from Buswangan, had come to the East and a marriage with Tiban's daughter, Nemi, had been arranged. Then just ten months after the wedding, Rikardu became ill and died, leaving Nemi with their unborn child. Uneasiness spread through the village. Not only because Rikardu was from the remote West, but also because everyone thought of the demands of their old customs.

Such a baby when born is *fobun*, "belonging to the dead." Like the deceased's fields, crops and possessions, it is to be abandoned. Even if the mother would try to keep the newborn alive, "it was doomed to die because it had no father." We had experienced the tragedy of this taboo many years before in Pangalkagan.

It was the believers' first testing on this particular custom. In faith we wrote home asking prayer for "peace of heart and protection from Satan as believers defy old customs and follow the Lord's ways of love."

Just at that time, a middle-aged widower, Mr Spirit-Fence, moved from the interior to Dalandan, the village of his believing sister and her family. Wanting to listen to the gospel and hoping to find a wife, he faithfully attended the daily services. Later that year, at the same Easter feast where Lanikaw and Berting were married, he was baptized and took Nemi as his wife. A healthy boy, Linyu, was born three weeks later, and although there was an initial period of difficult adjustment for Nemi, the baby was lovingly cared for and God was honored.

After Easter, news came from the West that Dagadafug and two of his daughters were very ill. To regain his health, he finally returned to the East, requesting that the church elders send another family. After much prayer, and waiting patiently until Dagadafug was completely recovered, they lovingly suggested that he return and finish out his year. He humbly accepted their decision, and for his remaining six months had no more problems with his health.

Just before our furlough it was our turn to be tested. A garbled telegram arrived from Rick and Vicky in Hawaii stating that there had been an accident with "broken hips and femur." We didn't know what kind of accident or who was hurt. Quickly we packed a suitcase and took the seven-hour trip by bus and boat to Batangas City where we could make an international phone call. The connection was perfect and Vicky told us that Rick, riding his bicycle in a bike lane on the Navy base, was struck by an illegally driven car that suddenly turned left across the lane. He was in the hospital with a shattered hip. Sick at heart, we returned to Pinamalayan, comforted by the thought that only seven days later we were scheduled to leave for furlough with a ten-day stop in Hawaii.

Busily packing, we didn't pay much attention to the storm warnings, until Wednesday when Typhoon Atang plowed a direct path across Mindoro. Mopping up the floors while we continued to sort and pack, we were still able to keep on schedule. Then Saturday Faguguanun, leading Safa church elder, arrived with the upsetting news that our Safa house had lost its corrugated iron roof in the fierce winds.

Not until Monday were the rivers low enough for us to hike to Safa. We were shocked by the sight of the walls of our home standing bare and roofless while the sheets of twisted roofing lay scattered and abandoned. The sympathetic believers told us, "We rescued all of your things from the house, and are keeping them for you in our homes."

Amazingly, the day was bright and dry, so we were able to spread our books and bedding on woven sleeping mats in the hot sun, and by early afternoon pack them away again for the believers to store. Even though we had to take some still damp items with us, our steps were light as we returned to Pinamalayan that same day, for we knew the believers would quickly repair the house for Ann's use. By 3:30 am Wednesday morning, just one day later than we had originally planned, we were able to leave Pinama-layan for furlough. The joyful reunion with our children, families and friends included a recovering Rick who one day would even be playing soccer again.

Back in Safa in May 1979, after our rewarding year at home, we were delighted to see Linagum's tiny boys, David and Ane, the first twins born to Tawbuid believers and therefore the first twins allowed to live. According to their old customs, the second twin is not considered a person, but simply part of the afterbirth which is wrapped in leaves and taken to the jungle. I could visualize these twins becoming young men, an indisputable testimony of God's love and care to all their heathen neighbors! But my aspiration to show off God's trophies was shattered when Ane died at age two, just like Baltugangan's rescued baby girl.

Believers as well as unbelievers were experiencing new difficulties as a determined lumber company was bulldozing its way into the interior. Making wide ugly roads that spoiled the natural beauty and usefulness of the land and gave easy access to outsiders, it was bringing in its own personnel who were taking advantage of the timid interior people.

During our stay in the hills, eight of these lumbermen arrived, inviting themselves to use the church as their headquarters while they spent a week scouting for suitable trees. Their backpacks and gear in the church took up needed room. Their smoky cooking fires and loud conversation during the daily devotional meetings were disturbing, especially at prayer time. And their attempts to lure the young girls by serenading them at night and being too friendly in the daytime caused much distress.

Village leader Butuan warned the girls to stay at home after dark and only go in twos and threes during the day. And everyone prayed for God's protection and intervention. It was three months before God's answer came. Three months for the believers to witness to and encourage their frightened unbelieving neighbors. And then, sudden relief! With five days of cloud-burst rain wreaking havoc on the equipment and washing deep gullies down the lumber roads, the operation was brought to an abrupt halt. Athough the lumbermen then began building a "campo," planning to repair the road after the rains stopped, it and the lumbering attempt were soon entirely abandoned, and never resumed.

Another demonstration of God's power with far-reaching effects occurred at tiny Masakbe village where thirteen of Yudgulian's relatives were "listening", an answer to his ten years of faithful praying and witnessing. His brother, Linakungan, came to Safa bringing his very pregnant wife.

"What can we do," asked the prospective father, "so that this baby will live?"

Close beside me someone said quietly, "His wife has given birth five times, but none have survived."

"We will all pray for you," I said. For we had no idea, even after many probing questions, why her babies had died. Within two months healthy Foyungan was born, delighting her parents and all the praying believers.

Then one afternoon the "listeners" from Masakbe arrived at our little Safa home, came up our ladder-stairs and perched on the porch, asking if they could talk to the "*rikurdur*." Always eager for unsolicited text, Russell heartily agreed to put their stories on tape, secretly amazed that these shy interior folk had volunteered.

Their words were composed entirely of songs, myths, spirit chants, and curses. Each man took his lengthy turn, and wouldn't stop until he was completely finished. Then with a satisfied grunt, he would sit back on his heels and pass the "steel ear" to the next speaker.

This was not the first time someone had asked to record chants and poems, but Russell had supposed they merely wanted to hear their own voices. After this visit, however, we began to piece together various conversations and observations, and the significance of their desire to record began to dawn on us.

When anyone wanted to follow the New Teaching, he could refuse to make any more sacrifices to the evil spirits for sickness or for death. If he had any spirit paraphernalia, it could be buried or hidden in the jungle. It was never burned, for that in itself was a form of cursing an enemy and might be misunderstood by unbelieving neighbors. But how could he dispose of the chants, songs, poems, myths, curses and other forms of verbal power used for controlling the evil spirit world? How could he rid his mind of the old customs when he had decided to trust only in *Funbalugu*? Recording was their method of burying in the jungle their spirit paraphernalia of the mind.

At the Thanksgiving Feast that year, we watched baby Foyungan's parents along with six other believers from Masakbe as they declared their faith publicly by baptism. Afterwards Russell and I were marveling at God's amazing work among the Tawbuid, when Suklinyan came over and began chatting with us.

He had accepted the challenge of a widow in interior heathen Ngawe who had said, "You can make fields near me, if you want. But you're not to be always harping about *Funbalugu*!" After he and his family had moved there as missionaries, people occasionally came to see him in twos and threes, but they did not want to meet together. Now he told us, "Takumi and the six other leaders have met, and have decided the New Teaching is not from *Funbalugu*."

"What'll you do?" we asked, knowing how discouraging his witness to his heathen neighbors had been.

"Just keep living there, and witnessing," he replied with determination.

Although those seven village leaders had decided not to "listen," he hoped to be able to reach powerful leader, Sikfufu, who had taken Sumsumagan's place over them, and had once expressed interest in the New Teaching.

"How is it," I wondered out loud, "that so many Tawbuid are now trusting and obeying *Funbalugu* and yet these men do not want to 'listen'?"

"Has anyone ever told you about the prophecy handed down from our fathers?" Suklinyan asked us.

"Do you mean when Tiban's father told him to follow the New Teaching that would come into his area?" I asked.

"It wasn't from Tiban's father, but from Taliugan,

many, many generations before that," Suklinyan answered.

"Tell us about it," Russell invited.

"It was handed down from father to son, father to son, for many, many years," he began. "And because of the prophecy our own Dalandan leader, Tree-Branch, decided we should follow the New Teaching. The men now living in Safa village as well as the men in Tiban's group also heard it from their own fathers."

"What was the prophecy?" I asked.

"Our fathers told us that white teachers would come into our area and we were to listen and obey their teaching," he answered. "And we would be able to recognize them because they would know our language."

A strange thrill went down my spine. I turned toward Russell and we looked at each other, speechless. We knew of no other outsider who could speak Tawbuid, although our co-workers were quickly learning it. Now the reason was apparent for those eight "fruitless" years in the West learning the language. God had it all planned from the beginning.

That was why, here in the East, gentle Gorio had told Caroline he wanted to see those teachers who knew his language! And although he did not come and listen in those early days, just before his sudden death he told his wife and children to be sure to follow the Teaching. All are now believers in Safa village.

Sometime later when Russell was in the West, he told the believers at Balani about the prophecy. Yagundai, a Balani believer, then gave the version passed down to him. "The elders told us not to forget that there will come teachers, big people, *em kalag-bean*, 'like our cousins,' who will be white. And even though they come from a far country, they will know our language." This reminded Russell of the Tawbuid at Pangalkagan who called him *lagbe*, or cousin.

When Russell asked about Taliugan, or Long-Neck, he was given names from the genealogical record which is remembered by the shaman as part of their spirit control structure. Between Taliugan and the present Dalandan village leader there were sixteen generations, more than three hundred years. That is how long the Lord had been preparing the Tawbuid for the coming of the gospel!

Back in Pinamalayan two more surprises awaited us. The town's electric current had been restored and a special letter from George had arrived. During our furlough he had broken his leg in the growth area. Because of the continual danger of imperfect development, the doctor wanted it X-rayed every six months until he had stopped growing. But our friends at home and the Tawbuid here were praying. The latest X-ray showed nearly two inches of firm, straight growth since it had been broken the year before, amazing the doctor and making further X-rays unnecessary.

On a rainy afternoon several weeks later in Safa, we were shaken to hear the news that raced through the village.

"Berting has disappeared!"

No one knew where he had gone. He had not returned home the night before, and was still missing. Young Berting had come from the West to find a wife and had married Lanikaw, Bumblebee's daughter. Solemnly everyone began gathering at the *Funbalugu Bale* for the evening meeting. The musical sounds of the light rain on the metal church roof were to me in a minor key.

Village leader Butuan slowly got to his feet to explain the situation. A number of men from Safa had gone to work for a lowland farmer, and after work had gathered on his porch waiting for the evening meal. The farmer's dog began to bark furiously at the tribal men, frightening his tiny child who fell off the porch. He was so incensed at the dog that he dashed out of the house and across the porch, chasing the fleeing animal with his raised *bolo*.

Berting was petrified, especially when the farmer passed right between him and Butuan. However, he stayed long enough to eat and then left immediately. "Even though I had carefully explained to our men," said Butuan, "that it isn't the Tagalog custom to rush off right after a meal."

And that was the last anyone saw of Berting, except for Katumpis who was on the trail. Berting had rushed by without recognizing him or slackening his pace. No one knew where he was. But they knew what to do when faith is tested. The evening meeting became a prayer meeting.

Later that week men from an interior village reported that Berting had passed their way, acting very strangely and heading toward the interior. It was surmised that he was trying to find the interior trail to the West, a trail he had heard about but never used. But I thought of Squint and Dawa's lonely deaths, and shivered.

The following week Uan and Gunye returned from instructing the school teachers in the West.

Berting had not shown up there. With no companion, no food, no shelter and no personal knowledge of the trail, we all wondered what had happened to him.

The day before we left on a planned visit to our co-workers Anita and Larry in the West, we were busy stapling the cheerful orange plastic covers on newly-translated Romans and the Question Booklet, and finishing the 1980 Tawbuid Scripture Calendars to take with us. But we ached for the day when the Western believers would no longer have to struggle with the Eastern version of God's Word but would have their own translation. (Sadly, even to this present day only James has been translated into the Western Tawbuid language.)

On that visit while Larry and Russell were in the hills at Balani, Berting suddenly appeared! He was thinner, quieter, more subdued. Three weeks of wild, often trail-less, solitary jungle slogging to cross the center of the island had taken its toll. And he never wanted to return to the East again! However, he willingly wrote a letter to his wife for Russell to deliver. Then the Western church leaders surprised Russell by giving him a note they had written to Faguguanun, Safa church elder who had been a missionary in Berting's village. They were suggesting that someone from the East, perhaps Faguguanun himself, as well as Berting's father-in-law, come to the West to talk to (and bring back?) Berting. All of us were sorry to see this East-West problem, but were rejoicing in the loving fellowship and prayer it evinced.

The letters were delivered, and a week later seven adults and four babies arrived at our house in Pinamalayan on their way to see Berting. Faguguanun not only brought his own wife and baby, but also Berting's wife, Lanikaw, and baby Simun, along with four other young marrieds.

They had a meal and stayed half the night, catching the 2:30 am southbound bus. At Bulalacao they would save money by hiking across the southern tip of the island to the West, reaching Balani in time to join Berting for the Christmas feast and services.

When they returned at the end of the month, five Western men were with them on their way to MBS which had now graduated twelve Tawbuid. But Lanikaw and Simun stayed behind in the West. It was not hard to imagine her, quietly with her sweet shy smile, taking her place beside Berting, the man she had promised never to leave, always to obey, to cherish and to care for in sickness and in health.

Two months later we took sad news to Lanikaw. Her brother, Sikamawayan, had returned home exhausted from a strenuous day gathering rattan. After a refreshing bath in the river, he collapsed and in two days was dead.

Those from Buswangan especially, grieved to hear their children's first school teacher was dead. But the dark foreboding of the old days was gone, for they sorrowed with hope, knowing he was with the Lord. We wondered if Lanikaw would now be anxious to return home.

But Berting found it impossible to think of returning to the East. Intense fear was holding him back. We learned that on a previous trip to the East he and his Tawbuid companions had been robbed at knife-point. In terror he had fled to the unfamiliar interior, making his way alone back to the West. Perhaps that explained his irrational behavior when he fled from the farmer's porch.

In that same month Durfu lost his wife after healthy baby Esse was born. She died while being carried out of the hills to the hospital in a rattan swing on the back of one of the believers.

Again East and West mourned the death of one who had lived and served on both sides of the island. How we would have loved to rush to the comfort, help and encouragement of each of those families, scattered from East to West. But we could not always be there. Our part now was to prepare God's Word in their own language, mimeographing each portion, giving it a strong binding, and putting it into their hands. The Lord could be their comfort and guide through His Word, whether their paths were rough or smooth, and whether we were there or not.

At Easter time 1980 news quickly spread across the island that Durfu with his seven children and Bayanyus, Sikamawayan's widow, with her four, were being married! We smiled as we recalled that she had taken care of Durfu's new baby Esse for many of those first difficult nights after Martina had died. On our next visit to Safa we were delighted to hear all the happy sounds of crowded but joyous living that came from their big house next door.

That summer we, too, had happy sounds of crowded but joyous living coming from our big house in Pinamalayan and our little house in the hills. Bob and George were with us for two months, and then Rick, coming under water on his Navy sub, and Vicky and Tina by air visited us, much to the delight of the Tawbuid in East and West.

Ideal East-West travel for the Tawbuid believers

would be the trail over the mountains across the center of the island in their own territory. It held fewer dangers and fears for them than the lowlands, and no fares had to be paid. Many attempts had been made to encourage the interior leaders to reveal that trail, but they could not be persuaded. And the believers did not want to antagonize leaders who someday might be willing to listen to the gospel.

No one had been able to locate or follow this trail, although Russell and an American companion had crossed the rugged central area of the island some years earlier by laboriously chopping their way through the almost impenetrable jungle!

Then one sunny day during field clearing time at the end of January 1981, Biolang, leader of Balani Village, and five Western believers arrived in Safa, having hiked across the center of the island! They were not sure they had followed the main trail on their three-week trek to the East, but it was a beginning. Overland travel was possible, and with more experience this route might prove useful. We wanted as close a tie as possible between East and West because we soon would be going to the States for an unexpected three-year home-staff assignment.

We also wanted to leave more Scriptures in Tawbuid. Two months before our departure, we had finished James. Now we were concentrating on those fifty long chapters of Genesis, as well as the huge Reading-Guide Question Booklet with three to four questions on every verse in Genesis. And Second Corinthians was partially completed.

As our friends at home prayed, we worked and God supplied. By Easter, just three weeks before we left, Genesis was finished and distributed in the East.

It was amazing how exactly the Lord had it planned.

The stencils we had on hand were just enough. The paper was more than sufficient. When we unexpectedly ran out of ink, we found the special Gestetner type was available (and fresh!) at the tiny local school supply store! And while we ran about 30,000 sheets through the mimeograph, then cut, assembled and bound the pages, the electricity did not fail, nor did the mimeograph or the missionaries break down. Repairs for both would be available only in faraway Manila.

The Western Tawbuid received their copies several weeks later, after our co-workers took the stapled pages to the West, bought the heavy material and covered them. So while we, and even our co-workers were gone (for they left the field permanently soon after we departed), East and West not only fellow-shipped together, but were reading the same Scriptures for over a year on both sides of the island.

While we were on the home staff in the States, thoroughly enjoying the precious privilege of three years with our children, we received over fifty letters from the Tawbuid which revealed their continued growth and obedience. We even finished Second Corinthians during a six-weeks' visit back to Mindoro in the middle of our time at home. When our assignment was completed we were able to return to the Tawbuid with a God-given contentment, for our children, as well as Russell's elderly father, were well settled at home.

Rick, Vicky and their three children were in New York where he was an electrical engineer. Becky and King were operating their own private elementary school in Corvallis, the same town in Oregon where

Bob and George were living in an attractive mobile home and attending Oregon State University.

Our thankfulness for God's provision for our family was combined with our rejoicing to be back in Mindoro. Not only could we continue Tawbuid Bible translation, using the research and first drafts Russell had done at home, but we also could again join the believers in joyful fellowship.

Chapter 18

REJOICING

Splashing through the last river crossing in happy anticipation of the coming weekend, I looked up to see five neat, brightly-dressed tribal girls perched on the huge boulder beside the path into Safa village. As they returned my smile I automatically greeted them in Tawbuid, *"Bagu ami kadasug.* We have just arrived." With chagrin I instantly realized my mistake. This attractive rainbow would not understand my words. They were not Tawbuid. They were from one of the other tribes attending the annual Mangyan Believers Conference being hosted in 1985 by the Safa church.

Embarrassed, I smiled apologetically, trying to think of an appropriate Tagalog greeting. Suddenly my attention was diverted by the frolicking, laughing children racing toward me down the river path, tiny giggling brothers and sisters hanging precariously on their backs.

A warmth of joy swept over me, seeing Tawbuid children and their young visitors romping delightedly together. With light steps I quickly went up the slope into the village clearing, and again my heart was touched. Clump after clump of people, thick as bamboo, were talking, laughing, bouncing babies, and watching other clumps of talkers. Tawbuid believers blending with their visitors from the other five Mindoro tribes.

As I went from group to group greeting old friends and new, catching snatches of conversation, the words *Sharing, Caring, Fellowshipping,* and *Rejoicing* took on a new and deeper meaning. Now it involved all six tribes. But this was only the beginning of my soul-stirring day.

Later that afternoon when the tractor-tread bell began its loud pealing, the clumps of people flowed toward the church, still continuing their bubbling conversations.

Flashing a smile at my translation helper, Sikiagum, I sat down beside her on our usual section of the split palm-trunk flooring. As I leaned back against the wall and glanced down the length of the crowded church, I was amazed. The building had now become four times as long as it was wide. Somehow from the outside this had escaped me.

The grass-roofed addition made months ago to accommodate the growing congregation, now had a temporary palm-leaf extension beyond that. And still the grassy clearing at the side of the church was needed for the overflow, *How will they ever get everyone organized for sleeping places, cooking areas and sufficient food?* I wondered. I had forgotten that while we were in the States for those three years, the Tawbuid believers were continuing to develop.

Like our own children, we had watched them grow so slowly that we hardly realized they had become adults. Then suddenly they were mature, independent, in positions of leadership and responsibility, and even, I would find out today, doing things better than we could.

The pages of everyone's small Tagalog hymn book began flipping when the first hymn was announced. As the singing began, I suddenly sat up and took notice, for like a huge organ, the volume rose in unison in the Tagalog language:

Oh Lord my God,
When I in awesome wonder
Consider all the works thy hands have made.
I see the stars,
I hear the rolling thunder,
Thy power throughout the universe displayed.

Awesome wonder, as I thought of His power and was overwhelmed. More than five hundred voices from the six Mindoro tribes were majestically praising our Great Creator God in beautifully-blended harmony, even though their customs, dress, languages and experiences were so different.

Awesome wonder, as I listened to the opening prayer. "Lord, we are so happy you are here with us. Help us be quiet and able to hear your words. Open our minds to what you have to say to us. This is our prayer."

Awesome wonder, even as announcements were made. First Uan and then Dagadafug rose to explain the arrangements to the guests. "If any of you need to buy rice, we've brought in a big supply. Just over at the house," Uan stated. He knew some had preferred not to carry heavy loads of sweet potatoes, green bananas and root crops on their long trip to the Tawbuid area.

"And anyone who has not yet found a place to sleep or cook, see either me or Kalafe or ..." Dagadafug added, mentioning the members of his committee.

Here were Tawbuid men taking positions of leadership and responsibility, combined with servanthood, among the six tribes. Was it possible that this was the tribe which had been *Unknown, Hidden, Fearful* and *Suspicious*? Who fled in terror from the outside world and were even afraid of those in their own culture? Who had no faith in Christ and no ability to read His Word? Who had no thought, let alone boldness, of teaching others, leading a meeting or praying to the Great Creator God? Who were so uncertain and mistrusting of the future, that only the present received attention?

They had been planning this big event for months, arranging, organizing, managing. They were also prepared to take part in leading, speaking and interpreting. My eyes were opened to a new appreciation of the Tawbuid. Quiet, unassuming, faithfully carrying out their responsibilities, but secure, relaxed, completely unconscious and unconcerned about any impression they might be making on others. Just being themselves.

Awesome wonder at what God had done. He not only had given them freedom from the tyranny of fear, but also a freedom to be what they were with no pretense.

As I glanced around, I had to suppress an appreciative grin. The relaxation, unconcern and obvious security of the Tawbuid believers was so evident, even by the individual ways they were dressed. Uan, with his back straight so it wouldn't touch the dusty wall, and with a grin of enjoyable fun spread over his face, was decked out in a second-hand white embroidered Tagalog dress shirt and long trousers. In spite of the handkerchief needed to frequently mop his brow, he was thoroughly enjoying his new elegance! By contrast, Durfu, like Falakan, Kulas and a number of others, was cool and comfortable in spite of the heat, relaxed in his normal everyday wear: a simple, neat G-string. In between the Well-Dressed and the Comfortable were as many variations as purse and personality allowed.

Tigansi's bright green shorts and flaming orange T-shirt picturing a *Kalesa*, was set off by a pair of tall rubber boots when he first arrived at the meeting! Yaws-crippled Budiawian, who goes everywhere on one foot and one padded knee, was completely oblivious of the call of his gray T-shirt proclaiming "SOS." (I couldn't help thinking, he was the brother of evil Balinguy and his wife was the daughter of gentle Gorio, and now this couple were devoted believers.) Many there had short pants and no shirts, while others like Sibnai in his brilliant red, white and blue striped T-shirt, wore shirts with the traditional G-string.

The women were just as varied. At Durfu's side his little daughter was in a flour-sack sarong. Like that of some of her elders, it was knotted tightly under the arms. She was quietly absorbed in a tiny string-tied baby lizard, while the playmate beside her was occupied with a looped rubber band necklace. Inday, Rikardu's daughter from the western side of Mindoro, now married to a young Safa believer, had added a colorful flowered blouse to her flour-sack skirt. Near her Dariayi was sitting, attractive in a bright red polka-dot dress. But when I smiled at her, she looked down, grinning shyly in apology for her shaved head, a sure method of eliminating lice! Her husband, in long trousers and T-shirt, sat with his arm around her.

Dariayi's step-sister was outfitted in an orange dress, and from her shoulder hung a wide flour-sack strap to keep her baby comfortably supported while riding on her hip. Beyond her, Yudgulian had put on his reading glasses, and I noticed several others in the crowd had done the same. There was even a sprinkling of wrist watches. But again I thought in *awesome wonder* how free these Tawbuid believers were of the tyranny of material possessions.

One of the Buhid men was called to the front to give an account of progress, praise and prayer requests from his churches, followed by the report of the Alangan representative. Other requests were mentioned and everyone was invited to pray simultaneously, each in his own language.

That's a mistake, I sighed to myself. *No one will be able to enter into the spirit of anyone else's prayers!* But as the subdued beginning soon became a gentle continuous rumble of thunder, I was strangely moved. Showers of blessing, I suddenly realized, would have to be the result as God answered the prayers of these five hundred who, with bowed heads, were talking personally to Him in their own languages on behalf of the Buhid and Alangan. Quietly I joined them in English.

Awesome wonder at this smooth blending. This praying, working, caring, serving, fellowshipping together. Who would be able to fathom the depths of joy, help and encouragement this interaction was bringing to the believers in every tribe!

Thirty years had now passed since the day of the Great Darkness. Quickly reviewing those earlier days,

I realized that every one of the other tribes had made a significant contribution to the faith and spiritual growth of the Tawbuid believers.

The Tadyawan, braving the black magic and curses of the Tawbuid, had been the first to make a direct and conscious effort to teach them "Our Father's Words," building a special meeting-house at the riverside for that purpose. I felt a glow of warmth for those faithful Tadyawan believers.

Two years later the Alangan encouraged the Tawbuid. Although just babes in Christ, the Tawbuid had gone to Ayan Bekeg to help construct the first Mangyan Bible School buildings. Working and worshipping with the Alangan believers, seeing their church in action, and realizing there were others following the Lord strengthened their faith.

Hanunoo hospitality was another pleasant experience several years later when six Tawbuid men went with us to visit them. As they fellowshipped with the believers and saw their faithfulness in taking God's Word regularly to several outreaches, they were blessed and challenged.

The Buhid believers influenced the Tawbuid in two ways. While crossing the island together, the Tawbuid watched them witness in Buhid homes along the way by phonograph and conversation, and later copied their methods. In the Buhid church they saw for the first time an offering being taken for the Lord, a practice which they promptly adopted on returning home. They learned how those offerings could be used when Buhid believers from Apnagan gave a gift for the transportation of the Tawbuid attending the Preparatory Bible School. Another practice which they also emulated.

The Tawbuid first met the Iraya believers as hosts at the Mangyan Believers Conferences, and later as their teachers at the Bible School where their influence was most keenly felt and appreciated.

Suddenly my mind was brought back to the present as the special conference speaker was being introduced, the pastor of one of the lowland churches. As he stood, a Hanunoo took his place at the pastor's right and a Tawbuid at his left. Three speakers?

Then the leader explained. The message would be interpreted into two Mangyan languages, for someone had suggested that those who did not understand Tagalog would understand either Hanunoo or Tawbuid! Strictly speaking that was rather ambitious, but everyone happily accepted the arrangement.

As the sermon began, phrase by phrase in Tagalog, both enterprising interpreters were quick and able. I marveled at Tawbuid Yanigia's ability in Tagalog. It seemed only yesterday that we despaired of ever teaching the Tawbuid enough to attend Bible School!

Then the speaker used the phrase "strangers and pilgrims." Maligday, in Hanunoo, sailed right through, but sweat droplets began to form on Yanigia's brow as he tried to think of a Tawbuid equivalent for pilgrims. He grinned apologetically and wiped his damp forehead with his hand, before finally being able to explain the concept of a homeless wanderer, so the sermon could continue.

It came to me with a new force that the phrase which stumped him came from a passage of Scripture not yet translated into Tawbuid. But in Hanunoo the whole New Testament was finished now, and so these words had already been discussed and used, giving little trouble to their interpeter.

My theory was reinforced when the speaker, bringing the message to a close, enumerated the sins of the flesh and contrasted them with each fruit of the Spirit. Now Yanigia was instant and accurate, for those verses had long ago been put into the Tawbuid Thick Book and memorized by all the believers. This realization was another jolt, urging us to a quicker completion of God's Word in their language.

Silently I pledged to do all I could to help complete the task God had given us and to pray for the translators in the other tribes still striving to finish their New Testaments. With a sudden pang I realized that translation for the Western Tawbuid believers was not being done at all! As everyone bowed in closing prayer, I asked God to send someone soon to translate His Word for those isolated believers also.

Quickly the chatter began as the believers spilled out from the front doorways and from the back wall-less addition into the cool evening air. Dagadafug grinned as he passed me, and I thought, "There goes our cheerful Tawbuid MTCA representative!" MTCA, Mangyan Tribal Church Association. How official and competent it sounded! And it was. Now. But the process toward that goal had taken years.

I climbed the pole stairs to our little hill house and in the kitchen began to scrub someone's gift of sweet potatoes for our supper. *How far Dagadafug and the Tawbuid believers have come*, I mused. In those early days when the paths of the Tawbuid believers occasionally crossed those of other tribes, they had no thought at all of a formal inter-tribal association. Nothing in their culture could presage such an all-enveloping idea.

To help the believers and their young churches eventually stand on their own feet in a non-sympathetic world, the missionaries had begun to work toward an association that would declare their unity, but not impose uniformity. As brothers and sisters in Christ they rejoiced in that unity. But their individual tribal customs and languages which governed the expression of their meetings, their worship, their giving, their evangelistic methods and even their church buildings could never be uniform without a serious loss of their God-given individual identity.

How well I remembered escorting Bumblebee and Kalafe to that first council session, even though the Tawbuid had no idea what a "representative" was. Two years after that initial meeting, the MTCA was legally registered with the Philippine government, and five years later the MTCA churches joined the national Association of Bible Churches of the Philippines, or ABCOP.

Taking down my blackened cooking pot, I filled it with the potatoes, put in a dipper of water and hung it over the clay fire-table where the short pieces of dry wood, with some coaxing, soon began to blaze.

I thought of how we had prayed that this integration into the outside world would come slowly enough so the Tawbuid, originally the most backward of all the tribes, could absorb it and not be absorbed by it. During our furlough three years later we were delighted to get a letter from Ann showing how God had answered that prayer.

A group of Tawbuid believers, hearing that the ABCOP churches were having their yearly assembly in Manila, decided that they would attend. Weren't they part of ABCOP? In spite of the extremely high cost of transport, a group of them saved their money, dressed in their best clothes, and took a bus to Calapan to brave the unknown. Along with delegates from the lowland churches, they boarded the ferry and crossed the channel to Luzon Island for the first time in their lives. At the other side one of the waiting buses hurtled them for three hours through crowded cities and masses of frightening traffic. Finally arriving in Manila, they astounded those at the conference by their unexpected appearance.

Attending the meetings, purchasing books, and visiting with other believers added to the adventures they had to tell when they returned to their hillside homes in the jungle. The outside world certainly had not absorbed them, but with lively fascination they had absorbed some of that outside world!

Suddenly I saw the potatoes were bubbling over, so I removed several sticks of wood from the blazing fire, pushing the remaining ones closer together.

During those early years of MTCA organization, the Bible School and its farmlands were gradually put under its jurisdiction as the missionaries quietly began stepping back. *And now*, I thought with satisfaction, *the Principal and all the teachers are Mangyan.*

Then in 1978, two years after the MTCA joined ABCOP, the Council learned of the unreached Negrito tribes in Camarines Sur and accepted the challenge to reach them, even though that mission field was across the inter-island sea, a trip of more than 250 miles from Mindoro. The Eastern Tawbuid who had planted churches in the mission field of Western Mindoro were enthusiastic, though none felt qualified to go. Special offerings were taken, regular gifts were pledged and prayer support was begun by all the tribal churches for the Hanunoo couple, Jeremias and Monling, who were chosen to be the first Mangyan missionaries to the Negritos.

On his recent furlough Jeremias visited Safa. How eager the believers were to hear first-hand how their gifts were being used and their prayers answered over those past seven years.

"We first went to San Ramon in April 1979," Jeremias began. "Our house was very tiny, but it was all right for the four of us. But I did not know what to do to reach the people.

"For several days they would not even look at us! They were often drunk or angry or they threw stones and chopped at each other. They were very set in their ways, very stubborn. So I began to go with them to their work. I helped them plant cassava, or rake and prepare *abaka* (Manila hemp). I didn't know anything about *abaka* at first, I had to learn. Sometimes I went fishing with them, using a net in the river, and I even went with them to harvest for the lowland Bicolanos.

"Just one month later, some began to listen, so we asked Felix if we could use his house. We began teaching them about heaven and hell, and telling them stories from the Bible.

"For the first two months we could only speak in Tagalog which was not well understood. By the third month we were mixing Tagalog with Naga Bikol, which they know, until we learned enough to use only the Naga Bikol language.

"By Christmas 1981 ten, including Felix, were ready to be baptized..."

The Tawbuid rejoiced to hear the details of the joys and sorrows, the difficulties and triumphs. Not only were Negritos believing now, but also lowland Bicolanos, because of the witness of Jeremias and Monling and their Buhid co-workers, Dangin and Saynay. At the end of Jeremias' meeting, the Safa believers decided to take a special offering. In a church whose normal Sunday giving is just over thirty pesos, they put 135 pesos into the coconut-shell offering plates.

While I cut off the stems of the sweet potato tops, washing them and putting them on top of the boiling potatoes, I thought of the MTCA's third main respon- sibility, the Mangyan Development Program, inaugu- rated with a generous gift from the West German government. Initially OMF planned and supervized the activities, employing qualified lowland believers to head the departments of Public Health, Adult Education and Scholarships, Agricultural Develop- ment and Marketing, and Legal Assistance with Land-Securing.

Tribal men were gradually given more responsi- bility until one became head of the project under MTCA, working with lowland and tribal personnel as well as several OMF missionaries.

The Tawbuid were not involved at first because they already had their own simple programs. For example, each family had its first-aid kit of useful remedies, with one person in each village keeping a supply of replacement medicines to sell. For serious illnesses, a sympathetic local doctor was not far away. They now had goat herds and were slowly acquiring water buffalo. They continued to try a variety of new crops from time to time, and had found local markets for their produce of bananas and various root crops. All new "listeners" were taught to read by the believers, and for the young people, Ann's four-year elementary schools followed by the three-year MBS course was all the education they felt was necessary to work for the Lord.

The Tawbuid did need Legal Assistance, however, for obtaining the elusive title deeds to their hill lands. Before the program was begun, Russell had tried to help them make out the land-holding descriptions they needed to file with the government. Surveying their acreage was a new experience! With a hundred-meter length of rattan and a compass he was guided around the boundaries of the group's claim. Starting at the river and surveying "over hill, over dale" for more than four kilometers, he came back to the beginning. When the readings were plotted, the starting and ending points missed meeting by only twenty meters! Years later the Tawbuid were able to hire the licensed surveyors contacted by the program, so there is now hope that titles will soon be granted.

The most recent project is SALT (Sloping Agri-cultural Land Technique) for hill lands where surface erosion and over-use has depleted the soil. The Tawbuid land, because of their regular forest-fallow agricultural cycle, is not as depleted as many other tribal areas. However when the project was introduced it was the Tawbuid who showed a willingness to take the five weeks from their busy field-clearing schedule and spend two hundred pesos each from their meager pockets to make the trip to Mindanao, on the southern tip of the Philippines, to study this new technique.

I lifted the lid of the cooking pot with a short narrow bamboo slat, and my probing knife told me the potatoes were done. As six of us missionaries sat on stools and trunks in our tiny sala eating the simple meal from enamel plates on our laps, we began to discuss the new SALT project.

"How many will be making the special plots?" I asked.

"Seven," was the answer. "The six who went to Mindanao as well as Suklinyan."

"Have they planted the *ipil-ipil* seeds?" I wanted to know.

"Not yet. But that will be the next step, after the land is cleared and the level contours are made."

The fast growing *ipil-ipil* trees would help control erosion, and their leaves could be dug into the ground to add nutrients to the soil. Vegetables or other crops planted between the rows would flourish and supplement the income or the diet of the Tawbuid. The work would be time consuming, as the newly-sprouted trees would need thinning, transplanting, and constant trimming, and the crops would need weeding.

That night, just before going to sleep, I wondered if the Tawbuid cooperation would encourage other needy tribes to try the SALT project. The Tawbuid seemed to have a heart for helping and giving to others, I thought happily as I drifted off to sleep.

I was not so enthusiastic about their giving spirit when suddenly at 2 am on Sunday morning the night's peaceful silence was shattered by the loud squeals of chased pigs and the voices of laughing excited men. Whatever were they doing at this early hour? Immediately the familiar early morning crowing began and I thought, "Where else would you find people waking up the roosters?"

As I lay quietly listening to the ruckus, I wondered at which annual Believers Conferences the Tawbuid had been present. Probably every one since 1967. In the following years they had been so enthused by the joy and courage they received from fellowshipping with such a wide spectrum of believers that they were determined to bring some of the newly-reached western Tawbuid to attend.

My most poignant memory of Tawbuid enthusiasm for these conferences was in March 1980. We were in Pinamalayan, and knew that several Tawbuid planned to attend the Conference which was to be held in the Buhid village on the Batangan River, forty miles south of Safa. On Sunday, five days before the conference was to begin, winds from an unseasonal tropical storm began to rage. By Monday the rains had arrived in cloud-burst torrents, coming right through our upstairs wooden plank walls and in around the windows. As we mopped the flooded floors, I began to think of the hundreds of tribal believers who would be traveling to the conference on Thursday. Roads would be churned into muddy bogs, rivers flooded and trails obliterated. If they did not travel in large groups the trip would not only be difficult but hazardous.

So it was with great delight that we saw a jeep stop in front of our house on Thursday morning crammed with Tawbuid from Safa, Dalandan,

Masakbe and Fandung. Several of them came to tell us they were the first of two jeeps on their way to the conference! Completely on their own these believers had chartered both jeeps to go all the way from the end of the road near Safa to the Buhid village on the Batangan River, so that more than fifty Tawbuid could attend. Nothing, it seemed, could dampen their eagerness to have another five days of joyful, memorable fellowship.

And now, after years of enjoying others' hospitality, the Tawbuid were able to reciprocate. I was glad even if it did make it hard to sleep at 2 am. As I lay there, snatches of conversation I'd heard the day before began to come back to me, and I felt sure they must be preparing a feast. *For everyone?* I wondered incredulously. *For five hundred people?* It sounded like something the Tawbuid would do!

Ann's Mangyan Christian Elementary Schools were one example. After Uan in Safa and Gunye in Dalandan had both taught the Tawbuid schools for a number of years, Ann trained them as school supervisors and teacher-trainers. In this capacity they served the other tribes. Even though all their expenses were paid, including a very small allowance, they were not working for a salary. Typical of the Tawbuid believers they gave their time and talents freely for the Lord, whether at home or in another tribe.

It wasn't all easy sailing. On one trip to instruct the teachers in the West, Uan's box of school materials was stolen from the boat on which he had traveled. With heavy steps he had to hike up to the Western Tawbuid villages with the news that the teachers could not be trained nor the new term begun on schedule.

What rejoicing followed when in answer to prayer the box was found. Its scattered contents had been collected from the beach and returned by the police. All that was missing was a coin display for the math class, so the teachers were trained and school did begin on schedule!

Turning over I slept a bit more before the bright Sunday dawn brought me fully awake.

Gunye led the first service, and again the organ blend of voices sang from the heart "Praise Him, Praise Him," [and I did!]. "Give of your Best to the Master," [they did!]. "Great is Thy Faithfulness," [we could all see it!]. And "All Hail the Power of Jesus' Name," [such majesty as everyone joined in!]. On the lighter side, for a special number Linagum and Lumidi regaled the congregation with the lilting rhythms of Manobo believers' choruses learned while studying SALT agriculture in Mindanao. And then as we listened in the morning heat to the message from God's Word, a mercifully cool breeze sprang up making concentration easier and more enjoyable.

At noon each family cooked its own large pot of rice as is the Tawbuid custom for feasts. These were brought to the church along with great wide banana leaves that served as table and plates on the floor of the church or on the grassy area outside where everyone was asked to sit by tribal groups. With much lively bantering and teasing laughter the huge caldrons of meat were taken off the outdoor fires and, after a hymn and prayer, the dishing began. Tawbuid flitted here and there filling and refilling the coconut shell bowls with steaming pork and savory broth.

There was plenty for everyone!

How had they managed it? Later I learned that every Safa family had given 35 pesos so that several fat pigs could be purchased. If noise and bustle, high spirits and laughter were any indication of everyone's enjoyment, the Tawbuid had helped produce a perfect day.

But it wasn't over yet, even though the men studying at the Mangyan Bible School did have to return right after the feast for classes the next day. That evening Uan in his humorous style led the meeting and Yanigia gave an excellent message. The Lord's supper followed and though I was startled to see Pepsi-cola and bread being used as the elements, evidently a conference tradition, the disposable folded-leaf communion cups and the thoughtful spirit of the observance made me feel at home.

In a special ceremony the newly-elected MTCA council was introduced and the new Buhid missionary to the Negritos, Ihit, was commissioned. He apologized that his wife could not come because of their new baby, but they looked forward to beginning work with Jeremias and Monling and Dangin and Saynay in June.

And then Berting came up to me after the meeting asking if I could give him the words of "My Tribute," a special number sung in Tagalog by the lowland pastor. He wanted to learn it! Berting, who had fled in fear, who had wandered alone in the jungle for nearly two weeks, who said he never would leave the West again. Now he was always the first at every meeting, ready to urge the early ones to sing a few songs before the meeting started.

Early Monday morning as everyone gathered

their rice kettles and sleeping mats, their baskets and children and began the trip back to their homes, the Tawbuid did not relax their diligent reaching out to others. In their own tribe the still unbelieving Bintuk had attended some of the conference meetings and now the believers were making plans to teach in his village if he would agree. Others were planning another trip into the interior to try to contact powerful leader Sikfufu.

Five years ago Yudgulian, alerted by the muddy water in the Banos River, had gone upstream and found 43 Tawbuid dam-fishing. They had said they would listen to the New Teaching if Sikfufu agreed. In the intervening years, although he has been almost impossible to contact, he has softened enough to allow those under him to listen to the gospel. But he told the believers that if he would listen and obey the New Teaching, "the earth would come to an end!"

At the conference the Tawbuid had been able to share these prayer requests. They knew, as they continued to give God's Word to fellow tribesmen, the believers in the other tribes were praying for them. So that in the words of Paul to the Corinthians, when God answers "many will give thanks," truly rejoicing together.

More challenging reading from OMF Books

TO A DIFFERENT DRUM
What brought a physiology Ph.D to work with delinquent boys? Why had *Pauline Hamilton* chosen to march to a different drum from her contemporaries, to experience danger and hardship in China and then Taiwan rather than security and prosperity in the USA? Only because the God who had saved her from suicide and given meaning to her life had called, and as she obeyed she found Him faithful beyond all expectation.

THAT GREATER FREEDOM – Margaret Kirk –
At a time when Muslim extremists rebelled against the government of Indonesia, Ari and his small community were caught in their trap. As they struggled to keep true to values that were precious to them, they sought and found a freedom that was more than political. A beautifully told, sensitive and moving story.

SOMETIMES I PREFER TO FUSS – Verda Peet –
Stifling heat, cultural blunders, laundry, tropical sicknesses, separation from children, leeches, Christians who trade in opium, noisy neighbors, slow or dangerous transport ... yes, opportunities for fussing abound when you are a missionary in North Thailand. This book is sometimes painfully honest, often very funny and always realistic.

GOLD FEARS NO FIRE – Ralph Toliver –
The panoramic story of the Lee family and their life in Communist China. A true-to-life novel of a Christian family from 1949–1980.